D1616097

A Green Band in a Parched and Burning Land

A Green Band in a Parched and Burning Land
Sobaipuri O'odham Landscapes

DENI J. SEYMOUR

UNIVERSITY PRESS OF COLORADO
Louisville

© 2022 by University Press of Colorado

Published by University Press of Colorado
245 Century Circle, Suite 202
Louisville, Colorado 80027

All rights reserved
Manufactured in the United States of America.

 The University Press of Colorado is a proud member of
the Association of University Presses.

The University Press of Colorado is a cooperative publishing enterprise supported, in part, by
Adams State University, Colorado State University, Fort Lewis College, Metropolitan State
University of Denver, Regis University, University of Alaska Fairbanks, University of Colorado,
University of Northern Colorado, University of Wyoming, Utah State University, and Western
Colorado University.

∞ This paper meets the requirements of the ANSI/NISO Z39.48-1992 (Permanence of Paper).

ISBN: 978-1-64642-296-8 (hardcover)
ISBN: 978-1-64642-297-5 (ebook)
https://doi.org/10.5876/9781646422975

Library of Congress Cataloging-in-Publication Data

Names: Seymour, Deni J., author.
Title: A green band in a parched and burning land : Sobaipuri O'odham landscapes / Deni J.
 Seymour.
Description: Louisville, CO : University Press of Colorado, [2022] | Includes bibliographical
 references and index.
Identifiers: LCCN 2022025044 (print) | LCCN 2022025045 (ebook) | ISBN 9781646422968
 (hardcover) | ISBN 9781646422975 (epub)
Subjects: LCSH: Sobaipuri Indians—Arizona—History. | Sobaipuri
 Indians—Arizona—Antiquities. | Land settlement patterns—Arizona—History. |
 Excavations (Archaeology)—Arizona. | Arizona—Antiquities.
Classification: LCC E99.S662 S485 2022 (print) | LCC E99.S662 (ebook) | DDC
 979.1004/9745—dc23/eng/20220608
LC record available at https://lccn.loc.gov/2022025044
LC ebook record available at https://lccn.loc.gov/2022025045

Cover illustration: watercolor of the Acequias Hondas Narrows on the lower San Pedro River
by Marilyn French-St. George

To Canito and headmen Humari, Coro, and Bajon, and their councils and villagers, who occupied this era of history. Their sound intentions in the late 1600s have resonated through the ages and now touch their descendants at Wa:k (San Xavier del Bac).

Contents

I would like to thank a number of people for comments and input, including Todd Bostwick, Phil Halpenny, and members of the Wa:k community, including David Tenario, Tony Burrell, and Felicia Nunez. I am appreciative of the access provided to private land from Diana Nash of Circle Z Ranch, the Nature Conservancy of Sonoita Creek, Ellen Brophy Williams of the Babacomari Ranch, Bill Bergier, BHP, Mike Massee at the City of Nogales, and many others. Finally, this work could not have been completed without the continued assistance of a host of volunteers and the cooperation of members of the Wa:k community as we rediscover their heritage.

A Green Band in a Parched and Burning Land

The Sobaipuri O'odham (soh-BY-per-ee, or sometimes pronounced soh-by-poohr-ee, and *AH*-tum)[1] were a principal force in Expeditionary and Colonial Arizona history and arguably the most influential and powerful Indigenous group in southern Arizona in the Terminal Prehistoric and Early Historic periods. They are also one of the least understood and lesser-known farming groups to have occupied the American Southwest. In the following pages I discuss their geographic distributions, way of life, and ethnic differences that have been clarified in the past few years through archaeological, ethnographic, and ethnohistorical research. The implications of some of this research are also discussed. With this exploration of Sobaipuri O'odham landscape use comes an understanding of the sources of and basis for many of the inferences drawn about this ethnic group in the past as well as where ideas stand currently. New readings of old sources combined with new archaeological evidence provide a baseline from which to discuss and revise our understanding of these people and their pivotal role in history. Conversations with the descendants of these historical people also provide a concurrent way to assess and interpret long held but poorly understood information.

The Sobaipuri O'odham were irrigation farmers, first and foremost, and so they occupied the verdant strips along southern Arizona's main rivers. They were Akimel or River O'odham. This may be a surprise to many because today they are not called Akimel

Those Who Sing of the Green Band

https://doi.org/10.5876/9781646422975.c001

3

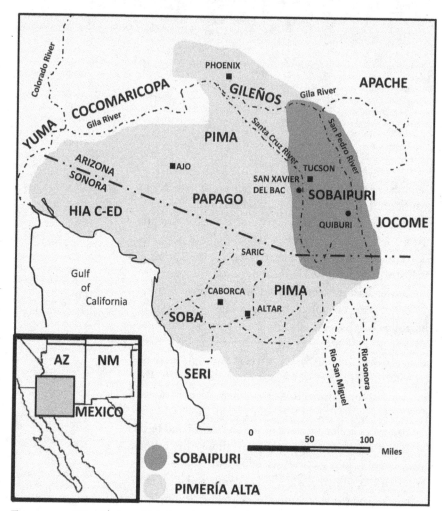

FIGURE I.I. *Distribution of Sobaipuri in southern Arizona in the 1600s. Figure prepared by Deni Seymour.*

O'odham by outsiders, and in fact, other people are called Akimel O'odham. But historically the Sobaipuri occupied all the major rivers in southeastern Arizona, including a portion of the Gila River (figure 1.1; see chapter 3), and they were an archetypical and a quintessential River O'odham in the sense that they were year-round farmers with permanent settlements. The distinctiveness of the riparian zones of southeastern Arizona made the river margins a critical niche and consequently, their contrast to the surrounding desert has been recorded in traditional stories and songs. A Badger song,[2] collected from the Gila River O'odham, goes as follows:

The land is parched and burning,
The land is parched and burning.
Going and looking about me
I see a narrow strip of green.

(Russell [1908] 1975:322)

This narrow band of green was the focus of Sobaipuri life and other O'odham who resided along the rivers, while those who lived in the desert, full or part time, would have come seasonally or periodically from the parched and burning land to these riverside oases. But not all portions of the river margin were equal with respect to resources, river flow, or other values important to the O'odham. Dependency on irrigation agriculture meant that the Sobaipuri selected suitable segments of these rivers for their occupations so that their villages were near—generally overlooking—their fields and canals (Seymour 1989, 1993a, 1993b, 2011a, 2020a; Seymour and Rodríguez 2020). Another implication for this choice of settlement location was that they were along travel and trade routes so the O'odham encountered people from all over their world (Seymour 2007a, 2008b, 2011a, 2020c; Seymour et al. 2022a, 2022b). They were the first to obtain information and new trade items, and to encounter trouble. Trouble came because they occupied the choicest land and produced bountiful harvests, making them the focus of both raiding and beneficial trading. Newcomers coveted their land and the coresident mobile peoples (Jocome, Jano, and Apache, among others) would have also valued the locations with reliable surface water and desired the stores of food that bridged the lean times. These factors required the Sobaipuri to defend their land and their supplies as well as their people—the warriors defending their women, children, and elderly. These factors also explain why the O'odham were notable warriors, consummate diplomats, and accomplished irrigation agriculturalists who lived in sizable permanent settlements.

Before initiating discussion about new understandings relating to Sobaipuri landscape use, this chapter provides some background information for those not familiar with the Sobaipuri and past research related to them. A revised baseline of understanding was included in the book *Where the Earth and Sky Are Sewn Together*, which was built on a quarter century of new and focused research on this group (Seymour 2011a). That book summarized past research and changes in understanding through time that influenced perceptions of the Sobaipuri, as well as research findings from work I had undertaken between

1985 and 2010. Like the current work, that book was based largely on my research because so few have studied, and currently no one else is studying, the Sobaipuri. Since then, I have continued investigations with a steady flow of new findings that are included in this book. I have made archaeological, documentary, and ethnographic study of the Sobaipuri my life's work, so I expect to continue to build on these results, revising ideas and correcting misimpressions as new data become available.

When I began my research, only five Sobaipuri sites were known (AZ BB:6:9, ASM; AZ BB:11:20, ASM; AZ BB:13:14, ASM; AZ DD:8:128, ASM; AZ DD:8:129, ASM; AZ EE:2:80, ASM; AZ EE:2:83, ASM; AZ EE:2:95, and ASM; AZ EE:8:15),[3] while a few others that were recorded as Sobaipuri have since been shown not to be Sobaipuri (Harlan and Seymour 2017:186n2; Seymour 1993a, 2011a, 2011b; Seymour and Sugnet 2016). Now over 110 archaeological Sobaipuri sites/components have been recorded, with many more O'odham sites known. These Sobaipuri village sites are situated along all the key rivers and tributaries in southeastern Arizona, with a couple in the foothills (e.g., at Barrel Canyon and Pima Canyon, not illustrated) and most cluster along certain river segments (figure 1.2). This increase in numbers of known sites and components is important from several perspectives, not least of which is that the twentyfold increase in sites allows us to understand more about Sobaipuri archaeology and the relationship between information conveyed in the documentary record and in archaeology and, consequently, more about the Sobaipuri themselves. In turn these data are regularly presented to descendant populations, who evaluate the information from their unique perspective and use this information to enrich their community. The strong correlation between landscape attributes and the distribution of Sobaipuri sites is both a product of this increase in archaeological sites and at the same time has contributed to the ability to predict where more should occur, thereby, through this process, strengthening the perception of the pattern. In turn, when this pattern was revealed, the many hints provided in documentary and ethnographic sources became apparent and relevant, providing an even richer understanding of the O'odham past.

This decades-long research has allowed a more faithful connection between the documentary and archaeological records than past efforts were able to achieve, as will be shown throughout the book. Most of the key places north of the international line visited by important historical figures—such as Fray Marcos de Niza, Francisco Vázquez de Coronado, and Father Eusebio Francisco Kino—have been identified. What this means is that definite Sobaipuri sites have been found after extensive thematic-based survey that

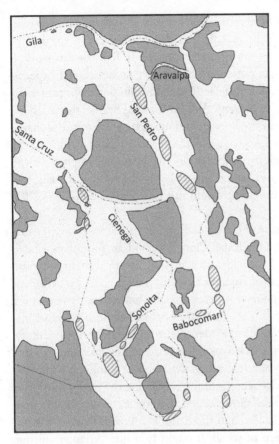

FIGURE 1.2. *Sobaipuri site distributions and historical clusters of known villages are grouped along certain river segments downstream from narrows and along wide expanses of arable land. Figure prepared by Deni Seymour.*

chronometrically date to the correct period, match the documentary record with respect to location, and contain artifacts and features diagnostic of the Sobaipuri; often, they reveal European items connecting them to the Expeditionary and Colonial periods. I have excavated a few of these sites as well, and through that process learned substantially more than was perceivable from surface evidence alone. While some of these place identifications remain controversial, it is important to understand that much of this debate is founded largely on rivalry rather than any consideration of the facts. In most instances there is only a single option when location, size, chronometric dates, and material culture assemblages are paired with texts and maps. There is no alternative data set by which to cogently dispute the known facts, and the existing data set improves and gains robustness each year as new data are contributed. Notably, this work has been undertaken in a systematic and targeted way, and, in most instances, I have resurveyed areas at least three times as conditions change (such as along the middle San Pedro and Santa Cruz Rivers, where erosion gradually exposes additional evidence). In light of this work, I invite you to consider the facts presented, based, not on outmoded expectations, ad hominem attacks, or political-factional considerations, but rather on what the record has available to present. As I have noted before, there can be substantial disjuncture between the meager and modest nature of the archaeological record and what researchers have expected based on later historical and earlier prehistoric manifestations, and also on the historical importance of the people who wrote about and visited these places.[4] In many instances, the importance of the places investigated would not be apparent were it not for the historical record.

The documentary record from the Colonial period in this area is extensive, but all accounts, and those from the Expeditionary period, are narratives, which many historians consider less than ideal for use in historical archaeological analysis (see Seymour 2009c, 2011a, 2012a, 2014, 2020a, 2020b, 2021). Nonetheless, this is the nature of the documentary sources available and, despite their issues, they have proven informative in the study of Sobaipuri archaeology and history. When paired with other forms of evidence, the meanings of documentary passages become apparent, often in surprising ways, bringing a richness to the study of the past and opening our analyses to new ways of thinking. Kino was among the first to leave extensive records of the area, being the most prominent Jesuit missionary among the Sobaipuri charged with their conversion. He first entered what is now Arizona in 1691 and thereafter ventured inland on fifty or more journeys, at least fourteen of which brought him into Arizona; during his travels he established several missions and visiting stations until his death in 1711 (Bolton [1932] 1986:52, [1936] 1960:588). His records have become some of the most important, in part because ethnohistorians have focused mostly on the discovery, translation, and retranslation of his accounts, making them available for study. Military figures, including Kino's escorts, also left important records, many of which have been translated, including those of Captain Juan Mateo Manje, Lieutenant Cristóbal Martín Bernal, Captain Diego Carrasco, among others (Kino in Bolton 1948:I and F. Smith et al. 1966; Carrasco in Burrus 1971; Manje in Burrus 1971; Karns 1954; F. Smith et al. 1966). Earlier, in the mid-sixteenth century, Marcos de Niza and Vázquez de Coronado passed through the Sobaipuri area in southeastern Arizona (see Flint and Flint 2005; Seymour 2008a, 2009b, 2011a, 2017a), and their actual route is being rediscovered as this book is published. In fact, the first Coronado-related site discovered in Arizona is at an important Sobaipuri village site. Other key documents are also available that are both contemporary with and after Kino. Other and later missionaries—such as Felipe Segesser, Jacobo Sedelmayr, Luís Xavier Velarde, Ignaz Pfefferkorn, Bartholomé Ximeno, Bernardo Middendorf, Diego Bringas, Joseph Augustín de Campos, and Ignacio Xavier Keller—left often-detailed accounts of the Indigenous peoples of this area and their cultural practices and the environment, as did later missionaries, military men, inspectors, and visitors.

Information contained in the ethnographic record has also been used to fill in many of the information gaps, but regrettably much of the work was carried out among neighboring O'odham with different histories and heritage, rather than among Sobaipuri descendants themselves (e.g., Russell [1908] 1975; Underhill 1938, 1939:41, 1946, 1968, 1969). While ethnographic analogy was commonly used as a way of understanding the then-meager archaeological record and deep past, researchers did not realize that an inappropriate ethnographic model was being applied, despite the fact that it was often contradictory. A substantial degree of inconsistency therefore arose when the direct historical approach was used to link past and present. The work of both ethnographers and archaeologists reflects this limitation as they tried to make sense of the larger picture but lacked sufficient data to seamlessly connect all the dots, with few data points there at the time. This deficiency continues to this day as absorption and acceptance of new archaeological and ethnographic findings lag years behind discoveries, as traditional knowledge from one area is uncritically applied by researchers to another, or, as occasionally occurs, O'odham in one area insistently urge that their point of view be applied to all. Some traditional knowledge from the past has been lost and continues to be lost, and so that knowledge retained in one area is sometimes transferred to another as an active part of the revitalization process and also as a demonstration of the living character of traditional practice. This transference is likely how it has always been, especially at those points in the prehistoric record at which fundamental shifts can be seen and are defined as phases or periods. In-depth scholarly studies or layperson familiarity with one area or cultural attribute, such as dialect, is all too often presented as if applicable to the O'odham in general, past and present without critical assessment. Many linguistic studies suffer from this practice, with translations and spellings from one area assumed applicable in the adjacent area (e.g., Geronimo 2012; Winters 2012). The lay public sometimes harvests information from the one O'odham they know, while not understanding the influence of geographic and cultural differences, subjects that should be more familiar to the anthropologist. In practice, someone asks for a translation or spelling from an O'odham they encounter (or perhaps someone they know), and the resulting answer permanently enters the record, whether that O'odham consultant is knowledgeable, from the correct area, conscious of the implications of their answer, or motivated by an undisclosed objective in their response. Sometimes this data-reporting practice is driven by the assumption that knowledge is limited and therefore must be collected in any form available. While this point may be valid, it does not justify uncritical acceptance of a practice or information as applying to all O'odham historically or presently. While it is true that knowledge is not always readily available and informants are not always forthcoming, the information collected from specific reservoirs of knowledge should be applied thoughtfully and appropriately after thorough analysis by the trained professional. Care taken in the collection and analysis of information might reveal that the O'odham consultant is not being asked if that is the way something is said locally or by all O'odham, but rather they are simply being asked what they think. This is a distinction they should not be expected to convey unless asked, often because they had not thought of it that way or do not appreciate the significance to scholarly investigation. The more in depth the interface and more focused the questions, the more likely these distinctions will become apparent or be revealed. When comfortable, O'odham individuals occasionally comment that they did not feel like explaining or they were just providing the response expected or one that they thought the questioner would understand. They recognize the difference between engaged investigation, curiosity, and hit-and-run data collection. The latter (hit-and-run investigations) being where the researcher comes into a community with a pre-existing notion and leaves with the expectation fulfilled, regardless of the integrity of the information or the gradations discernable from more concentrated listening. Different answers sometimes result when the O'odham consulted assess that the effort to explain will be received, understood, or appreciated.

Early ethnographic studies, especially those of ethnographer Ruth Underhill, were oriented broadly and combined the practices of diverse O'odham groups, while for the most part studying deeply only those who practiced the two-village system. As Underhill (1939:v) wrote: "Most of the time was spent on the Sells reservation . . . though a few weeks were spent at San Xavier." The results were nonetheless extrapolated to the Sobaipuri (and their descendants at San Xavier del Bac), such that the Sobaipuri and their descendants became a political subset of the Tohono O'odham, rather than the Akimel or River People they were. To her credit, she did discuss the Sobaipuri at length in an effort to understand their seemingly anomalous history (1939:15–23).

By the 1930s the moniker "Papago" had already permeated perspectives others had of the Wa:k community at San Xavier del Bac and its Sobaipuri past. Underhill's work emphasized this "Papago" (now generally regarded as a derogatory term) or Tohono O'odham contingent within the community, probably as a result of the short time spent at Wa:k and likely also to the faction willing to converse with her during that two-week period (possibly the one that had the most to gain by broadcasting their story or who were related to people further west). This calculated eagerness for the ear of the ethnographer by factions is not uncommon when people of different backgrounds occupy the same physical and political space. Often one faction prevails, especially when a single cohesive narrative is sought by the community or the anthropologist, despite being among populations where multiple narratives have survived. Underhill's work among the O'odham further west was assumed, even by her, to also apply to those who initially resided further east along the San Pedro River and the Santa Cruz River and their tributaries, that is, the Sobaipuri. This approach was driven by a lack of comprehensive understanding of the fundamental differences between community clusters, differences that were based on the ways in which their lifeways were shaped by their specific connections to the land and were made distinctive by their geographic separation from one another. In her defense, she did acknowledge the greater complexity in the O'odham world, and she conveyed her partial understanding of the situation: "It is realized that to gain a full understanding of regional differences and therefore, perhaps, of the past history of these people, an even more intensive study should be made in each locality" (1939:vi). With this comment she was acknowledging the diversity within the O'odham area, while at the same time she recognized the impossibility of constructing a single cohesive representation: "As often as possible various people were consulted, and the variation in their accounts was usually found due to regional differences" (vi). She also wrote: "Even among the American Papago it was found that there were decided differences in dialect, customs and ceremonies and an effort was made to get data from each of the three important groups" (e.g., "American Papago" [mostly Tohono O'odham in the area surrounding Sells and also the "Hia C'ed," or "Sand Papago"], "Mexican Papago" [O'odham south of the border] and "Pima" ["Gila Pima"]) (vi). She noted, with reference to these three distinct groups, that "one of these was often completely ignorant of traditions known to the others, so that it was no uncommon experience to have an informant in one village deny with amusement the possibility of some practice which those in the next village acknowledged as traditional" (v). This is a common occurrence today as O'odham both from Wa:k and elsewhere laugh lightheartedly at the differences in practices between themselves. A good example of this is when an O'odham from Sells laughs at and disparages

Wa:k O'odham interpretation of the origins of the name "Sobaipuri" and the name of the village of Gaybanipitea.

Researchers also sometimes use the information to discredit the results of other researchers or engage their unsuspecting O'odham informants in an information war or influence/power struggle, a practice all too common today among research factions. In other cases, as noted in the preceding paragraph, O'odham engaged from one area convey their opinion or understanding while the investigator may neglect (or be unable) to place the information in the larger O'odham context. Ethnographic summaries sometimes describe practices or beliefs as if they are applicable to all so as to construct a satisfying and cohesive narrative at the expense of understanding the often-important distinctions between O'odham groups.

There are more than just the three divisions noted by Underhill, and since her time more communities or reservations have been distinguished. These new reservations and the many communities are an indication of the differences between geographic areas, and many more distinctions are warranted, according to individuals in various O'odham communities. The overarching political structure known today as the Tohono O'odham Nation was never a feature of O'odham life in the past, which seemingly explains its poor fit today. The farther from one's community an O'odham goes, the fewer distinctions seem warranted by them as outsiders because of lack of specific knowledge. One the other hand, the merging of distinct communities of practice within one O'odham's own area is a basis for much consternation. One way modern Wa:k O'odham view the organization is that there are the Gila and Salt River O'odham, formerly one group that split from the other. Ak Chin and San Lucy are two additional separate and distinct communities. Wa:k is its own community with its very unique heritage and history related to the Sobaipuri who dominated southeastern Arizona and is reflected culturally in so many ways (Seymour et al. 2022a, 2022b). Then from Wa:k's perspective there are those in the West (roughly equivalent to Underhill's Sells reservation) and those in the Far West (Hia C'ed). There are also those south of the border, who today correspond geographically with those on the north, who are Hia C'ed. Within each of these larger areas, however, there are smaller clusters of communities who share commonalities, including ways of thinking, traditions, and ceremonies, and who interact on a regular basis and therefore share dialect variations. Underhill's desire was to capture the past of a vanishing race, as was a common view at the time. What she attempted was to convey "a picture of Papago life as it must have been just before the coming of the White man. In many parts of Papago county, it is still very much like that, though changes are coming fast" (1941:7).

The academic and bureaucratic homogenization of O'odham south of the Gila River resulted as well from the assumption that the people closer to Tucson were "Papago"/Tohono O'odham and had simply lost their traditions and that those residing at Santa Rosa (Gu-Achi, "Place of the Burnt Seeds") and other villages in the vicinity of Sells represented a purer and more complete representation of the preservation of past ways (Underhill 1938:5, 1939:30, 1941:7, 1946:4–5, 1974:311–318, 1979:32). This assumption is conveyed by Underhill's conception of Santa Rosa as one of the most isolated and traditional villages on the reservation and her opinion that the center of the reservation was less changed than other areas, while also acknowledging that the O'odham were "by no means a homogenous group" (Underhill 1946:4; see also 1939:v, vi, 20, 30). This perspective of a more standardized version of O'odham that more purely reflected the past and the true O'odham way was reinforced by political factors originating in the federal government, wherein San Xavier was subsumed into the Tohono O'odham Nation (or, as Underhill referenced it at the time, the Sells Reservation). Placement of San Xavier (and other communities now referenced as districts) under Sells or Indian Oasis resulted from bureaucratic expedience that disregarded cultural differences noted by some government workers and academic researchers at the time (Seymour et al. 2022b). There were also both a misunderstanding that the people of Wa:k were "originally from [the] parent village [sic] of Santa Rosa and San Lorenzo" and an incorrect assumption that the designated grazing districts represented "ancient sub-divisional lines" (Collier 1936 in Fontana 1993; Hall 1936; McQuigg 1913, 1914; also see Fontana 1993:13–14, 22–23, 45–65; Hoover 1935:259–262; Underhill 1938, 1939:60–61). The narrative was strengthened when Robert Hackenberg (1974a:272,) citing Underhill (1939:23), incorporated research results into land claims testimony about the disposition of the Wa:k community, stating that the original Sobaipuri occupants had died out during an epidemic and by other means. This position of extinction was reiterated in newspapers and by later historians (e.g., Hackenberg 1974b:76, 272, 275; Joseph et al. 1949:22; "Last of Indian Braves Tell Story Out of Rich Long Life"; "Last of Sobaipuri Tribe Passes with 'Red Evening'"; "Soba Puris Once Ruled Tucson Area"; Underhill 1938:16, 1939:23; also see Seymour 2011a; Seymour et al. 2022a, 2022b). This perspective has persisted for decades, despite the fact that many of Wa:k's current residents can definitively trace their heritage to the Sobaipuri. This book will demonstrate that the Sobaipuri were not from the west but that they once occupied the margins of every river in southeastern Arizona.

This assumption about all those residing between the Santa Cruz River and Santa Rosa being essentially similar only confused the understanding further.

It ultimately led to archaeologist Emil Haury (1976) referencing the prehistoric Hohokam as Desert Farmers and using the Tohono O'odham analogy rather than one more appropriate to the Akimel O'odham. This confusion was so deeply embedded that it has persisted today because people have referenced the existing ethnographic material while not understanding how inappropriate and misleading it could be. One consequence of this is that up until recently there has been debate as to whether the Sobaipuri were year-round irrigation farmers or part-time farmers with a heavy reliance on wild foods. Thus, when scholars cited the earliest documentary evidence, they assumed that the mobile groups encountered (e.g., those small groups presenting gifts of little value, e.g., Seymour 2016a) were descriptive of the Sobaipuri, who, in contrast, practiced a very different lifeway as irrigation farmers and therefore left very different archaeological evidence. Because of the seeming contradiction in the records, Sobaipuri research remained at a stalemate with little progress until a sufficiently strong archaeological record began to serve as an arbiter (e.g., *Where the Earth and Sky Are Sewn Together*). The confusion was heightened because as a result of Apache attacks, Spanish policy, and disease, most of the Sobaipuri moved from their original villages to live at the Wa:k community at San Xavier del Bac. Furthermore, the baptismal records from 1768 document "Papagos," that is, Tohono O'odham, at Wa:k (Matson and Fontana 1977:148–150). This record indicates both that more Tohono O'odham were moving in (e.g., Matson and Fontana 1977:66, 72) and a seeming record of a shift in the way these villagers were perceived and referenced by outsiders. The term "Papago" gained prominence as the Franciscans took over after the Jesuit expulsion, apparently because these missionaries lacked the temporal depth of cultural understanding held by their predecessors or perhaps were more interested in acculturation than understanding distinctions. Formerly, such as in 1764, it was recognized that the "Papagos" inhabited "the sandy, barren plains of the northwest" or "the sterile wilderness" (Nentvig in Pradeau and Rasmussen 1980:54, 99), but shortly after the mid-eighteenth century, the missionaries were exploiting the political imbalance produced when Tohono O'odham moved into Sobaipuri settlements. As the O'odham were referenced, so they became, in name at least. Furthermore, assumptions introduced into the historic record and public opinion in the mid-1800s by rude and uneducated travelers, politicians, and land-grabbers contributed a great deal to defining who the Wa:k O'odham were from a public perspective. Yet, that they were not "Papago"/Tohono O'odham is reinforced by the report that when urged to be obedient in 1764 the Sobaipuri residents of Tucson commented: "Maybe you think we are Papagos?" (Pradeau and Rasmussen

1980:99). In the first third of the twentieth century Carnacion Mamake of the Wa:k community at San Xavier del Bac told stories about her Sobaipuri ancestors that other residents did not believe because by then, so many residents had been indoctrinated, taught in school and in public for decades. Yet, even the Tohono O'odham at Santa Rosa spoke of themselves as the "real Papago," which Underhill (1974:311) took to mean that "all others have elements of foreign or mixed blood." But rather, in fact, what they were likely saying according to today's O'odham is that the people to the far west and far east were a different kind of O'odham (and were initially referred to as such) than those from Santa Rosa, with different lifeways, more mobile and more sedentary, respectively. And of course, it cannot be denied that communities through the millennia tend to think of themselves as the true conveyors of their culture, being the only real people or the most traditional.

These are the ways in which the ethnographic record had been collected and incorporated into studies of the Sobaipuri. The fact that today we are able to incorporate but critically evaluate Underhill's important and monumental work is a testament to how much has been learned and to the congenial interface between O'odham and anthropologists who seek to understand the differences found throughout O'odham territory. As the Wa:k O'odham have stated, they knew they were different; they just did not understand why, in part because they were "brainwashed" (Tony Burrell, personal communication, 2018).

ARCHAEOLOGY COMES FROM BEHIND

The documentary record originally dominated study of the Sobaipuri because so few Sobaipuri sites (and O'odham sites in general) were known. What little archeological evidence was available for those sites thought to be Sobaipuri was contradictory, as initially each site documented as Sobaipuri presented quite different kinds of evidence. Yet, the astute reader will notice that one of the sites included in the list of five initially known Sobaipuri sites at the beginning of this chapter does include one recorded by Charles Di Peso (1953) of the Amerind Foundation. Di Peso can be credited with recognizing and recording the first-ever documented genuine Sobaipuri site (AZ EE:8:15, ASM; figure 1.3). At the time he thought he was investigating Santa Cruz de Gaybanipitea, whereas, in fact, he excavated Santa Cruz del Pitaitutgam (Seymour 1989, 1990, 1993b, 2011a, 2014). Since then, the actual Santa Cruz de Gaybanipitea village site has been identified. Indeed, it was the first of many sites I recorded along the middle San Pedro in 1985 and after (Seymour 1989, 1990, 1993b, 2011a, 2011b). Di Peso (1956) also erroneously recorded a prehistoric

FIGURE 1.3. *Places mentioned throughout this book. Figure prepared by Deni Seymour.*

site with a late O'odham component as being the important Sobaipuri village of San Cayetano del Tumacácori. He also thought he had identified San Salvador del Baicatcan as being the archaeological site of Solas Ruin (Di Peso 1953), but this site has since been shown to be a prehistoric site without a Sobaipuri component, as I have inspected it more than once myself. He had assumed Kino's maps were wrong and that Kino had plotted Santa Cruz de Gaybanipitea and San Cayetano del Tumacácori on the wrong side of a key tributary drainage and river, respectively. He assumed this error despite that Kino was an expert cartographer and his maps have been shown to be quite accurate, especially for the time, particularly with regard to the side of the river a village was on.

Di Peso (1953) also excavated Santa Cruz de Terrenate, a Spanish presidio occupied between late 1775 and early 1780.[5] At this place he also thought he had identified the important Sobaipuri site of Quiburi, visited by Father Kino in the 1690s. Yet, the material culture he identified and associated with the Sobaipuri at that site was indictive of later activity, and the occupational sequence was much more complex, with the much-later O'odham artifacts that dominate the record associated with the presidio. Organic-tempered O'odham plainware and redware do not appear on the scene until 1775 or so. Regrettably, many of Di Peso's inferences are propagated today by researchers not familiar with the history of ideas in this area (see discussion in Seymour 2011a). As Rex Gerald (1968) argued then, and as I have since shown, the setting of the presidio was never the location of Quiburi. No one today would make that association based on the documentary evidence now available, and, even at the time, some of the primary documentary evidence had to be dismissed to make that early argument for that location being Quiburi. The common practice at the time of ignoring inconvenient data that do not fit sometimes continues to this day.

Di Peso made the connection between the place (Santa Cruz de Terrenate Presidio) and the documentary record (Quiburi) for two key reasons. First, Bolton ([1936] 1960:361) had claimed that Quiburi was located at Santa Cruz de Terrenate, and so Di Peso accepted this inference and believed he had found supportive evidence (see chapter 9). Di Peso so readily accepted this inference most likely because the documentary record only referenced a handful of Sobaipuri villages. Kino's earliest map (*Teatro*) only showed four villages in this immediate area, and the textual record from the 1690s only mentioned two (see Bolton 1948:I; Burrus 1971; F. Smith et al. 1966). Consequently, it was a reasonable inference that if two of these sites had been found (Di Peso's Gaybanipitea [now Pitaitutgam] and this one), they must be these two Kino-period sites (Seymour 2011a). At the time it was also assumed that the Sobaipuri presence in the area had a shallow time depth, appearing right before Kino entered on the scene, but this assumption of a late arrival has since been discredited with abundant new chronometric evidence (Harlan and Seymour 2017; Seymour 1989, 2011a, 2011b, 2014; Seymour and Sugnet 2016). This assumption of a recent O'odham arrival also accounts for why it was at the time most reasonable to assume Kino's maps were incorrect with respect to the placement of Santa Cruz de Gaybanipitea. It was not known that there were around three dozen Sobaipuri sites along this stretch of the river alone, something my research three decades after Di Peso would begin to reveal. Nor was it considered, and there was no real reason to think, that village locations shifted every couple of decades, leading to a proliferation of sites and components that could be associated with a single historically referenced placename. This trend was not ascertained until later when I published this as an explanation as to why there were so many Sobaipuri sites (see Seymour 1989, 1990, 1993b, 1997, 2003, 2007b, 2011a, 2011b), and later when J. Darling and others (2004) recognized the movement of villages—both they and I relying on Paul Ezell's (1961) seminal work along the Gila wherein he mentioned village drift (also see Segesser in Treutlein 1945:158; and regarding daughter villages, see Underhill 1938:16). Nor had it yet been revealed that not all the Sobaipuri moved out of the San Pedro Valley during their forced removal to Tucson in 1762 (Seymour 2011c; Seymour and Rodríguez 2020) and that a much longer, earlier and later, occupation could be demonstrated on the San Pedro and elsewhere.

As it turns out, my field excavations at Santa Cruz de Terrenate Presidio (1775–1780) revealed evidence of a Sobaipuri village. The material culture evidence matches that found at Santa Cruz del Pitaitutgam and Santa Cruz de Gaybanipitea and all the other Sobaipuri sites now known. Yet, my excavations and documentary research indicate that the Sobaipuri village at the presidio was Santa Cruz, not Quiburi. This explains why the presidio was called Santa Cruz or Santa Cruz of/de Terrenate, with Terrenate referencing the initial presidio further south of the modern international line. Before that, Ternate was the name of a settlement near the headwaters of the San Pedro River. The Sobaipuri village at the Santa Cruz de Terrenate Presidio location (that preceded the presidio) was called Santa Cruz and was the successor of Santa Cruz de Gaybanipitea, established and occupied after that village was attacked in 1698 and after the people from there and Quiburi moved for a few years to Sonoita (Seymour 2014; see chapter 6, this book). When the people from both villages returned to the San Pedro shortly after 1700, they reestablished their villages in new locations and Santa Cruz was placed at the future site of the presidio, while Quiburi was a bit north. This shift positioned both villages within earshot of one another, without a hill between them, so that if future violence erupted and either village was attacked, the warriors from the other village could easily and quickly come to the aid of the victims. Even in 1775, when Hugo O'Conor sighted the location for the planned presidio he noted that it was to be established in the location known as Santa Cruz. The criteria that made the location acceptable for a Sobaipuri village made it suitable for a Spanish fort and included that it be defensible with water, wood, and arable land (Croix in Thomas 1941; Seymour 2011a, 2023). Quiburi was never known as Santa Cruz, but rather Quiburi's daughter villages of Pitaitutgam and Gaybanipitea (derived from O'odham placenames) were prefaced by that saint's designation, as was the post-1700 village that preceded presidio construction. The village was sometimes called Santa Cruz of/de Quiburi because it was in the Quiburi Valley, along the river sometimes called the Quiburi River, and was a smaller settlement that was politically subordinate to Quiburi, and so was "of Quiburi." But Santa Cruz and Quiburi were always different places, which is why today no reputable scholar familiar with the documentary and archaeological records would suggest that Quiburi was at the later presidio location.

At the time, Di Peso was just beginning to define the material culture attributes of the Sobaipuri, and the available documentary record was not as extensive. Consequently, much of what Di Peso concluded has since been revised, despite the incredible importance of his work. Nonetheless, his collections provide valuable information that has since been used in concert with modern excavations to revise our understanding of this place. Material culture defined as Sobaipuri at the presidio that was actually Sobaipuri (such as Whetstone Plain pottery) has now been shown on the basis of its spatial distribution to be associated with the earlier Santa Cruz village that occupied only a portion of the presidio footprint (Seymour 2023). So, while there was a Sobaipuri village at the spot of the presidio, its historical identity was misinterpreted and the evidence for it was confused with artifacts from the later presidio occupation. One could argue that the now-identified Sobaipuri evidence that relates to Santa Cruz at the presidio could be included as evidence of a sixth Sobaipuri site attributable to this early period of knowledge (list provided toward the beginning of this chapter). But since the evidence and the placename were initially misidentified, the evidence was legitimately dismissed or at least questioned for decades by most knowledge scholars until the recent twenty-first century work conducted there produced definitive proof.

The purported Sobaipuri component at the four sites investigated by Di Peso in the late 1940s and early 1950s varied considerably, leaving archaeologists confused, without a clear material cultural basis from which to work. It was not until some quarter century after Di Peso's investigations at Santa Cruz del Pitaitutgam that the series of actual Sobaipuri villages (the second through the fifth) were defined (Doyel 1977; Franklin 1980; Huckell 1984; Masse 1980, 1981). For some time after this, and even when I first began work, scholars who expressed an interest in the Sobaipuri were few. Those who could recognize Sobaipuri evidence in the archaeological record could be counted on one hand and mostly included those just mentioned who had encountered Sobaipuri evidence in the field. Little has changed in this regard, to the detriment of the resources themselves. Components are usually found on larger multiple component sites, and these are routinely damaged and destroyed by archaeologists and historians who are unfamiliar with the subtle nature of the evidence and the specific ways in which they need to be recorded and excavated (Seymour 2011a, 2017b). Some researchers are also not interested in these late components and commonly disregard and therefore destroy them when looking for earlier material, despite their importance and rarity (Seymour 2017b).

Most of what we knew back in the 1980s (which was extraordinarily little) has since been revised in light of new evidence. The greatest challenge has been addressing the question as to how we would know the specified sites were Sobaipuri as opposed to some other group, such as Jocome or Apache. Some researchers even questioned whether the distinctive attributes were protohistoric because they were so often found as components on Hohokam sites, and chronometric dates sometimes placed them much earlier than the Kino period (Ravesloot and Whittlesey 1987). The logic at the time was that they might not be Sobaipuri and that they surely had not been proven to be protohistoric. Today the perspective has changed, and because of hundreds of carefully selected chronometric dates we know that the Sobaipuri pattern overlaps temporally with the Hohokam. The Sobaipuri were present much earlier than previously thought, long before the arrival of Europeans. Because of past confusion and doubt about the existing archaeological or material cultural definition of Sobaipuri, it became clear that in addition to correlating on-the-ground evidence with the Sobaipuri documentary record, it would be necessary to define the Jocome and Apache in the archaeological record. This took me on a decades-long search for evidence of these other groups, which resulted in the gradual definition of these other complexes (Seymour 1995, 2002, 2004, 2009a, 2011a, 2014, 2016a). The results of this effort established a basis to distinguish between Jocome, ancestral Apache, and Sobaipuri, and I was soon able to distinguish each, even on multiple component sites, because I had deconstructed their diagnostic assemblages throughout the greater Southwest. Originally, Sobaipuri experts thought that the small triangular indented- and flat-base points and fine-grained chert bifaces and stone tools were as diagnostic of the Sobaipuri as were their elongate stone-ringed houses (see Masse 1981; Seymour 1993b). Yet, many of these apparently diagnostic attributes that were once assigned to the Sobaipuri have since been shown to be Jocome, or Sobaipuri with an overlying Jocome component (see Seymour 2011a, 2014, 2016a). Some are even assignable to other groups, such as the Jano and Suma, which are among a number of mobile groups documented intermittently in this area. So, while many of these tool forms are distinctive and pertain to the "Protohistoric" period, these unique stone items found on Sobaipuri sites often represent a later Jocome occupation. This is apparent with the Jocome and Jano occupation at and near Sobaipuri sites in the vicinity of Quiburi that were mentioned in the documentary record from 1686 (AZ EE:4:36, 169, 178, 179, 181, ASM; see Seymour 2016a:166–167, 2020d) and one along Sonoita Creek (AZ EE:6:106, ASM; Seymour 2015a). Some of these items are found on Sobaipuri sites because they were weapons left on battle sites, such as at the 1698 battle at Santa Cruz de Gaybanipitea (Seymour 2014, 2015b). The Bechtel burial encountered in Tucson (AZ AA:12:98, ASM; Brew and Huckell 1987) is another site defined as Sobaipuri that instead was likely Jocome.

Through concerted and ongoing efforts at defining all the primary groups known to have occupied southeastern Arizona in the early Historic period and before, it has been possible to isolate with certainty the Sobaipuri archae- ological signature from that of the Jocome and ancestral Apache (Seymour 2002, 2004, 2009a, 2011a, 2012a, 2014, 2016a, 2017b). The Sobaipuri archaeologi- cal signature as previously defined was only partially correct. Foremost among the diagnostic attributes are the unique elongate rock-ringed house outlines, that are distinctive from the often-rounder ones used by more mobile people (figure 1.4). The Sobaipuri also covered their houses with mats and dirt or adobe, whereas those O'odham from the desert and mobile people of other origins tended to use only brush and poles or branches. The Sobaipuri-specific site layout, with houses paired and arranged in linear rows, is not known for any other groups, including their Tohono O'odham cousins. Whetstone Plain pottery is the hallmark type of the Sobaipuri but has been insufficiently stud- ied to know whether other O'odham groups shared this technology and made similar wares and what the differences among them might be. Small triangular arrow points that were made on fine-grained material are also representative of the Sobaipuri, but these are A-shaped (with U-shaped and flat bases) rather than the many other forms that characterize other groups in the area at the time (for example the Eifel-tower-shaped ones of the Soto complex, which are probably Suma; Seymour 2002, 2014, 2017c; also see Harlan 2017). Some of the village sites that have produced chronometric dates from the Kino period and later have also revealed artifactual evidence that confirms these dates, including glass trade beads (seed beads and larger multifaceted glass beads), iron knives and crosses, and other gift and trade items (see, e.g., 2007b).

The distinctive Sobaipuri pattern continues into the nineteenth and twen- tieth centuries, when various aspects of their material culture are modified or are replaced with those of other groups. By 1775 manure-tempered plain- and redwares supplement Whetstone Plain, as do red-on-brown wares and other types produced for the tourist industry and for non-O'odham household use in the mid- to late 1800s. Nonetheless, luminescence dates on Whetstone

FIGURE 1.4. *Outline of Sobaipuri house after excavation and two historical images of River O'odham houses. Upper photograph by Deni Seymour. Middle photograph: Middle photo: National Anthropological Archives and Human Studies Film Archives, Smithsonian Institution, 2696-a-1; Arizona State Museum Photo Collections. Bottom photo: public domain.*

Plain indicate that this pottery type began at least as early as the late AD 1200s and continued in use well into the twentieth century. Their distinctive houses were gradually supplemented and then replaced with adobe-walled structures in the late nineteenth and early twentieth centuries.

The addition of a robust archaeological data set has advanced our understanding of the Sobaipuri because it provides insights into information not available in the documentary record. There are many more sites than ever imagined. Sobaipuri occupation is temporally much deeper than originally thought and overlaps with the Hohokam, indicating that they played a role in the events that transpired within the Hohokam world. The archaeological record also provides information on the location of key historical places, which in turn allows us to understand so much more about how the Sobaipuri used the landscape, which is the focus of this book. Archaeological data provide a different perspective on what the documentary record might be conveying and a broader perspective from which to interpret the ethnographic record. Thus, rather than simply supplementing the documentary and ethnographic records, in this instance the archaeological record takes the lead in providing a context for understanding so much more about the Sobaipuri lifeway and for resolving conflicting evidentiary source materials. On-the-ground evidence so often provides explanations for something stated in the documentary record that was interpreted one way but was in fact meant in another.

In the following chapters, archaeological sites and ethnohistoric data are examined that relate to each of the primary drainages used by the Sobaipuri, addressing long-held notions and poorly understood aspects of Sobaipuri landscape use and settlement patterns. The reader will note that the chapters of this book cover topics not discussed elsewhere. I have continued to research the Sobaipuri O'odham since the 2011 publication of *Where the Earth and Sky Are Sewn Together*, which established a new understanding of the people called Sobaipuri. This current book relates some of the new findings, filling in some of the many questions that remained upon the writing of that book. A number of questions were raised decades ago, and only recently have data been available to answer them or to examine them in new ways. Each of the chapters addresses at least one of these questions. In fact, this book addresses some of the longest-standing questions for the Sobaipuri and reorients the discussion in new directions. This book may be viewed as an overview of current understandings of Sobaipuri landscape use, including their unique way of using the river valleys. We now have archaeological evidence of Sobaipuri occupation in the Sonoita Creek drainage and along the Babocomari River. We have dozens more chronometric dates for individual Sobaipuri sites and also dates that parse some of the complex building episodes and occupational sequences of mission and presidio sites. This book addresses the topic raised by prominent Borderland historian Herbert Bolton ([1936] 1960:248) years ago about the apparent dividing line on the middle San Pedro and Santa Cruz Rivers between Sobaipuri on the north and Pima to the south. It addresses the ethnic identity of people at the headwaters of the San Pedro and on the middle Gila. Placenames are positioned within the context of the larger O'odham landscape. The cumulative nature of occupation in Sobaipuri villages is discussed along with the complex chronometric results obtained from missions and presidios, the occupation of river valleys and places long after they were said to be abandoned, and, briefly, the way village movement has influenced a range of factors, including the final survey and ultimate land ownership within the San José de Sonoita land grant. Hopefully, new research will continue to fill in our understanding of these important prehistoric and historic peoples because this academically neglected group was critically important in the course of historic events and remains important to descendant populations.

NOTES

1. The words "Pima" and "O'odham" are used interchangeably in this book, though "Pima" is usually a general historical reference to the O'odham or today it specifically references the Salt River Pima.

2. A Badger song is one of many medicine songs, which is one of the principal groups of O'odham songs (Russell [1908] 1975:271, 322).

3. A reviewer requested a mention of how site numbers are designated within the state. The main repository that oversees the assignment of site numbers is the Arizona State Museum (ASM), affiliated with the University of Arizona in Tucson. As its web page points out: "The ASM site number system is a modification of the one originally developed by Gila Pueblo in the late 1920s. Both systems systematically and increasingly subdivide areas to ultimately designate site numbers. The ASM system uses a five-part designation that includes a political designation (e.g., AZ), a quadrangle designation (e.g., U), a rectangle designation (e.g., 15), a site-in-rectangle designation (e.g., 2), and a suffix (i.e., ASM). These examples would form site number AZ U:15:2(ASM)."

4. See discussion in Seymour (1989), for example.

5. Ternate should not be confused with Santa Cruz de Terrenate, though the original and subsequent presidios took their name from a location nearby that was sometimes spelled Ternate and so the same name is likely being transferred through time. Referenced here is to Ternate, which is not the later presidio.

2

This chapter explores some concepts relevant to Sobaipuri landscape use, including what it meant for a river segment to be suitable for irrigation agriculture and how the Sobaipuri successfully managed the rivers for their use and settlement. These factors explain why their villages were situated where they were and the reasoning behind why and how they periodically moved short distances along the river margins. These understandings make Sobaipuri village locations predictable from an archaeological standpoint and explain why their villages were placed only in certain locations.

The Sobaipuri Landscape

SELECTIVE SETTLEMENT AND RIVER FLOW

Europeans have known for some time, and O'odham have known for even longer, that only portions of the Santa Cruz and San Pedro Rivers (as well as the Babocomari River, Sonoita Creek, and Aravaipa Creek) have reliable surface flows (Seymour 2020a). Each of these rivers originates in springs that have been fed for millennia by precipitation falling on the adjacent mountains that flows into the aquafer. A substantial portion of their flow is underground. Surface flow is visible where the water table intersects with the river channel bottom (Webb et al. 2014). In 1780 lieutenant of the infantry and engineer of the Royal Armies Gerónimo de la Rocha y Figueroa, noted this characteristic of the river flowing on the surface, then going underground, only to reemerge further down channel.

https://doi.org/10.5876/9781646422975.c002

He even colored the bands of rivers on his map with green and tan to reflect where the flow was on the surface and where it sank below (Rocha y Figueroa 1780b; Seymour and Rodríguez 2020). His late eighteenth-century exploratory visit was during an especially dry year and was also during the driest season, so even river segments that tended to have water during normal years were either dry or short of surface water. Nonetheless, portions of these rivers maintained surface flow throughout the year. By the 1780s farming in modern-day Sonora, Mexico, seems to have already impacted the flow of the Santa Cruz in the downstream settlements near Guevavi and Tubac. These zones of previously reliable surface water were completely dry and (temporarily) abandoned, as at Guevavi, or they received such low flow that the residents of Tubac requested that they be allowed to relocate owing to insufficient water to farm (Seymour and Rodríguez 2020). This variability in flow is likely one reason Sobaipuri settlements shifted so frequently as well, as will be discussed below.

This characteristic of the river flowing on the surface in some areas and not others was noticed even earlier by Jesuit Father Eusebio Francisco Kino, when he noted verdant portions of the river where fields were amply irrigated while other parts of the river were dry (Bolton 1948:I:passim; F. Smith et al. 1966:14–15). His military escort Captain Juan Mateo Manje also made mention of this attribute when in 1697 he noted the condition of the Santa Cruz River when traveling south from the Gila and Santa Catarina de Cuituabagu:

> traveling nine leagues south down [*sic*: up] the river, (which submerges some distance, coming out again and then flowing to join the Jila [*sic*] River to the west and near the last settlement we came from), we came to the settlement of Calle de Correa, where the Indians obtain their drinking water from a well made by hand in the bed of the river. These lands are seasonable. (quoted in Karns 1954:92, see Seymour 2020a)

Seasonally, during the summer rains, each of these rivers may rage in a torrent, either spreading wide beyond its shallow banks or racing confined through a narrow, entrenched channel that often collapses under the force of the flow. Surface flow rate decreases as water backs up upstream from where the channel constricts in locations where bedrock outcrops are located near the surface (figure 2.1). Sometimes these constrictions result in upstream marshy conditions, as was apparently the case at Tres Alamos in late historic times, and the camping location referred to as Los Alamos by Padre Kino in the late 1600s (chapter 10). This outcome is also characteristic of the formerly extensive marshes at Wa:k, at Tucson, and along the Babocomari. Downstream from these narrows, as they are called, the underground water is forced to

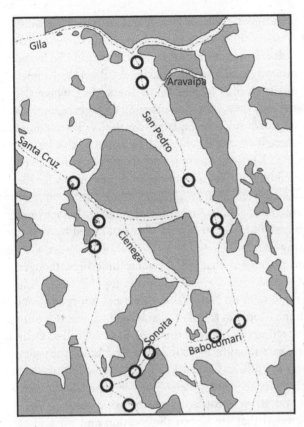

FIGURE 2.1. *Location of many of the narrows along river channels of southeastern Arizona relevant to Sobaipuri village locations. Figure prepared by Deni Seymour.*

the surface, even in the dry season, producing a reliable flow. Canal headgates placed just downstream from these narrows captured this flow, transporting it downstream through extensive irrigation canals and laterals, distributing it to fields on the broad floodplain. These bedrock outcrops also shielded canals to some degree from washouts, lessening the labor involved in maintaining these irrigation systems and increasing the value of infrastructure that could be retained and improved rather than seasonally replaced (Seymour 1989, 1991:12, 20–21, 2003, 2011a:193, 237, 2011b, 2020a).

O'odham placenames often convey important features of this Sobaipuri landscape, capturing the salient attributes of a location that make it suitable for settlement and farming. "Wa:k" means "come in" or "goes in" or "enter," which is a reference to the submersion of the river's surface flow in this area where the ancient village was located (Tony Burrell, personal communication, 2007). As O'odham elder Tony Burrell states: "The O'odham understand

Wa:k refers to San Xavier, but the meaning itself does not say where the water goes underground. Maybe 'where the water goes back in.' I think this is what is understood with the O'odham," if it were "su:dagî wa:k it would be 'water comes in.'" Thus, this community name for San Xavier del Bac (Wa:k) references this characteristic of the river as it goes below the surface where the ancestral village was located and then later, downstream, emerges again as a surface flow (Seymour 2019a). This attribute explains why the Wa:k settlement at San Xavier is located where it is, why it remained anchored to this stretch of the river, and why it has such a great temporal depth of occupation. Even large prehistoric sites focused on this river segment as well, presumably for the same reason, and investment was made in two hilltop retreats with *trinchera* constructions (walls constructed of cobbles and boulders on the hill slopes and tops), which according to oral and written history were later used by Wa:k's residents to flee from enemy attacks.

Guevavi is an O'odham placename that has for some time been thought to be derived from the O'odham word *gi-vavhia*, meaning "big well," "big water," or "big spring" (Kessell 1970:49; National Park Service 2007; Seymour 2011a:46). Yet, this is a Tohono O'odham translation and spelling, and there are other possibilities for interpreting this name in the local dialect. Until recently all these other possibilities were thought to be inappropriate labels for valley locations because they refer to cliffs and bedrock, which have been perceived as mountain characteristics. Consequently, these likely interpretations were dismissed as possibilities. Yet when considering the bedrock outcrops present at Guevavi (e.g., Guewawi) that are key to the location and survival of the Sobaipuri village, one of these other interpretations for the name makes greater sense (figure 2.2a and 2.2b). With this new understanding of how important these terrain features along the rivers were to Sobaipuri settlement placement, it is now thought that Guevavi derives from *ge: waw*, meaning "big cliff/bedrock." This derivation is also consistent with the local dialect, which uses *w* instead of *v*. Linguist to the O'odham, the late Jane Hill agreed, based on a photograph shown to her, that the outcropping at Guevavi near where the canal's head is a pretty decent size, good enough for "*gue* . . ." (*ge:*) (Jane Hill, personal communication, 2013). This interpretation was confirmed by Wa:k O'odham community resident and linguist Felicia Nunez (personal communication, 2021). Even historic canals head at this bedrock outcrop (figure 2.2a; also see Seymour and Rodríguez 2020:fig. 6.5) and follow some of the same courses as those inferred to be remnant segments of earlier canals (Seymour 1991c, 1997; figure 2.3). It was common for later farmers to reuse and modify existing ancient canals for their own use, since most of the work was already

FIGURE 2.2. *(a) Bedrock and canals at Guevavi, where canals have headed for centuries. (b) Aerial of bedrock at Guevavi that pushed the water to the surface, making it available for use and giving the name to the village. Photographs by Deni Seymour.*

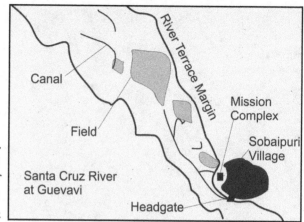

FIGURE 2.3.
Canals and fields related to the Sobaipuri village of Guevavi. Figure prepared by Deni Seymour.

completed, the best courses were already established, and their courses went to fields that were already leveled and cleared. Thus, the importance of Guevavi as a Sobaipuri village, and then a mission, relates to its placement with respect to bedrock outcrops that made irrigation farming viable and reliable.

The historically referenced Sonoita, or Los Reyes del Sonoydag, is also descriptive of its setting. Sonoydag likely means "Spring Field" or "Field at Point Where Rocks Emerge" in O'odham, both of which reference the important role river constrictions and bedrock outcrops play in river behavior and therefore the ability of the Sobaipuri to manage their canals and water their fields. The Point Where Rocks Emerge would in fact be where water would be pushed to the surface, thereby becoming available even at the driest times. In the Sonoita Valley this bedrock constriction is the vicinity of Patagonia, which explains why Sonoita Creek is seen as originating here and why water flows year-round from this location.[1] This bedrock outcrop is not as visible or dominant in this location as many others, because of the rockiness and roughness of much of the terrain in this valley and the thoroughness of vegetation cover, but to the experienced Sobaipuri eye the river channel characteristics would have been obvious.

This place also demonstrates the difficulty sometimes encountered with determining the meanings of old O'odham placenames. Different interpretations of old words may arise based on who is asked and which O'odham dialect they may speak. In Wa:k community discussions many possibilities are often suggested before the most likely interpretation is chosen. It is also important to consider that the Spanish wrote down each term as they heard it, which was not always an accurate representation of the original O'odham word. Moreover, the spelling of this word often changed through time. Modern speakers and linguists are then challenged to determine what the original word was and what it meant then. Even the dialects have changed through time, such that many words in the old language differ substantially from those in use today. With regard to the term "Sonoita," one Wa:k O'odham resident suggested that it likely derives from the term "Shon," at the "bottom," "base," or "where everything begins," that is, perhaps "where the spring waters begin." In this interpretation Sonoita would derive from *shon oidag* or *son oidag* and so might mean "fields at the base" (Dennis Ramon, video interview, January 27, 2016). In essence, this is just another way of saying "Field at Point Where Rocks Emerge" because the bedrock is the basis for the water being pushed to the surface, allowing it to be used for growing crops in the floodplain.

It is for these reasons that bedrock outcrops and the resulting constrictions in river margins are important to Sobaipuri settlement distributions. Sobaipuri canals headed near these constrictions and their fields were located downstream, where the river once again broadened, providing ample and fertile lands for crops (figure 2.4). While canals headed at a constriction in the channel, downriver segments had to be broad enough for fields to be fed by these canals. On the other hand, once the channel was too broad, streamflow tended to become sluggish, causing the riverbed to become marshy and unsuitable for irrigation and unhealthy for habitation. Sobaipuri villages were situated adjacent to the fields, generally overlooking them from land that either could not be farmed or that was only suitable for certain forms of dry farming. Quiburi of the 1780s (see chapter 7 for the progression of sites named Quiburi), San Joachín on the Babocomari River, and Wa:k (chapter 4) were all situated near marshes, the first being situated in the midst of one (Ciénega de Quiburi) owing to the dire need for defensive positioning. Three archaeological examples of canal and field systems likely used by the Sobaipuri, but clearly modified later, are present in the area around Guevavi on the Santa Cruz, on the Babocomari near Santa Cruz de Gaybanipitea and Santa Cruz del Pitaitutgam, and at Quiburi on the San Pedro (Seymour 1991c, 2004, 2011a). The system on the San Pedro originates in the Santa Cruz Narrows, which is just south of and upstream from Santa Cruz de Terrenate Presidio and the Quiburi of Kino's time, as well as upstream from a series of Sobaipuri villages that were occupied from the beginning of their occupation of the region. The modern and historic Wa:k community in the Santa Cruz River Valley is surrounded by centuries of irrigation canals.

As shown in figure 1.2, Sobaipuri site distributions and historical clusters of known villages are grouped along certain river segments. Between these

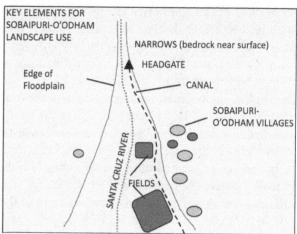

FIGURE 2.4. *Schematic model of use of Sobaipuri riverside landscape, with a narrows where canals water a downstream field with a terrace-top village overlooking it. Figure prepared by Deni Seymour.*

clusters, there are long expanses with no Sobaipuri occupation. The areas with evidence of Sobaipuri settlement conform to the simple rules just outlined that ensured the presence of surface water, protection of canals and head gates, ample fields, and adjacent topographic features for settlement. The areas devoid of occupation correspond to areas with unreliable surface flow.

These attributes of lack of surface water and inappropriate channel characteristics explain long expanses of unsettled land on all the rivers, including the Santa Cruz River between Tumacácori and San Xavier del Bac as well as north of the Tucson/Marana area. While Sobaipuri presence on the Santa Cruz is addressed in detail in chapter 4, it is important to point out here that Sobaipuri settlement is more restricted along this river than on the San Pedro, owing to these river channel characteristics. In fact, the model of Sobaipuri landscape use relative to river channel characteristics explains the general absence of Sobaipuri villages along key portions of the Santa Cruz noted, but heretofore not explained, by Kino on his maps and in his writings (see Seymour 2020a; Seymour and Rodríguez 2020). An illustration of this point is provided by a substantial gap in Sobaipuri settlement north of a small relatively unknown settlement shown as San Martín on the east side of the river in the crease of Kino's *Teatro* map (*Teatro de los trabajos apostólicos de la Comp. de Jesús en la América Septentrional*, 1695–1696) (figure 2.5). Examination of this map illustrates this settlement north of San Cayetano del Tumacácori, but which is not shown again in this location on later maps. No mention of San Martín is made in Kino's letters, reports, or memoir, and no evidence has been found archaeologically (possibly owing to widespread bulldozing and construction activities),

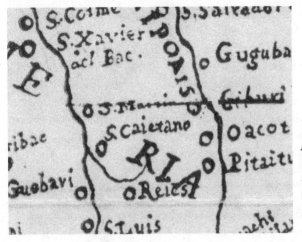

FIGURE 2.5. *Close-up of a portion of Kino's 1696–1697* Saeta Martyrdom *map showing San Martín on the crease, which is the last settlement upstream from San Xavier del Bac.*

yet Kino reports its presence on this map. Shortly thereafter, it seems that the residents of San Martín may have moved to Arivaca, because on Kino's next map San Martín is to the west, farther from the Santa María (Santa Cruz) River, and is called San Martín de Aribac. This change may indicate that this settlement was occupied by O'odham practicing a more mobile existence or perhaps one in which their village location shifted seasonally between the Santa Cruz and Arivaca drainages, as was recorded further north on the Santa Cruz River. The location and character of San Martín have remained a mystery, and because it is not specifically discussed in Kino's writings, this village has not assumed a historically important role in interpretation. Yet, as it turns out, this place is important for understanding Sobaipuri settlement between San Cayetano (del Tumacácori) and San Xavier del Bac.

Early in Kino's time, San Martín was the northernmost settlement on this portion of the Santa Cruz, with a lengthy gap between San Martín and San Xavier del Bac that has not previously been explained. Attributing this absence to a sparse Kino-period Sobaipuri occupation does not seem the most viable explanation. When river channel characteristics are taken into account, settlement distribution here and elsewhere makes more sense. On Kino's map, San Martín is on the east side of the river, a third of the way between San Cayetano (del Tumacacori) and San Xavier del Bac. This would place the village in the general Canoa vicinity (see Burrus 1965:pl. 8 after page 40). The streamflow character in this zone seems to explain the Kino-depicted settlement distributions. Modern-day Canoa was a historical place known by this name in the middle 1770s. It was referenced as a stopover place during the

1775 Juan Bautista de Anza expedition (see Bolton 1930b:6, also see page 211; Coues 1900:63). Both Anza and Padre Pedro Font stated that "we halted at the place which they call La Canoa" (Bolton 1930b:6, also see page 211; Coues 1900:63), which suggests that it had this name for some time. There was a spring here, and it was the last reliable waterhole between this spot and the springs just south of or upstream from San Xavier del Bac. Here, somewhere north or south of the former village of San Martín or Canoa, the river's flow sank underground (except for seasonal flows). On October 28, 1699, Manje mentioned the disappearing water eight leagues (twenty-one to twenty-four miles) north of San Cayetano del Tumacácori, noting:

> we spent the night in the bed of the river which submerges and runs along underneath the sands. At a distance of 8 leagues it comes out again and runs as far as the great ranchería of San Xavier del Bac. (F. Smith et al. 1966:81–82)

This distance is closer to Green Valley and Canoa than it is to Chavez Siding Road and Tubac, where the flow stopped in the later Historic period. The water is therefore unavailable for agricultural exploitation without pumping north of this location. Historically, water for use in fields may have been poured into irrigation troughs using a bucket-and-lift system, as was the case in portions of northern Sonora. Beginning at Elephant Head Road, a fault crosses the riverbed, and, thereafter, water descends underground until it resurfaces just south of Martinez Hill at San Xavier, where bedrock pushes the water to the surface. Being agriculturally oriented, this is the northernmost location where a Sobaipuri settlement could occur that was reliant on irrigation agriculture or, alternatively, where a Tohono O'odham village might relocate seasonally to farm along the riverbanks. This fault line is visible today on Google Earth upriver or south of the modern Canoa community (and just north of Amado), where the riverbed is green with irrigated land to the south (upriver) of Elephant Head Road and dry brown to the north (downstream) until reaching the community of Green Valley (figure 2.6).

The Spanish meaning of the Canoa placename could refer to a watering trough or perhaps even an irrigation flume (as the terms was used at this time to denote a specific type of irrigation feature; figure 2.7). The name may relate to the water being channeled from the small spring or from river flow, which here would still be at or near the surface but to the north or downstream would not be. Alternatively, canals may have been taken off at this last reliable point of river flow, before the water disappeared into the sands, water being funneled to the north (downstream) as well as the south (upstream) of this point via flume structures.

FIGURE 2.6. *Photograph of dividing line between irrigated fields and dry land at the fault along Elephant Head Road near Canoa. Right is to the north. Photograph by Deni Seymour.*

San Cayetano del Tumacácori and then the later Franciscan San José de Tumacácori are along a segment where water was reliably pushed to the surface. Situated against and somewhat parallel to the Santa Cruz channel, the Cayetano Mountains force water closer to the surface, making it available for human use. As Manje noted, San Cayetano del Tumacácori was also situated at a bend in the river, stating that "the land is suitable for planting . . . The town nestles in the half-moon bend of the river lined with shady cottonwoods" (Burrus 1971:251; Seymour 1993a, 2007b, 2011a:52; 2018a). The bend likely being referenced occurs north of and at the downstream end of the Cayetano Mountains.

This understanding of Sobaipuri landscape use as tied to river channel characteristics has been effective in predicting the location of Sobaipuri sites on the San Pedro, Santa Cruz, and Babocomari Rivers, and along Sonoita Creek. Site densities are high enough, development low enough, and research conducted just early enough that many of these sites on the San Pedro and Santa Cruz are still visible in those areas. In other locations, such as along the Babocomari River and Sonoita Creek, fewer settlements were present, so not all suitable residential locations were occupied. Moreover, more intensive modern use and private landownership make locating sites difficult, though much access has

FIGURE 2.7. *(a and b) Traditional-style irrigation flume or canoa near Las Trampas, New Mexico, with hollowed-out logs spanning the arroyo to convey water from one side to the other. Photographs by Deni Seymour.*

been granted and substantial progress has been made through the years identifying where these sites are not located, along with pinpointing the locations of a few villages. This model of village distribution can also be used to understand Kino's statements regarding Sobaipuri settlements along the Gila River and to predict where sites are located (see chapter 3).

When Sobaipuri settlements moved, every ten to thirty years or so, movements tended to be confined to a portion of the river segment that already had infrastructural improvements. While the Sobaipuri moved their villages up and down the river segments, sometimes shifting to the opposite bank of the river, they tended to remain within a particular segment. This meant that village movement occurred over a short distance and was dependent on the nature of the adjacent landforms and also on the course of the river. These shifts probably occurred as village populations grew too large to sustain all residents on adjacent farming lands, as social tensions rose, as the channel shifted, to allow fields to fallow, as segments of the river became dry, and as political stresses increased between groups (Seymour 2011a). All of these reasons are provided in the ethnohistoric record, and the variety of reasons explains the complexity of Sobaipuri settlement patterns. This pattern of movement by a sedentary population has confounded historians and archaeologists in their interpretations of Sobaipuri landscape use (as discussed in chapter 11).

The Sobaipuri also tended to occupy landforms that allowed them to live without fear that their homes would be flooded. These locations also doubled in their value as protection from the enemy. These settlement locations included the terraces above the river and low hills. A few settlements were on the floodplain, or at least on the older portion of the abandoned floodplain where normal river flows would not flood the village for the term of occupation. Villages may have shifted to these lower floodplain locations during drought periods because during high-flow periods these floodplain zones might have been inundated. Like people today, during extended periods of low flow the Sobaipuri probably had a short-term memory about the course of the river during nondrought years and the destruction possible during flood periods, thereby inhabiting areas that in higher-flow years would be inundated.

EXCEPTIONS TO THE RULES

Most Sobaipuri habitation sites known are along the major rivers (San Pedro, Santa Cruz, Babocomari, Sonoita Creek, and Aravaipa). There are exceptions to these distributions, and as is often the case these exceptions are in some ways the most interesting and those that prove the rule. Variations in this landscape use model relate to specific factors, including efforts to protect villages and activities from enemies, such as the Jocome and Apache, and from missionaries when viewed as hostile to O'odham traditional practices and religion. The earliest-known archaeological exceptions are the settlements documented in the foothills of the Santa Rita Mountains. These seem to be (a) seasonal hunting-gathering sites, (b) ceremonial locations, or (c) places of refuge noted in documentary sources where Pima (O'odham) went attempting to escape from missionaries or soldiers, either to carry out traditional ceremonies or to flee after hearing a frightening rumor (Kessell 1970:55, 57, 90–91; Treutlein 1945:156, 164; Wyllys 1931). There are ample descriptions of O'odham, including the Sobaipuri, fleeing mission settlements to avoid punishment, attack, or perceived retaliation. They also went to these locations to carry out ceremonies out of the view of the priests and during uprisings, as noted by Padre Felipe Segesser in 1737:

> Nocturnal dances are the reason for the many sorcerers. Indians take their children to these dances so that they see and hear with better opportunity what no eye should see and no ear should hear . . . They told me that if I forbade dancing they would return to their wilds where they could dance undisturbed. (Treutlein 1945:156, 157).
>
> On another occasion I wrote how at Guebavi the Pimas deserted me all at once, drove away horses and cattle, and left me alone with a boy who was too little to flee with them . . . The cause of this unrest was a false report given out by some uneasy Spaniards who wanted to frighten the Pimas. They alleged that Captain Don Juan de Ansa would come and slaughter all Pimas. Nothing more was needed completely to confound the Pimas of Pimería Alta and to cause them to flee to the mountains. (Treutlein 1945:164)

Use of outlying locations for traditional ceremonies occurred at San Xavier as well, where during the Franciscan period and within memory of modern Wa:k, resident families would travel first just south of the community and then later to the far southwestern corner of the district to conduct ceremonies in private. Stories linger about the maltreatment of medicine people. These types of areas were probably used during the late 1700s and early 1800s, when the defensive O'odham village of adobe-walled row houses occupied the plaza in front of the church requiring that non-Christian ceremonies be carried out in secret at some distance from the village (Seymour 2019b). A bit earlier, Segesser disapprovingly described seeing ceremonial features at Wa:k (Treutlein 1945:156), indicating that even then the ceremonial areas may have been separated from the view of intrusive outsiders:

When I was at San Xavier del Bac I took a walk with an Indian. We happened upon a place where the Indians had held a nocturnal dance. The place was full of circles, like a labyrinth, and my guide showed me, upon my inquiry, the spot where the devil in very terrible shape entered the circle, the Indians or Pimas then having to follow him into it. He also showed me where the devil again stepped out of the circle. I well perceived the great harm done by these nocturnal dances, but could not forbid everything lest the people flee into the mountains and wilderness.

The Santa Rita Mountain nonriverine sites are unusual in that they are some of the few O'odham habitation sites dating to the Colonial period (1691 through 1800) that are situated away from the river. The three Santa Rita sites have especially low artifact frequencies as compared to those found in riverine locations, but like their riverside counterparts, these too are situated on elevated landforms overlooking arroyos and are near springs.

Most archaeological surveys for Sobaipuri sites have occurred along the rivers, and so it is not surprising that few sites have been found in the hinterlands and foothills. However, I have conducted considerable survey in the foothills, mountains, and bajadas looking both for Sobaipuri and mobile group sites (Apache and Jocome) and have yet to encounter a Sobaipuri habitation site in these areas. The only other known example is represented by the residential loci found in Pima Canyon. Most of these are late dating with organic-tempered pottery and other historic artifacts suggesting a late 1800s date and seemingly represent seasonal gathering locations. Chronometric results on a Whetstone Plain sherd from a traditional style structure at Pima Canyon produced a date with a minimum age of 1820±20 (UW3455). Other such villages are expected in the mountains bordering the Avra Valley, where O'odham are known to have gone during the 1751 O'odham Revolt. Other O'odham from Guevavi and Tumacácori went to the northern portion of the San Pedro in the area of Tres Alamos when fleeing during the Pima Revolt, but these villages were situated along the margins of the San Pedro, as archaeological site distributions and chronometric dates indicate (chapter 10; Seymour and Sugnet 2016). Rock art sites away from the river are known in a number of places, but much work remains to be done to determine which elements are O'odham, and specifically Sobaipuri, rather than some other contemporaneous group.

Settlement patterns for some river-dwelling O'odham also changed in the late 1700s as a result of increased pressure from the Apache. Documentary evidence from the Gila River mentions movement of settlements away from the main river channel area to more defensible zones. During the 1775–1776 Anza expedition, Padre Font mentioned an interesting settlement shift along the Gila at La Encarnacion de Sutaquison (Bolton 1930a:46). This is the location along a stretch of the river formerly occupied by the Sobaipuri, and so these residents would presumably be Sobaipuri descendants (see chapter 3). Font mentioned why the settlement was placed so far from the river:

> The Indians were asked why they lived so far from the river, since formerly they had their pueblo on the banks, whereas now they had moved it to a place apart. They replied that they changed the site because near the river, with its trees and brush, they fared badly from the Apaches, but now being far away they had open country through which to follow and kill the Apaches when they came to their pueblo. (Bolton 1930a:46)

Major river courses were travel routes, not only for the Spaniards but also for Indigenous groups, as they had been for centuries. Villages in lower-lying areas along these routes had proven indefensible as animosities with mobile neighbors increased and O'odham population densities decreased. Thus, the age-old pattern of landscape use on somewhat raised landforms adjacent to the rivers, near their fields and water, was abandoned in some areas in favor of wider, more open, and therefore defensible locations that had longer views and that were remote from the key travel routes along the rivers.

Prior to this period, Sobaipuri along the San Pedro moved from riverside terraces to hills that had steeper sides and where views were not obscured by vegetation. This seems to be the case for the residents of Santa Cruz del Pitaitutgam, who, after their village was attacked, moved to Santa Cruz de Gaybanipitea, which was situated on a higher landform (Seymour 2014). When this repositioning proved ineffective, and the Sobaipuri were attacked in the famous 1698 battle, residents temporarily shifted their village to the Sonoita Valley to the west to avoid direct confrontation and inadvertent contact with the enemy. Selection of steep terrain was one option that continued to be open to these San Pedro Sobaipuri, and when Santa Cruz de Gaybanipitea's residents returned they inhabited the place that would later be the site of the Santa Cruz de Terrenate Presidio, while residents of Quiburi who returned occupied a village somewhat further north (chapter 8, this volume; also see chapters 7, 8, and 11).

The latest Sobaipuri settlement known from historical accounts on the San Pedro, Quiburi of the 1780s, was on a steep-sloped hill surrounded by a marsh for protection (see chapter 8).[2] This is one of two known instances where a Sobaipuri village was located at a marsh. The other is along the Babocomari River, where at least one of the settlements overlooks the marsh upstream from the constriction that forced the water to the surface.

TERRITORIAL BOUNDARIES

Many researchers think of the Sobaipuri as residing initially only in the San Pedro Valley, a misimpression that comes not only from Father Juan Nentvig's *Rudo Ensayo* (see Nentvig 1764, 1863; Pradeau and Rasmussen 1980) but also from the fact that this river was once referenced as the Valley of the Sobaipuris and River of the Sobaipuris (see Kinnaird 1958), whereas other river valleys were not (see Seymour and Rodríguez 2020; Seymour and Stewart 2017). Yet, as has become clear, the Sobaipuri occupation was much broader and encompassed all the key river valleys with reliable running water in southeastern Arizona. We also tend to think of the San Pedro River Valley as the eastern edge of Piman or O'odham territory. Yet once again, this impression is inaccurate. Nor was the San Pedro the western edge of Jocome or Apache territory, as early evidence of both groups is found much further west, including in Ventana Cave and Nuestra Señora de la Merced del Batki village, respectively. Territories were not exclusive, and each of these groups mentioned lived in and traveled through territories often viewed today as that of another group. They tended to use different niches, which meant that their residences were often in different environmental and geographic zones (see Seymour 2012b). Even so, Jocome and Apache residential sites are found along the San Pedro (and other rivers; Seymour 2016a), and as just noted, Sobaipuri residential locales, as well as hunting-and-gathering camps, sometimes occurred in the foothills and mountains and other nonriverine zones.

An important distinction is to discern when a site was occupied by the Sobaipuri as opposed to just their pottery being present. Whetstone Plain (most characteristic of the Sobaipuri) and organic-tempered plainwares and redwares, made by the Sobaipuri at various times, are present at Whitlock Cienega (AZ CC:7:9, ASM), which is at the northern end of the San Simon Valley, in an area far outside that recognized for the Sobaipuri. These wares may be present because this area was along a well-used trail for trade and probably also for raiding and was close to a reliable seasonal water source. More pertinent to this case, however, is that the ruins of an old ranch and stage station are located nearby, suggesting that these items were tradewares made for use by non-O'odham residents. Nineteenth-century organic-tempered wares are known from as far east as the Sapir, New Mexico (James Ayres, personal communication, 2007), and probably result from movement down the railroad as utility wares for the regional non-Indigenous market.

On the other hand, there is historical evidence of Piman interest in, travel through, and use of valleys to the east of the San Pedro. This might be surprising because Kino noted the San Pedro as the Pimas' territorial boundary when he stated that they went "down the Rio de Quiburi, to the last Sobaipuris of the northeast" (Bolton 1948:I:168). But there is evidence of a much more expansive distribution, even during Kino's time. In one instance there is evidence of what were implied to be Sobaipuri living in an eastern valley. In 1697 Lieutenant Cristóbal Martín Bernal, who had accompanied Kino and Manje on a journey down the San Pedro, noted: "A Captain arrived who lives in the eastern part in another valley called Babitcoida, bringing with him 71 men without arms and 31 women and some boys to render obedience to me" (F. Smith et al. 1966:39). Manje also mentioned the presence of this headman, presumably Sobaipuri, arriving late in the afternoon at Ojío with people from "two settlements called Busac and Tubo, located on a small creek which runs from the east and joins the river" (Karns 1954:83). This reference clearly places Sobaipuri residences in a valley east of the San Pedro, likely the east end of Aravaipa Creek or somewhere in the Klondyke Valley. During the 1795 José de Zúñiga campaign, there was also mention of a Pima Canyon in one of the ranges east of the San Pedro (Hammond 1931:62), presumably north of the San Simon or Sulphur Springs Valley and probably south of the Gila River. This canyon may have been in the Pinaleño or Santa Teresa Mountains or may represent the north end of the Klondyke Valley where Aravaipa Creek ends. Further research may reveal more about this location.

Along these lines, it is probable that Pima origin stories relate to this area east of the San Pedro. A Pima origin story recorded by ethnographer Underhill (1969:11) states that the Pima originated in an alkali flat east of their territory: "They emerged at a placed called Smooth Ground, an alkali plain at the extreme east of the present Papagueria, near Benson." Where this is has been lost to history, written and oral, but there are several hints as to where at least some O'odham might have conceived this place as being. Historically there was a canyon (as just noted) and a playa named after the Pima in the Sulphur Springs Valley. While the history is vague, it is worth reconstructing what is known so that more may be found. Willcox Playa was historically referenced as Playa de los Pimas. Will Barnes ([1935] 1982:57) stated that in 1854 Lieutenant John G. Parke named Willcox Playa "Playa de los Pimas." Yet the name had already been applied by 1834, when Manuel Escalante, governor of Sonora, wrote of a campaign against the Apache (McCarty 1997:44, 46). Even earlier, when Captain José de Zúñiga campaigned into the Gila region in the spring of 1795 he referenced the "Playa de los Pimas" (Hammond 1931:54). How much earlier the name was applied to this location is as yet unknown, but future research may reveal an even earlier reference to Playa de los Pimas. It is intriguing to consider that this might have been the mythological alkali flat where the Pima are said to originate.

The Sobaipuri were also a bit more widespread along the rivers than many people think. Chapter 3 discusses information suggesting that at least in Kino's view, the Sobaipuri also lived along a short segment of the Gila River. Chapter 4 discusses their distribution along the Santa Cruz, and chapter 5 examines three villages at the headwaters of the San Pedro that were Piman, and perhaps Sobaipuri. From an archaeological perspective, we can only document the distribution and character of sites and from this work draw inferences regarding identity, as noted in historical documents and ethnographies, and as correlated to material culture characteristics (pottery, points, housing characteristics, and layout). Much work along these lines remains to be done in the areas at the margins of Sobaipuri territory.

RANCHERÍAS AND DEFENSIVE VILLAGES

Archaeological research has shown that Sobaipuri village layout is very different from that recorded for O'odham groups historically and also differs from that of their prehistoric predecessors. Village layout is uniquely Sobaipuri beginning with the earliest sites recorded and does not conform to the widely held notion of the *ranchería*. Site layout changed through time both as a result of Apache attacks and probably of attacks from rebellious O'odham, a change that is clearly seen in the late 1700s at Guevavi and noted in Rocha y Figueroa's 1780 diary for Tumacácori and San Xavier (see a little later in this section; see Seymour 2019b; Seymour and Rodríguez 2020:104, 105).

The term *ranchería*, as used in the Spanish documentary record of northwestern New Spain, is generally conceived of as a scattered accumulation of houses (or *ranchos*), in contrast to the aggregated *pueblo* (village). One of the many implications of this term *ranchería* is that the structures comprising these settlements were widely spaced. Structures included in a single settlement were thought to have been distributed across the terrain with considerable open space between them. For example, Edward Spicer ([1962] 1981:12) suggested that "houses were scattered as much as a half mile apart" (also see Ezell 1961:113). This authoritative position provided a rational basis for erroneously inferring that site distributions initially encountered on the upper San Pedro in the 1980s and 1990s were a tangible representation of this model, especially when coupled with the assumption of a shallow time depth, then thought to be limited to the late 1600s and a portion of the 1700s until their supposed removal in 1762 (but see Seymour 2011c). Documentary data from mid-eighteenth-century Sonora reinforced this notion of the sprawling ranchería, when Father Joseph Och indicated that "they generally erect their houses so far apart from each other that the padre had to do much running and perspiring" (Treutlein 1965:151–152).

Yet, despite use of the term in the historical record, archaeological data demonstrate that this model is inappropriate for the Sobaipuri, while still applicable for the Tohono O'odham (or "Papago" of the time) and other western O'odham. The numerous spatially discrete Sobaipuri archaeological sites encountered on survey in the mid-1980s I initially thought might represent segments of a larger widely dispersed ranchería.[3] This visualization was used initially to account for the unexpectedly large number of Sobaipuri archaeological sites in an area where Kino-period historical records indicated to Di Peso that there were only two (or six if the varying locations and movement of some settlements were considered; Seymour 1989, 1993; see chapter 7). Yet, this view held by Di Peso, myself, and others at the time rested on a diachronically shallow perspective wherein the Kino-period documents were given undue weight, as they continue to be, when characterizing Indigenous populations.[4] Consideration of earlier chronicles and collection of chronometric dates from sites along this and other rivers indicate a substantial presence from as early as the late thirteenth century (e.g., AD 1280) that diminishes in scale by Kino's time, contracting down to two villages on the middle San Pedro by the late 1690s (Seymour 2007c, 2009b, 2011a). It is now clear that the numerous sites along the river represent temporally discrete and substantial village occupations beginning in the late AD 1200s, not scattered loci within a single ranchería.

The archaeological record reveals that the Spicer model of the idealized ranchería-type settlement is incorrect for this area and for the Sobaipuri in general and that it contrasts with what is reflected in on-the-ground archaeological evidence. First, Sobaipuri sites are more compact than the ranchería model allows. Moreover, clear site boundaries are demarcated on the ground that often correspond to topographic divisions. Further, settlements are spatially separated from other contemporaneous settlements, and considerable open space occurs between archaeological sites that differentiate distinct settlements.

The Spanish conception of "scattered" and "far apart" is different from our own, each being a relative term that is now corroborated by archaeological data. Different regions may also have had different patterns of landscape use, which, when considered, allow for contrasts between areas and a more accurate view of the Sobaipuri compared to other Piman groups.

Most Sobaipuri scholars of the past were of the impression that Sobaipuri houses were freestanding single constructions without order or plan in placement (see Masse 1981; Seymour 2011a). Again, archaeological data obtained over the last couple of decades show that this perception is also incorrect. All Sobaipuri houses, on the over 110 sites I have recorded with a subset excavated, are paired, though only one in each pairing may be currently visible on the surface. In such pairings, one house seems to have been a general-use structure or dwelling, while the second is usually devoid of features inside and out and often smaller, seemingly to have been used for storage. The dwelling unit usually has a fire area inside and out, along with predictably situated work areas indoors and out (Seymour 2007b, 2009d, 2011a, 2011b).

Archaeological data suggest that a Sobaipuri settlement, really a village rather than a ranchería, is a localized occupation of one or several households in a clustered arrangement. Rather than being scattered willy-nilly across the terrain, houses are arranged in an orderly fashion in spatially discrete clusters that formed distinct and organized settlements. In addition to being paired, houses are arranged in rows, and on larger sites they are often arranged in two parallel rows, as at Santa Cruz de Gaybanipitea, and sometimes in multiple stacked parallel rows as at Santa Cruz del Pitaitutgam. The arrangement depended in part of landform shape and the size and temporal depth of occupation (Seymour 2011a).

The unique Sobaipuri layout of paired structures continued through time and was in evidence for seven centuries, but the pattern exhibited sometimes varied between drainages. For example, paired houses are side by side or end to end in sites along the San Pedro and Santa Cruz Rivers (rows two and three in figure 2.8). Yet along Sonoita Creek a different pattern is visible, with paired structures slightly offset from one another, in essence, combining the end-to-end and side-by-side pattern (row three in figure 2.8). These differences may indicate ethnic differences between drainages or at least distinct populations whose isolation from one other led to the development of valley-specific practices (Seymour 2015a; also see discussion of ethnicity in Seymour 2011a). It is also possible that fewer suitable and smaller landforms in the Sonoita Valley required a modification to the normal end-to-end or side-by-side layout with more space between structures exhibited in other valleys.

Moreover, the spacing between structures within and between households varied considerably through time. From the AD 1200s though the mid-1700s or so, paired houses are a couple of meters to five meters apart with about double the distance between the pairs of one household and another household. Yet by the late 1700s defense became paramount, and as such there is a corresponding change in spacing in some of the latest occupations at Guevavi (figure 2.9). There paired structures were spaced between fifty centimeters and a meter apart with adjacent households mostly less than double the distance.

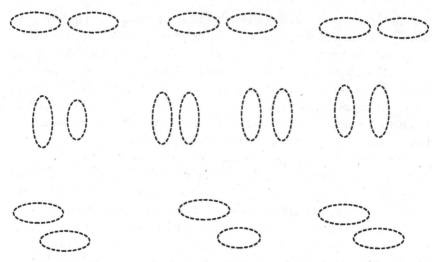

FIGURE 2.8. *Various layouts of houses at Sobaipuri villages. So far, the configuration in the bottom row is unique to Sonoita Creek. Figure prepared by Deni Seymour.*

In 1780 the engineer Rocha y Figueroa described similar patterns for San Xavier (figure 2.10) and Tumacácori (2.11), describing them as follows:

> The said San Xavier forms a square shape with its own houses, and it only lacks a few small gates to be entirely enclosed. In the four corners are a kind of towers with rounded gun holes. (Seymour and Rodríguez 2020:105; also see Seymour 2019b)
>
> Tumacacori Pueblo is almost surrounded by a wall in a quadrilateral shape to which are being added several small houses so that they may live in greater security [within]. (Seymour and Rodríguez 2020:104)

The consistency of layout for hundreds of years before this period suggests that by the late 1700s conditions had deteriorated in this region to the point where such spacing concessions were required for survival in the face of excessive violence from hostile groups. Soon after these changes at Guevavi, the residents moved to larger settlements and eventually all moved to the largest villages, where these new fortified layouts ensured some degree of defensibility.

These original patterns of house layout and landscape use are distinctive for the Sobaipuri, who were river dwellers, who were fully reliant on agriculture, and who constructed extensive canal and field systems that supported their sizable populations. When in 1539 Marcos de Niza came through one of these valleys, he commented that it was all "irrigated and is like an evergreen garden"

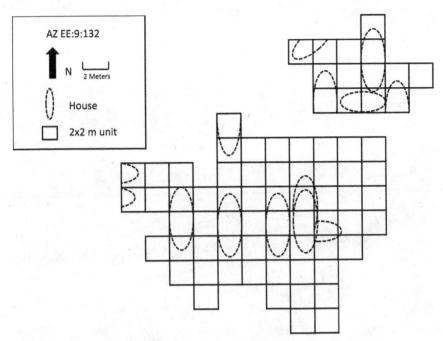

FIGURE 2.9. *Excavation units (2×2 m) in one portion of Guevavi showing house orientations, layouts, and overlap. Figure prepared by Deni Seymour.*

FIGURE 2.10. *Adobe-walled and wattle-and-daub houses formed a square at San Xavier del Bac between 1780 and the early 1800s to aid in defense. William Alexander Bell's photograph from December 2, 1867, facing west northwest. One of the two earliest-known photographs of the village and church.*

FIGURE 2.11. *Adobe-walled housing was placed inside an exterior adobe defensive wall at San José de Tumacácori as illustrated in the mid-1800s. This figure by James Mann shows the backs of houses forming the wall. Courtesy of National Park Service–Department of the Interior.*

(Flint and Flint 2005:72), which was an apt description of these lands tended and held by the Sobaipuri O'odham (see Seymour 2011a, 2017a).

All of these basic factors influenced where the Sobaipuri settled and how their villages were distributed and arranged on the landscape. Because they occupied the Sonoran and Chihuahuan deserts, they were dependent on the river valleys—the green bands—to provide water for irrigation and other life's needs. Through time, some of their settlement locations and house arrangements changed to accommodate the ever-present stress of enemies and nature. Some of these modifications and shifts can be seen in the archaeological record, proving tangible evidence of the ways in which the Sobaipuri adapted to their natural and political environments through time.

NOTES

1. There is also a constriction and therefore surface flow at Cottonwood Spring north of where a second set of Sobaipuri sites cluster (see chapter 6).

2. Archaeological research has identified Sobaipuri settlements on the San Pedro that date to much later in time, when historical accounts consider the location to have been abandoned by them (see Seymour 2011a).

3. In archaeology it is common to distinguish between the archaeological context (the site) and the behavioral or systemic context in which people lived (the settlement or village). Use of this dichotomy helps avoid confusion when switching back and forth between the archaeological record, on the one hand, and the documentary and ethnographic records, on the other.

4. Reliance on Kino-period documents at the exclusion of others is common practice among O'odham scholars because it has been believed that Francisco Vázquez de Coronado was the first to mention populations in the area and either did not mention the Sobaipuri or described them as "poor Indians" offering wild plant foods to the visitors. Stepping further back in time, we see that in fact Marcos de Niza's 1539 chronicle describes an entirely different demographic and organizational view of the Sobaipuri, and now with new archaeological evidence we see that Vázquez de Coronado was also describing the Sobaipuri O'odham.

3

https://doi.org/10.5876/9781646422975.c003

Documentary Clarification of the Gila River Sobaipuri Pima in Kino's Time

Considerable uncertainty has surrounded the issue as to whether the Sobaipuri O'odham resided along the middle Gila River when Jesuit Father Kino first visited them in the 1690s (see figure 1.1).[1] Many scholars cite the movement of Sobaipuri to the Gila in the first half of the eighteenth century, perhaps when some of the Sobaipuri left the lower San Pedro (Hackenberg 1974a:122; Spicer [1962] 1981:127, 146; Wilson 1999:42, 51). Some suggest Sobaipuri from the middle San Pedro migrated there after 1762, when the Spanish required that they move from the middle San Pedro (Ezell 1961:21), but no evidence is provided to support this move to the Gila in the materials referenced (also see Seymour 2011a). In fact, other places are mentioned in the record that received the subset of inhabitants that left in 1762 (e.g., Tucson, Santa María Suamca, and Sonoita; Officer 1987:40). Even earlier, Father Jacobo Sedelmayr complained that in 1747 "a number of whites, Indians, and apostates retired from our mission [Tubatama in Sonora] to the Gila River" (Matson and Fontana 1996:12; Wilson 1999:47), but the Sobaipuri were not likely among them. Others cite an augmentation of the Gila River populations with Sobaipuri migrants in 1770, and in doing so they reference a letter from Juan Bautista de Anza that discusses concern about an impending Sobaipuri movement from San Xavier del Bac on the middle Santa Cruz to the Gila, and the fact that three families had already left (Anza 1770:120; Dobyns 1959, 1976:31; Ezell 1955:2; Kessell

1976:56; Officer 1987:48; Wilson 1999:10, 51, 52). Available documentary evidence does not divulge whether they moved in 1770, because discussion indicates an attempt to intercept them and so suggests they did not move.[2] Even so, these sources indicate that movement to the Gila (and other areas remote from Spanish settlement) was a viable option for the Sobaipuri then and at other times. Movement away from areas with relatively heavy populations and desired by the Spanish was one of multiple alternatives available to the Sobaipuri in an effort to adjust to the Spanish incursion, their takeover of waterholes and prime land, and the resulting conflicts. The Sobaipuri were intensive farmers, so the lands they needed were also those coveted by and often the first taken over by the Spaniards. As part of their mode of accommodating, in some cases, the Sobaipuri moved. They could not move away from the rivers, because farming was their lifeway, and thus they still practiced intensive agriculture; consequently, for those on the Santa Cruz and areas to the south the option was to move to the Gila, San Pedro, Sonoita Creek, or the Babocomari River, where European population levels along the rivers were low. The San Pedro remained a place of refuge from Europeans through time owing to the danger because of its position in relation to enemy populations of Jocome and Apache that kept Europeans further west and south. Yet, Sobaipuri populations stayed there when everyone thought they had moved, and some groups spread there anew when conflict arose with Europeans, such as during the 1751 Pima Revolt (see chapter 10; also Seymour 2011c). By the 1800s, once the Apache had become their enemies and Sobaipuri population levels had dropped, moving into such remote areas was no longer an option.

The *Rudo Ensayo*, written by Father Juan Nentvig in 1764, places the Sobaipuri ancestral home only along the San Pedro, but this document is known to contain errors and misimpressions, and there is clear evidence (including archaeological) that the Sobaipuri also lived all along the upper and middle Santa Cruz, Sonoita Creek, Aravaipa Creek, and the Babocomari River during, after, and prior to Kino's times (Pradeau and Rasmussen 1980; Seymour 1990, 1991, 1992, 1993a, 1993b, 1993c, 2011b; Seymour and Sugnet 2016).

But when Kino first arrived and during subsequent trips to the Gila River, did Kino encounter Sobaipuri and, if so, where? The answer is important because the issue of Sobaipuri on the Gila serves as a baseline for understanding this period from which other inferences may be drawn. Kino's reference to Sobaipuri on the Gila is one example considered, and sometimes cited, by scholars who suggest that the Sobaipuri designation is applied indiscriminately by these early Europeans or that there was general confusion about group identity. Yet, other Pimans, including those along the Gila and Salt

Rivers, and the Tohono O'odham, viewed the Sobaipuri as distinctive, calling them, respectively, "Spotted People," "Jackrabbit Eaters," and "Being Like Apaches/Enemies" (see Seymour 2011a, 2014:47, 2017a). Descendants, such as at the Wa:k community (San Xavier del Bac) where many Sobaipuri initially resided and ultimately congregated, also view themselves as distinctive. As noted in chapter 1, one of the last either self-identified Sobaipuri woman (or identified as such by outsiders) Carnacion lamented the fact that other community members who came from the desert West made fun of her when she discussed the Sobaipuri because the differences were so substantial that others did not believe her (Oblasser 1931:98). Consequently, even though Kino and others did not specifically state what made the Sobaipuri distinctive from other O'odham, the prevailing evidence suggests that they were in fact so. Their agricultural way of life, using irrigation canals, made them distinctive from others in the region along with other attributes. This aspect of their adaptation and their name indicate that this ethnic group was defined in part on the basis of their position relative to the enemy and their status as the best warriors. Being along the river meant that they occupied the most desirable land and its resources and therefore they would have had to protect them, thereby becoming successful and formidable warriors. My research with the modern Wa:k O'odham, descendants of the Sobaipuri, indicates that there were many other differences as well, such as dialect, mannerisms, the way houses were built, and so on.

One thing that seems apparent is that among the O'odham the term "Sobaipuri" referenced the condition of being on the border with the enemy, with taking on characteristics of and being like the enemy. Then enemies were many, but later the term *o:bi*, or enemy, became synonymous with the Apache. *O:bi* is the basis for the *obai* in the term "*Sobai*puri." Thus, at least initially the name "Sobaipuri" referenced a condition or circumstance (perhaps its resulting behavioral modifications), rather than (or perhaps in addition to) an ethnicity or way of making a living (e.g., farmer) (Seymour 2014, 2017a). As one O'odham recently noted, those positioned on the southwest, bordering the Yaqui/Yoeme and the Seri/Comcaac were also called in the local dialect a version of Sobaipuri (Morning Light, personal communication, 2018). Thus, it might not be surprising that the people to the north, along the Gila who bordered other enemies might also be called Sobaipuri. Whether or not they were the same ethnic group or even the same population that had shifted to that location is another question, because Spanish records do not seem to convey this nuance in use of the term, but rather they apparently assumed it was (or adopted it as) an ethnic identifier. Yet, in a few important instances Europeans captured, perhaps inadvertently, what it meant. For example, Nentvig commented: "The most battle-hardened of all the Pimas are commonly called Sobaipuris for having been born and raised on the border of the Apaches" (Nentvig, in B. Smith 1863:105). Whether he understood this description as the basis for the name or only as the character of a people called Sobaipuri is not known. Notably, however, this observation highlights that concurrently there are different ways of categorizing others and ourselves depending on the issue at hand or point of concern and perspective.

A review of the available documentary evidence does show that when Kino traveled north in the 1690s, he noted the presence of a Piman group he referenced as Sobaipuri on a portion of the Gila. Based on these few passages, Bolton ([1936] 1960:247) describes Sobaipuri distributions during the Kino period as follows:

> Of the Sobaípuris there were three groups: one living all down the San Pedro River northward from the vicinity of Fairbank; another on the middle Santa Cruz between San Xavier del Bac and Picacho;[3] a third on the Gila River from the Casa Grande westward nearly to the Bend of Gila River. These last, then called the Gila Pimas, occupied a region corresponding to the present day Pima Reservation.

In this summary Bolton equates the modern term "Gila Pima" with that of the Sobaipuri, designating as Sobaipuri territory much of the length of the middle Gila where the Gila Pima were noted. At the same time Bolton excludes much of the eastern portion of their territory along the Gila, where Kino actually placed the Sobaipuri. Elsewhere, when Bolton describes the distributions of various Upper Piman groups, he again incorrectly states that all the Gila Pima were referred to frequently as Sobaipuri: "The Gila Pimas, because they are the ones best known to modern ethnologists, are now designated as the 'Pimas proper.' But in Kino's day they were frequently listed as Sobaípuris, or Soba y Jípuris (Bolton [1936] 1960:248n2)." Because of these statements by Bolton, many subsequent scholars have also assumed, seemingly incorrectly, that all the Gila Pima were Sobaipuri:

> Kino referred to Indians living along the San Pedro River from Fairbank northward, those of the Santa Cruz River between San Xavier and Picacho, and those on the Gila River from Casa Grande to Gila Bend, as Sobaipuri, *Rim*, p. 247. (F. Smith et al. 1966:13n42)

Proceeding with this same misunderstanding about all the Gila Pima being Sobaipuri, Hackenberg (1974b:100, 116–126) and John P. Wilson (1999:24) have stated that the Sobaipuri and Gila River Pima were not distinguished from one another by the Spanish during the Kino period: "Differentiation occurred through the divergent courses of events which befell the two groups in the Eighteenth Century" (Hackenberg 1974b:124; Seymour 2011a:19–20n5). They cite a statement by Kino when at Casa Grande which places the Sobaipuri on the Gila River (see the section "Documentary Data: Sobaipuri on the Gila"), and from this both authors assume that all Pima occupants along the Gila River were Sobaipuri. Yet, early Kino documents occasionally make distinctions between the Sobaipuri and other Pima on the Gila, suggesting that our view of these divisions understood by these Europeans needs revision.

Rather than all the middle Gila River Pima being Sobaipuri, as Bolton and these authors suggest, and rather than being a late division of groups, as Hackenberg and Wilson propose, a review of the original documents reveals a different distribution.[4] These sources make it clear that in contrast to Bolton's claim, the Gila Pima (or all the Pima along the Gila) were not *frequently* listed as Sobaipuris by Kino or his companions. In fact, in his longest work, *Favores Celestiales* (Kino 1698a), there are only three references by Kino to the Sobaipuri residents of the Gila River; and his military companions refer to people simply as Pima. Nor does Kino refer to all the Gila Pima as Sobaipuri, but rather he occasionally mentions those specifically around Casa Grande and to the east (upstream) along the Gila as being Sobaipuri. Those to the west (downstream) were references only as generic Pima.

Not all Pima residing along the Gila, especially those along its western or downstream reaches, lived there full time or practiced irrigation agriculture. This statement is consistent with my (Seymour 2011a) and others' (Loendorf and Rice's 2004:59; Wells 2006:22–24) notion that there were many different O'odham subgroups during the Historic period. Thus, the just proposed division would also potentially address or at least rephrase the question as to whether the early historic Gila River Pimas were irrigation farmers (Hackenberg 1983:165; Winter 1973:69), especially if the Pima to the west were seasonally mobile and part-time farmers, while those to the east were full-time farmers. Kino's maps also seem to reflect this distinction between Sobaipuri (seemingly farmers who were more formally organized) and a more generalized and at least partly mobile Pima (though not Pima proper, e.g., Bolton), along with a retraction of Sobaipuri territory from the Gila in the mid-1690s or early 1700s.[5] Indeed, Kino's Sobaipuri seem to represent what he perceived as (or perhaps was told was) an ethnic distinction within the Piman subdivision based on a more intensive form of organization required by irrigation farming and a warrior society; after all, these are often the types of things that form the underlying basis for ethnic divisions within societies. Clearly, however, distributions changed quickly within recorded history, or at least more quickly than the slowly produced historical documents.

As will be discussed further in the section "Clarification," the distribution of settlements referred to as Sobaipuri is in the Casa Grande (Blackwater Village area) area as well as to the east, a little downstream of the Gila–San Pedro confluence. This distribution presents a scenario that has the Sobaipuri occupying an eastern portion of the middle Gila River for a time, with other Piman groups (undistinguished from one another in Kino's writings by local name or more specific ethnicity) occupying the western portion of the Gila from west of San Andrés to about the big bend of the Gila River (Gila Bend). Thereafter, mixed settlements of Pima and Cocomaricopa (Maricopa/Piipaash, and presumably also various Pai groups) were noted before leaving Piman territory when traveling downstream to the west. Such a reconstruction of more than one O'odham ethnic group occupying different stretches of the Gila would explain Kino's vague reference to these western groups simply as Pima. It also accounts for variations in village sizes, subsistence pursuits, and village placement between and within the areas.

DOCUMENTARY DATA: SOBAIPURI ON THE GILA

To evaluate this issue, we must examine all period-specific text references to the Gila, isolating those that are specifically relevant. In Kino's first statement (1697) about Sobaipuri on the Gila (not his first trip to the Gila, which was in 1694), his exploration party was at Casa Grande, just south of the Gila River, after they had left the San Pedro and were heading west. The relevant portion of Kino's statement is "Pues ay mui serca seis o siete rancherías de Pimas Sobaipuris" (There are nearby six or seven rancherías of Pimas Sobaipuris; Bolton 1948:I:172; from original microfilm; author's translation.) This statement suggests that in all likelihood, Sobaipuri resided along the Gila given that the Sobaipuri were farmers, though Kino just placed them in the general area, not along the river specifically.[6]

The presence of Sobaipuris in settlements along the Gila River seems apparent also in a second passage by Kino from 1699. He stated:

> The captain of San Cayetano and the governor and twelve or thirteen other justices of the interior came to this pueblo of Nuestra Senora de los Dolores, *saying to me that Captain Humaric and the other Sobaipuris, of La Encarnacion and of San Andres* . . . (emphasis added; author's translation; also see Bolton 1948:I:202)

In this he clearly identified two of the largest Gila River settlements as Sobaipuri ("diciéndome que el capitán Humaric y los demás Sobaipuris de la Encarnación y de San Andrés"; from original microfilm) along with those widely recognized as Sobaipuri on the lower San Pedro under the leadership of Humari. This interpretation is consistent with settled farmers having larger settlements than those who are mobile or who farm only periodically during the time of year when they visited the river.

A third mention of Sobaipuris in relation to the Gila River accompanies a description of Kino's travels in which he stated:

> to the Rio Grande or *Gila River*, which flows out of the confines of New Mexico by the Apacheria, *and comes to these our Pimas Sobaypuris* and then exits more than 100 leagues to the west, by the Cocomaricopas and Yumas. (emphasis added; author's translation; also see Bolton 1948:II:243)

This third description also seems to place the Sobaipuri on the Gila River ("hasta el río Grande o río de Gila, que sale de los confines de Nuevo México por las Apacheria, y viene a estos nuestros pimas, sobaypuris"; from original microfilm; author's translation). Even so, this statement is not as definitive as the preceding two because it could be indicating the eastern boundary marked by the Sobaipuri on the lower San Pedro, currently thought of as being referenced when the Sobaipuri of the northeast are mentioned. Still, together these three statements seem clear that there were Sobaipuri on a limited portion of the Gila River at this time, at least as far as Kino understood.

Many more statements by Kino and his companions refer to the people between San Andrés and the San Pedro as generalized Pima, not specially Sobaipuri. Pima is a term the Europeans tended to use most often, no matter which subgroup or branch they were referencing (see chapter 1 discussion). They even sometimes referred to the San Pedro and Santa Cruz Sobaipuri as Pima, as they also often did for O'odham groups of other ethnic subdivisions.

Residents further west on the middle Gila were also referred to as simply Pima, yet in the case of these western residents, Kino, Juan Mateo Manje, Cristóbal Martín Bernal, and Diego Carrasco always referred to them as Pimas without a qualifier or local designation, never as Sobaipuri. For these Europeans, these westerners were a Pima undistinguished by local or ethnic identifiers. This mode of reference may be owing to European confusion, lack of knowledge, or multiple origins for these groups.

These more western Pima are sometimes referred to in modern times as the Gila Pima or, inappropriately, as the "Pima proper." Bolton ([1936] 1960:248–249n2; Wilson 1999:20) and others since him have referred to these Gila Pima as the

"Pima proper," Bolton says, owing to greater ethnographic knowledge about them (e.g., Russell [1908] 1975).[7] This name has been applied by scholars also because, as noted, Kino and his companions referred to them only as Pima rather than with some qualifier or more locally appropriate referent. The Gila River occupants were referred to by this vague referent of Pima largely because they were the least known to Europeans at the time, Kino having visited them less frequently and only later in his travels. Also, when Kino noted them, it was often in juxtaposition to other neighboring non-Piman groups so his reference to them as Pima was often to distinguish them from non-Piman peoples along the same river. The label Pima proper, applied later, conveys the notion that this group was most like the Lower Pima or was somehow more purely Piman than other groups, including the Sobaipuri or desert dwellers, such as the Tohono O'odham. The term "Pima proper" has led to the notion that somehow these were the consummate Pima with everyone else being a variation or subset.[8] This notion is incorrect, and for this reason the term "Gila Pima" is more appropriate than "Pima proper." Yet, even the term "Gila Pima" fails to consider the presently proposed division between western Pima (on the western-middle Gila) and eastern Pima that were Sobaipuri (on the eastern-middle Gila).

CLARIFICATION

Clarification of this issue of Sobaipuri distributions on the Gila seems to be provided by analyzing travel distances, places visited, and Kino's maps for the area in question. Examination of Kino's earliest map in the context of this 1697 statement about the "six or seven rancherías of Pimas Sobaipuris" located nearby provides some elucidation. The half dozen Sobaipuri rancherías mentioned in Kino's text may include those shown near Casa Grande along and north of the Gila River on Kino's 1695–1696 *Teatro de los trabajos apostólicos de la Comp. de Jesús en la América Septentrional* map, along with La Encarnación (Tusonimo or Tcurshonyi Mo'o) and San Andrés (El Coatoydag or Coatoidag; figure 3.1). Five dots representing settlements are shown north of the Gila in this segment, consistent with Kino's text, with La Encarnación and San Andrés south of the Gila ("Rio Sonaco o de Hila" on figure 3.1 map) and just west of Casa Grande. These therefore provide a reasonable explanation for the six or seven nearby Sobaipuri rancherías that Kino notes when at Casa Grande. These villages may have been noticed by Kino when in November 1694 he *discovered* this area and Casa Grande, as indicated in his journal (Bolton 1848:1:127–129) and by a notation on the *Teatro* map ("Descubierta en 27 de Nov 1694"; figure 3.2a and b).

FIGURE 3.1. *Kino's 1696–1697* Saeta Martyrdom *map showing Sobaipuri village locations.*

Significantly, prior to arriving at Casa Grande, Kino noted passing through seven or eight Sobaipuri settlements on the lower San Pedro within Headman Humari's domain. These and other settlements are shown on this *Teatro* map. Kino then mentions the "six or seven rancherías of Pimas Sobaipuris" in the vicinity of Casa Grande. After Kino left Casa Grande and headed west, he visited only two villages (La Encarnación and San Andrés, both labeled on Kino's map; see figure 3.3; also see figure 3.1), before turning south along the Santa Cruz River and on home to his headquarters at Nuestra Señora de los Dolores. Elsewhere, as noted, he referred to La Encarnación and San Andrés as Sobaipuri villages (Bolton 1948:I:202). From this it seems that the five dots shown north of the Gila, plus La Encarnación and San Andrés, were the "six or seven rancherías of Pimas Sobaipuris" near Casa Grande. Kino probably traveled along the south side of the Gila, which is why he did not visit those Sobaipuri villages represented by dots to the north and so mentioned no specific village names.

FIGURE 3.2. *(a) Drawing of the Casa Grande in the margin of Manje's original manuscript, Microfilm 143L. (b) Photograph of the Casa Grande or Big House, 1890; Published in the Bureau of American Anthropology 13th Annual Report, 1891–1892. (CG-0571).*

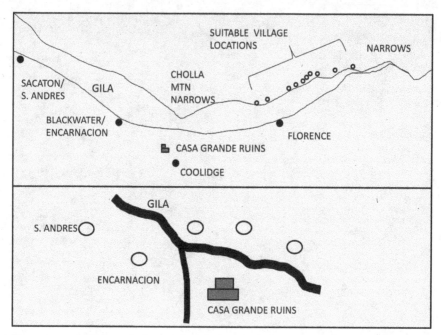

FIGURE 3.3. *(a) Schematic drawing of relevant places and river channel characteristics on the Gila. (b) Redraft of Kino's map showing the Sobaipuri villages depicted and discussed by Kino. Figure prepared by Deni Seymour.*

The designation of these villages as Sobaipuri and Kino's turn to the south at the western margin of his travels make sense if there was a cultural or ethnic boundary of some type, and perhaps a geographic break or change in river surface water in this location. The documents report that there were three to four leagues between La Encarnación and San Andrés, while the total distance indicated from the San Pedro to San Andrés suggests that there was an average of five leagues between each Sobaipuri ranchería in the forty-league distance encompassed by their seven settlements (although settlements tended not to be regularly distributed).

In 1699 Manje (Karns 1954:123–124) told us that there were ten leagues between San Andrés and the next Piman settlement (San Bartolomé del Comac, Comacson) to the west along the Gila, reinforcing the idea of a boundary between Sobaipuri and other Gila Pima settlements. This spatial gap is clearly visible on Kino's second map (*Saeta's Martyrdom*) as well, suggesting that perhaps this break has some relevance other than (in addition to?) simply geographic or streamflow characteristics, or that the latter provided a natural boundary for actual social divisions. In 1698 Diego Carrasco stated with regard to these additional Gila Pima settlements to the west: "There are another four rancherías that speak the Pima language." These four are shown and labeled on Kino's *Teatro* map as being situated east of mixed Pima and Opa villages, but west of those proposed here as being and specifically referenced as Sobaipuri. The question remains as to whether these divisions indicated by these Europeans were based on attributes or behavior that were important to the people and that can be distinguished archaeologically, and whether these proposed differences persisted through time and, if so, for how long.

Notably, during his travels, Kino turned south three times after visiting San Andrés and La Encarnación, perhaps supporting the notion that this was an ethnic boundary that denotes specific behavior, in this case stationary and sizable populations that were therefore predictably present for his visit. During the first trip in 1694 he visited these two settlements and then turned back south, though few details are provided. On another trip, with Manje and Bernal in 1697, and as was mentioned earlier in the Documentary Data section of this chapter, Kino traveled north down the San Pedro and turned west along the Gila, visiting Casa Grande and San Andrés, La Encarnación, and, according to Manje, a third ranchería named Tucsan or Tuesan (Bolton 1948:I:171–173; Burrus 1971:343n30; Karns 1954:85–88). This was a ranchería of 130 persons about a league from Casa Grande (Karns 1954:87), mostly likely to the north of the river where Kino's first map shows the closest riverside settlement (see five unlabeled dots just north of the river in figure 3.1). Kino states that Casa Grande was a league from the river (Bolton 1948:I:172), so this placement for the Tucsan or Tuesan settlement along the river perhaps to the north makes most sense for this initial visit, though the settlement may have moved over time, as O'odham and Sobaipuri settlements tended to do.

Wilson (1999:30) assumes this 130-person village is located to the west. Following Ezell (1961:111), Wilson states, "By the etymology of the name ('Tcuk Shon' = 'blackwater') this village should have been near modern Blackwater, probably west of it and a little more than a league north-northwest from Casa Grande (Ezell 1961:111)." Wilson suggests the 130-person village (Tucsan or Tuesan) is much more than a league from Casa Grande. Moreover, regarding the six or seven rancherías of Pimas Sobaipuris, Wilson (1999:24) also believes that these villages lay downstream or to the west. Yet, in contrast to Wilson's interpretation of this information, it seems, as I have just said, that from maps provided by Kino and the routes of travel taken that these unlabeled but plotted Sobaipuri villages actually lay upstream from Casa Grande, to the north and east, while Encarnación and San Andrés are to the west/downstream of Cholla Mountain and Casa Grande. Kino and his companions tended to mention villages in the order encountered, and he has yet to be proven wrong about which bank of a river a village was on. He was a skilled cartographer (see Seymour 2014 for a discussion). The unlabeled Sobaipuri villages were plotted north of the river, and while it was not uncommon for villages to move several miles from their original location, even switch sides of the river, these villages seem to have been distinct from Encarnación/modern Blackwater and San Andrés/modern Sacaton. Blackwater is located in the general vicinity of Encarnación, west of Cholla Mountain which meant it occupied a reach of the Gila downriver from Casa Grande and the Cholla Mountain narrows (see figure 3.3). This location is consistent with Chris Loendorf and others (2019), who indicate that the location of Blackwater is at one of the few locations where water "reefed" or came to the surface of the riverbed because of the presence of a bedrock outcrop. Tucsan and the unlabeled villages were seemingly plotted to the east of this Cholla Mountain narrows, placing them in a different irrigation district. This places Tucsan and the unlabeled villages in the general vicinity of Poston Butte or perhaps farther back from the river. According to modern O'odham S-cuk Son means "black base" (not "black-water") in its reference to the original O'odham village at Tucson, evidence of which has recently been discovered at the base of a black hill (Tumamoc Hill; Seymour 2022a). It follows, then, that this same term may also reference the 1694 village being at the black base. The 1694 Tucsan may have been in the vicinity of Poston Butte, the only black hill adjacent to the river in this area.[9] Incidentally, the modern Blackwater village is across the river from black outcrops that line the north edge of the river. It is likely that the location moved sometime in the Historic period, as villages do. The village, like so many others, derives its name from geological features that allowed them access to water in the channel and to farm (see chapter 2).

Support for this just-related interpretation is provided when Kino summarized the portion of his and Carrasco's 1698 trip along this portion of the Gila:

> In the rancheria of La Encarnacion, that of San Andres, and in those nearby, we were received with all kindness, with crosses and arches erected, and with many of their eatables, by more than one thousand souls, men and women. (Bolton 1948:I:186)

After San Andrés, the Europeans turned south and southwest away from the Gila River, and so Kino described entirely different O'odham groups, providing a summary of the next populations encountered. The inclusion of his second synopsis suggests that in the just-quoted passage Kino was summarizing the Sobaipuri population in the six or seven rancherías that include San Andrés, La Encarnación, and Tucsan. San Andrés was the furthest west and largest with 400 people, while Encarnación had 200, and Tucsan had 130. If, as it seems, Kino was referring to the total population of only these related seven Sobaipuri rancherías, then the other four Sobaipuri rancherías in this zone had a combined total of about 270 people, or about 70 people per ranchería, a size that was not uncommon for secondary-level Sobaipuri rancherías at the time. Kino would have known that the most important headmen tended to reside in the largest settlements, which were those he visited.

Notably, this comparison of texts and maps suggests that Kino recognized both Sobaipuri and other Pima occupations along the Gila River, routinely turning south at the western edge of Sobaipuri territory. This consistency indicates that some Sobaipuri in this period did in fact occupy this short stretch of the Gila River between its confluence with the San Pedro,[10] and San Andrés, probably near the Santa Cruz River confluence. The first of the non-Sobaipuri Gila Pima settlements may have been west of San Andrés (see figure 3.1). Kino could not necessarily depend on the Pima being present further west, given their practice of moving to and away from the river seasonally or avoiding the area when the flow was too high or broad.

The critical importance of the settlement dots on the *Teatro* map situated north of the Gila for understanding the far northern Sobaipuri occupation has not been recognized previously, probably because they are not labeled. It has been most reasonable to assume that these were drawn to represent the abandoned prehistoric ruins mentioned by Manje (Karns 1954:84–85). Alternatively, Kino stated: "As we journeyed we always had on the right hand and in sight, but on the other bank of the river, the very extensive Apacheria" (Bolton 1948:I:172). Consequently, another reasonable inference might have been that the five dots to the north of the Gila were symbolic of Apachean encampments, being situated north of the river in presumed Apache territory. Instead, this new look at the information suggests that these dots are the Sobaipuri settlements located, in Kino's reckoning, near Casa Grande. The Apachería is probably in reference to the mountainous areas (north of the Gila) west of the San Pedro confluence with the Gila and the first (easternmost) of the Gila Sobaipuri settlements in the Casa Grande/Blackwater/Florence area. This mountainous area would have been unsuitable for irrigation farmers.

Ezell (1961:111) did not consider these ranchería dots on the *Teatro* map when he stated: "Kino (Bolton 1948:I:172) wrote that 'there are nearby [the Casa Grande] six or seven rancherías of the Pimas Sobaipuris,' but the existence of only three in the eastern part of the Gila Pima territory can be substantiated by other documentary evidence." He is correct that the texts of various Europeans only named three, but this *Teatro* map and also the distributional implications of Kino's statements and those of his companions substantiate the remaining as Pimas Sobaipuris settlements.

Together Kino's statements about the Gila Sobaipuri seem clear that there were Sobaipuri on at least a limited portion of the middle Gila River, perhaps a portion of the forty-league segment (e.g., Bolton 1948:II:249) between the confluence of the San Pedro with the Gila, on the one hand, and San Andrés, on the other. Yet, most of this zone is not especially habitable for the Sobaipuri, owing to their irrigation adaptation and so probably only a short stretch was actually inhabited by the Sobaipuri on either side of the mountainous terrain, twenty miles or so west of Price, Arizona, in the general area of North Butte (and east of the current Blackwater community) and a five-mile stretch near the San Pedro–Gila confluence and the Dripping Springs Mountains in the Hayden/Winkelman area.

Kino's remarks regarding the western portion of Pima territory along the Gila are not particularly enlightening, however, because the Europeans consistently and interchangeably use the term "Pima" without modifiers. Still, from these passages and Kino's maps, it seems that there were likely two or three distinct population zones for Piman groups along the Gila; those to the east were Sobaipuri, while those to the west may have been a distinct Gila Pima or various neighboring groups, such as the Kohtak and others who tended to occupy the desert areas, returning to the Gila only seasonally (e.g., Bolton 1930b:33). At that time, the third grouping consisted of the mixed villages of Pima and Opa.

This geographically restricted Sobaipuri occupation was either early or short lived because by Kino's second map (1696–1697 *Saeta's Martyrdom* map), the villages north of the Gila are no longer shown.[11] These ranchería dots are not shown on this second map produced by Kino or any of his subsequent maps, indicating that perhaps these Sobaipuri settlements were soon abandoned.[12] These differences between the first and successive maps suggest that Sobaipuri political and occupational boundaries may have changed (retracted) in the late 1690s as they did along the middle San Pedro. The Sobaipuri occupants of these Gila villages may have moved owing to increased Apache and Jocome pressure (the Apache and Jocome would have been nearby in the adjacent mountains and also used portions of the river not occupied by others), conflicts with other Piman residents along the Gila, or washouts owing to unpredictable river flow, though streamflow charts from this period do not indicate a particularly high-flow cycle except for the period between 1689 and 1695

(Cook 2000). All are likely explanations because each of these processes is mentioned in the documentary record as responsible for the San Pedro River Sobaipuri contracting their political boundaries and shifting settlement locations (Seymour 2011a:153–156, 237–239). Such a move would explain Velarde's statement from 1716 that the Pimas of the Río Gila were separated by a small mountain range (Dripping Springs Mountains) from the Pima Sobaipuris, who were very numerous and had most of their villages on the west side of the (San Pedro) river (González R. 1977; Wyllys 1931; also see Wilson 1999:40). Kino's 1701 *Paso por tierra a la California* map shows only three villages in this zone along the Gila and they are immediately west of Casa Grande, perhaps suggesting a major change in settlement distributions and perhaps aggregation into fewer larger settlements.

This reconstruction of Sobaipuri along this limited portion of the Gila River is consistent with and explains Kino's short 1697 description of Sobaipuri settlements being near Casa Grande while at the same time maintains the clear distinctions between regional O'odham groups mentioned so often by these Europeans. Kino distinguished the Sobaipuri as a group separate from other Piman occupants of the Gila River who lived further west. It appears that a subset of the Sobaipuri lived in seven villages along a restricted portion of the Gila River, between the confluence of the San Pedro and Santa Cruz Rivers. Farther east the terrain was too rugged and channel too narrow, while the west was occupied by other people and the land became much more arid. Thus, Bolton and others after him have been incorrect in asserting that the Gila Pima west from Casa Grande to the Bend of Gila River were all or mostly Sobaipuri. Rather, just those six to seven villages lying along a short segment of the Gila River were occupied by Sobaipuri at this time, representing the northern edge of Sobaipuri distribution. Those to the west were Gila Pima and groups of Pima mixed with others. Whatever significance this term "Pima" had in this area with regard to ethnicity is not known for sure.

We might reasonably infer that this Sobaipuri cluster on the Gila was a distinct political entity, much like the lower San Pedro cluster under Headman Humari, the middle San Pedro one under Headman Coro, and so on. The leader for the Gila Sobaipuri was said to be Juan de Palacios, who resided at the largest Gila settlement of San Andrés (Bolton 1948:I:173). These Gila Sobaipuri residents may have then moved in among the lower San Pedro settlements, accounting for the large sizes of these San Pedro settlements a few years later, or perhaps to the Tucson–San Xavier area, where extra large settlements were positioned, or even into other Gila Pima settlements where their descendants reside today. The "recent" conflict between Humari's and

Coro's peoples and the retraction of Coro's to the south may have opened habitation and agricultural areas on the lower San Pedro that were unavailable a few years before (see Seymour 2011a:238, 2011b). Alternatively, they may have moved in with their Pima neighbors to the west.

CONCLUSIONS

This assessment of the meaning of Kino's observations around Casa Grande clarifies that the Gila River was probably occupied by the Gila Pima to the west of the Santa Cruz River confluence and by the Sobaipuri between the Santa Cruz River and the San Pedro confluence with the Gila. Both may be considered Gila Pima because that is where they lived. The stretch of the Gila occupied by the Gila Sobaipuri is immediately north of the Sobaipuri occupation on the San Pedro and Santa Cruz Rivers. The Pima along the Gila River from just west of Casa Grande to Gila Bend were other Gila Pima, who probably sometimes included a number of groups, including the Kohtak. This western portion of the middle Gila is north of various nonriverine or part-time riverine Piman groups, people later mentioned as visiting the Gila River and residing there seasonally. Later, Sobaipuri occupants initially from other rivers went to reside along the Gila, as historic documents convey and as inferences from documentary evidence suggest. No relevant documentary evidence is available for earlier in time.

Fortunately, archaeological data can be used to verify this interpretation, presuming these ancient sites have not been destroyed through development, farming, later reoccupation, or river washouts, or buried too deeply to locate. To my knowledge archaeological work has yet to be conducted on O'odham sites of this period in the areas in question. My limited investigations in this area east of the Gila Indian Reservation have not revealed evidence, but more extensive work is warranted. Investigations into the material signature of sites to the east and west of the Santa Cruz–Gila confluence would likely reveal some hint of ethnic differences or variations in adaptation, if, in fact, this division seen in the documentary record is valid, seventeenth-century European distinctions are relevant, and these distinctions indicated have material consequences.

Moreover, this issue of the presence of Gila Sobaipuri probably addresses the long-standing question as to whether the O'odham had irrigation before the Spanish (e.g., Winter 1973). Sobaipuri along the San Pedro and presumably elsewhere had irrigation as part of their early (pre-European) and post-European adaptation, and so it is assumed they did on the Gila as well.

According to Kino, who seems to be among the first to commit this term to paper, Sobaipuri settlements were present on the Gila. It seems Sobaipuri were all irrigation farmers, and this may have been one of the distinctions Kino recognized along the Gila in denoting Piman groups and that the O'odham themselves recognized. After all, different ways of life result in distinct behaviors that tend to have material and spatial consequences and often serve as the basis for ethnic divisions and identity. Sobaipuri possession of the best lands along the rivers, owing to their dependence of agriculture and a stationary lifestyle, meant they needed to defend their claims. Both irrigation agriculture and its resulting infrastructure and maintenance needs and a substantial warrior society can result in the need for more organized societal configurations, which in turn are often the basis for ethnic differences. In fact, this riverine adaptation may explain why they only occupied certain restricted portions of the Gila where fields and canals were less likely to wash out and where surface water was available. These Sobaipuri villages were arrayed with reference to portions of the river suitable for irrigation agriculture in the same way as other Sobaipuri settlements on other rivers (San Pedro, Santa Cruz, Babocomari, and Sonoita). As tensions heated up between the O'odham and the Apache and Jocome, the Sobaipuri likely had to withdraw from these locations, which were too close to the mountains, and consequently they inhabited fewer larger settlements for protection.

NOTES

1. This chapter was first written in 2011 and so the chapter includes modifications including additional interviews, such as personal communication from Morning Light in 2018.

2. Elsewhere I have stated that some families did leave, but this was based on Dobyns and Ezell (Seymour 2011b:19n5). After examination of the Anza letter, it seems that three families left to live with the Gila River Pima, but Anza's intent was to make them return. So, it remains a question as to whether their governor was able to convince them to return (Anza 1769; see also Dobyns 1959; Ezell 1955:55).

3. I believe Bolton was also wrong about the people living north of Point of the Mountain being Sobaipuri. At least some of those closest to Picacho were later said to be from the west and seemed to be part-time river residents (Pedro Font in Bolton 1930a:30, 32; Francisco Garces in Coues 1900:64). It is possible that Santa Catarina was Sobaipuri, but seemingly none of the settlements farther north were. My investigations of sites in the Pan Quemado area have revealed evidence of a much more mobile O'odham. These were likely Tohono O'odham who may have shifted seasonally

between the area around Chuichu and near the river at Pan Quemado. Research is still underway on this topic. See Seymour (2021).

4. This inquiry involved a search of all references to the Gila Sobaipuri in a pdf of Bolton's *Kino's Historical Memoir*, 1948:vols. I and II and then examination of these passages in the original microfilm, as well as examination of his other writings and those of his campaigns.

5. This change may reflect an expansion of Apache and therefore a movement of O'odham groups.

6. Regarding this, Christian Wells (2006:table 1) provides a summary of the diagnostic traits for identifying the Protohistoric period (AD 1400–1700) in the middle Gila River Valley, and he lists, among other archaeological traits, Sobaipuri Plain and Whetstone Plain pottery as well as Sobaipuri (Huachuca) projectile points. He indicates that four settlements in the middle Gila River—near Sacaton, Sweetwater, Casa Blanca, and near Pima Butte—were established on the remains of protohistoric occupations (Wells 2006:22–24). Yet conversations with Chris Loendorf (personal communication, 2013) indicate that no actual evidence of Sobaipuri habitation has been identified, and none of the O'odham sites investigated have been dated prior to the 1800s. However, Wells (2006:29) also notes that two archaeological sites on the Gila Indian reservation, GR 909 and GR 1139, seem to represent two different ethnic groups, with GR 909 dominated by straight-base triangular points (thought to be associated with the Pima), and GR 1139 dominated by U-shaped base triangular points. The latter are thought to be associated with Sobaipuri (Loendorf and Rice 2004:59). Yet, a similar range of point types has been found throughout the Sobaipuri area, indicating that perhaps these distinctions are related to use (hunting versus warfare) rather than ethnicity, and that they were also made by non-O'odham ethnic groups (Seymour 2011a:92–93). This issue clearly deserves further study.

7. In reality, there was less known about the Pima on the Gila to the west than those to the east, which is why those to the west were referenced in historical documents only as Pima rather than capturing the ethnic or other relevant subdivisions. Ethnographic work among the historic Gila Pima resulted in their traditions being recorded as representative of the Gila Pima as a whole. By then, many once-distinct O'odham groups may have then resided together in these settlements, but originally the Gila Pima on the middle and eastern portions of the river seem to have been Sobaipuri and full-time farmers.

8. Use of the term "Pima proper" is unfortunate because it implies that one O'odham group was somehow more O'odham than another, a mischaracterization that should be discontinued. Following this logic, however, if any O'odham of the time would be considered more properly Pima using Bolton's implied criteria, then the Sobaipuri would be the Pima proper rather than those to the west, who did not farm

full time. The different lifeways practiced by the O'odham then and now are just that, differences that characterize O'odham as a family of related people. One way is not more proper or more traditional than any other; they simply represent different ways of living based on the environmental conditions presented and the peoples' adaptations to that which make each subgroup different from the next in discernible ways.

9. The modern Sacaton community is adjacent to a couple of large black hills (at the southern edge of the San Tan Mountains) that are adjacent to the Gila, but this locale is situated substantially west of Casa Grande.

10. One site depicted on Kino's map is actually north of the Gila and east of the San Pedro–Gila confluence.

11. This potentially early presence (verifiable through chronometric studies) may also have implications for early O'odham accounts that discuss people coming from the east making the adobe walls of predecessors that we call Hohokam crumble before their magic (see Russell [1908] 1975; Underhill 1939).

12. The channel of the Santa Cruz River is drawn differently, especially in relation to Casa Grande and the O'odham settlements between the first and third maps as well, which may suggest that the Europeans followed a north-south canal or a nonriver route north-south the first few times but went all the way to the Santa Cruz–Gila confluence for the third map, which would be consistent with their more extensive trip to the west later. The third map shows what are probably La Encarnación and San Andrés to the east of the Santa Cruz–Gila confluence while the first and second maps show them to the west. We might suggest these villages moved during this interval were it not for the distinctive difference in the way the Santa Cruz River channel is indicated, suggesting the second map shows the channel while the first shows some other understanding, perhaps reflecting the cross-county nature of their turn and route to the south.

4

*Ethnogeographic
Evaluation of the Great
Principal Settlement of
San Xavier del Bac*

A fundamental and long-standing premise about sub-divisions of the Pima derives from historian Herbert Bolton.[1] Most discussions begin with his assertions because he was the most prolific early historian to write about the historical O'odham. Specifically, Bolton ([1936] 1960:248n2) provided a footnote comment in *Rim of Christendom* regarding the ethnogeography of historic O'odham or Upper Piman groups on the Santa Cruz River. This comment is widely cited, including by myself, and for decades has been the basis for discussing Sobaipuri distributions. Regrettably, however, Bolton's interpretation of the evidence is not quite accurate and has caused considerable confusion through the years regarding the historical names used for various Piman groups and their geographic distributions.

As a division of the Upper Pima the Sobaipuri occupied both the San Pedro and Santa Cruz River Valleys and their tributaries, and, as was just discussed, a short portion of the Gila (chapter 3) in the Terminal Prehistoric and Historic periods through to the late 1800s (see figure 1.1). This distribution, of course, conflicts with the *Rudo Ensayo* written in the early 1760s, which states that the Sobaipuri were initially only on the San Pedro (Pradeau and Rasmussen 1980).[2] Many modern scholars also think only of the San Pedro as being Sobaipuri territory. Yet, there should be no doubt that Kino referred to the people residing in substantial settlements along the Santa Cruz as Sobaipuri long before the movement of people there from other areas.

https://doi.org/10.5876/9781646422975.c004

For example, in 1700 Kino stated: "Having arrived at this great ranchería of San Xavier del Baac of these Sobaiporis of the west, which are those of the Río de Santa María [e.g., modern Santa Cruz River]" (Bolton 1948:I:234). This statement seems clear, but past interpretations of it have resulted in confusion.

In the passage in question in *Rim of Christendom*, Bolton states, as if describing distributions from south to north:

> On the San Pedro the Pimas proper, as they were then considered, ended with the village of Huachuca (on the site of Babacómari Ranch), and on the Santa Cruz with Tumacácori. The railroad from Tumacácori on the Santa Cruz to Fairbank on the San Pedro approximates the northern row of their settlements. According to Kino, the Sobaipuris began with Gaybanipitea near Fairbank on the San Pedro and with Bac on the Santa Cruz. ([1936] 1960:248n2)

This perceived distribution has the Sobaipuri as a bulge or wedge within the larger distribution of real or proper Pima found farther south and to the north along the Gila. Regrettably, Bolton does not specifically cite the basis for his statement nor provide further explanation. Instead, sleuthing by modern scholars is required if we are to identify the specific portions of Kino's correspondence that conveyed this message or, more accurately, to establish the passages from which Bolton drew his inferences. By identifying the original source or sources of, or impetus for, this view, we can evaluate whether Bolton's inferences have merit. It is my contention that taking these ethnic distributional data at face value has led to widespread misunderstandings. In the next chapter I will address the issue of Huachuca that derives from this understanding, whereas this current chapter focuses on the Santa Cruz River and the settlement of San Xavier del Bac.

Many researchers have adopted this perspective conveyed by Bolton as a matter of fact. For example, without reference, Spicer ([1962] 1981:129) refers to "the Pimas of the upper Santa Cruz and the Sobaipuris farther north around Bac" (also see F. Smith et al. 1966:13n42). The relevance of these misunderstandings can be found specifically in the archaeological literature, where researchers have attempted to correlate on-the-ground findings (archaeological sites, arrow points, pottery) to group distributions in the historic record. Others have pointed to Bolton's footnote as a basis for questioning the cultural affiliation of sites found and excavated on the upper and middle Santa Cruz River. For example, this was the basis for David Doyel (1977) suggesting that it was not possible to ascertain whether the sites excavated for the Interstate 19 construction were best attributed to the Sobaipuri or the Pima. Bruce Huckell (1984) also hesitated to draw affiliation conclusions for his sites in the shadow of the Santa Rita Mountains based on the then-slim body of evidence available from recorded and excavated Sobaipuri sites. My own work specifically addressed this question as well (Seymour 1993a:11, 2011a:33, 183–184).

VARIOUS RESOLUTIONS OF THE ISSUE

To resolve this issue, and to also clarify its validity as an issue, we can examine documentary sources and archaeological data, both of which have a bearing on interpretation. As noted, the past thirty-seven years or so have produced a relative abundance of data that assist in the effort, especially new archaeological data from the sites Kino visited. Moreover, consideration of the original texts in Spanish-period documents provides the most specific clarification. Thus, the first issue to be addressed is what Kino and others actually said. A separate question is whether these historical visitors understood distributions and identity correctly and whether they conveyed their understanding clearly and effectively. For archaeologists, then, the question is how these divisions might be manifest in a material culture signature (e.g., archaeological evidence), and what relevance the division and material culture signatures have for tribal affiliation or identity. For anthropologists in general the question is how these historical observations translate to human behavior.

Documentary Resolutions

We can scrutinize Kino's original use of the terms "Pima" and "Sobaipuri" to ascertain the meaning, relevance, and context of his statements. By examining every usage of the term "Pima," as opposed to or in combination with "Sobaipuri," in Kino's historical memoir (*Favores Celestiales*), we see that there is no basis in Kino's longest work for Bolton's inference. To begin, Kino clarified that Sobaipuris were a subset of Pimas, consistent with modern usage. Kino stated: "Here we began to obtain some information in regard to the many Pimas, both Sobaiporis and non-Sobaiporis" (Bolton 1948:I:290). Kino used the term "Pimas Sobaipuris" in a way that is also consistent with the Sobaipuri being viewed as a subset of the larger Pima "nation" (e.g., Bolton 1948:I:146, 162, 172). Yet, Kino also used the term "Pima" to describe groups indisputably known as Sobaipuri, for example, the Pima of Quiburi (Bolton 1948:I:168–169) and with regard to the victory of the Pima over the enemy at Santa Cruz de Gaybanipitea (Bolton 1948:I:178, 179). Thus, from this handling we see that Kino frequently referred to people as Pima that are now and were then known to be Sobaipuri, for example, distinguished from the nonspecific Pima as a whole or other types of Pima. This usage suggests that Kino's categories of reference were not always as exacting as we might wish them to be and thus should be used with caution when attempting to discern ethnic differences or to establish identities that were relevant to Kino, to the Sobaipuri themselves, or to modern scholarship. This issue was touched upon in chapter 3 as well.

Kino and Manje tended to use the term "Pima" in a generic fashion to subsume all other branches that were Upper Piman. Sometimes they did this as an expression of uncertainty about specific ethnic identification (as in Kino's earliest work and perhaps along the Gila River, as noted), while in other instances, their intent seems to be to unite all O'odham with the purpose of spreading the credit to all for the good deeds and loyalty of a certain village, local community, or branch. This last point is especially apparent in the above-cited reference to the great battle victory of 1698 in *Favores Celestiales* and in Kino's 1698 letter *Del Estado Gracias al Señor Pasifico y Quieto* (Kino 1698d) where the deeds of all Pima were lumped together for the political benefit of all. This lumping probably also resulted from a Eurocentric impression of the relevant level at which groups were politically and culturally interconnected. Kino and the other Europeans also made and revised distinctions as they learned more about Indigenous distributions, drew conclusions about ethnic differences, understood the way groups identified and differentiated themselves and their neighbors, and comprehended the fragmented nature of O'odham political organization.

Of direct relevance to our question regarding the Santa Cruz River, Kino's description of his first contact with the Sobaipuri of the north in 1691 suggested strongly that people south of San Xavier on the upper Santa Cruz were Sobaipuri. He indicated it was the Sobaipuri of both "San Xavier del Bac, more than forty leagues' journey, and from San Cayetano del Tumagacori" that came to meet him and Father Juan María de Salvatierra in El Tucubavia near Saric (Bolton 1948:I:119). This passage suggests that those at San Cayetano del Tumacácori were also Sobaipuri, but this evidence is rarely interpreted that way, probably owing to preconceived notions deriving from Bolton's initial inference.

Thus, in seeking the origin of Bolton's inference and examining Kino's original sources, we find a probable clarification for this issue. There seems to be little in the way of definitive evidence that Kino observed the distinctions on the Santa Cruz noted by Bolton or that the Pima were distributed the way Bolton suggested. Almost certainly, Bolton's notion originated in the variable use of identity terms used by Kino, Manje, and others that were drawn interchangeably from various levels of cultural, political, and classificatory relevance. Bolton's misunderstanding also probably arose because there was a substantial occupational break between the upper and middle San Pedro that he also attributes to ethnic differences, but current information indicates this break relates to surface water characteristics of the river rather than cultural, social, or political boundaries (see, e.g., Seymour 2020a; Seymour and Rodríguez 2020; also see chapter 2). On the Santa Cruz there is a long segment of river without Sobaipuri occupation between San Xavier del Bac and about Canoa (San Martín at the time), just north of San Cayetano del Tumacácori. As discussed in chapter 2, this gap relates to streamflow characteristics, not ethnic differences, though it is acknowledged that such geographic attributes can accompany ethnic differences or political subdivisions. While such an environmentally influenced break in occupation could also coincide with ethnic differences or territorial boundaries, in this case it does not.

This notion put forth by Bolton in a footnote regarding Sobaipuri occupation not extending to the upper Santa Cruz has persisted and grown in importance through the years, despite the meager data on which it was based. In all likelihood, the theory has been outwardly supported by other documentary data. For example, Smith's translation of Kino's *Relación Diaria* and accompanying footnote appear to support Bolton's vision. Kino specifically noted:

> Al ponerse el sol, salimos, como otras tres leguas de camino, a dormer en parte desde donde el día siguiente, con más facilidad, pudiéramos llegar a los sobahjípuris y a su primera gran ranchería, que es San Francisco Xavier del Bac. (Kino 1698c)

The relevant part of this statement is commonly read to mean where they encountered the Sobaipuri's "*first* [and] great ranchería." Fay Smith's (Smith et al. 1966:13) translation is that they slept "in a place where we could reach more easily the Sobaipuris and their *first* great ranchería, San Francisco Xavier del Bac" (emphasis added). In this way, Kino's statement has been taken to mean that San Xavier was the southernmost or, when traveling north from Sonora, the first Sobaipuri settlement encountered on the Santa Cruz River. This translation is consistent with Bolton's ([1936] 1960:248n2) supposition that the Pima lived to the south of San Xavier and the Sobaipuri occupied San Xavier and settlements to the north until Picacho (actually Marana, likely just north of Point of the Mountain). In fact, F. Smith reinforces this point in her footnote to this passage, as was noted previously:

> Kino referred to Indians living along the San Pedro River from Fairbank northward, those of the Santa Cruz River between San Xavier and Picacho, and

those on the Gila River from Casa Grande to Gila Bend, as Sobaipuri, *Rim*, p. 247. (F. Smith et al. 1966:13n42)

Yet, taking into account related and relevant factors, Kino's *Relación Diaria* statement is better read as if it says: "from where the next day, we would be able to arrive, more easily, to the Sobahjipuris [nation] and their *first great* rancheria, which is San Francisco Xavier del Bac." The implication, then, is that San Francisco Xavier del Bac was the first sizable or important settlement, while smaller Sobaipuri settlements were present to the south (also see Seymour 2011a:20n7, 30–31, 37n14). It was the initial great settlement, not the first settlement that was also great. This different emphasis to this translation is suggested both by a more critical and expansive examination of the literature relevant to the Sobaipuri and an acknowledgment of the inconsistent use of terms by various chroniclers of the period.

A statement by Manje has also been interpreted to mean that Bac was first settlement of the Sobaipuris nation: "We camped at the great settlement of San Javier del Bac, first of the Sobaipuri nation[s]" (to be encountered; Karns 1954:168; also see Crockett 1917:178). For the original Spanish, see "Llegamos a dormir al gran poblado de San Javier del Bac, primero de la nacion Sobaipuris" (Manje 1701 in Burrus 1971:481; Manje 1720). Yet *primero* in this context means the best, primary, or main: "We camped at the great settlement of San Javier del Bac, first [e.g., principal/lead settlement] in the Sobaipuri nation."

Similarly, translation of a passage in Captain Diego Carrasco's 1698 diary also supports my view, clarifying that San Xavier was the *primary great* ranchería, not the first to be encountered:

> Al poner fe el sol salimos como otras tres leguas de camino a dormir en parte desde donde el día siguiente con más facilidad que día a nos llegar a los Sobahipuris y a su primaria gran ranchería que es la de San Francisco Xavier del Bac.

In English Carrasco stated:

> Putting our faith in the daylight, we went about another three leagues so we could sleep where, the next day with more ease, we could reach the Sobaipuris and their primary great ranchería, that is that of San Francisco Xavier del Bac. (1698; author's translation)

With this statement, he means that San Xavier was the Sobaipuri's principal or primary great ranchería, not the first when traveling north or downriver. This statement is supported in a comment by Manje that refers to the "great settlement of del Bac" (Karns 1954:81) with "the largest population that, so far, we have seen" (Burrus 1971:378). This statement also matches census data taken through the years during this period (see Seymour 2011a:table 6.1), which also indicate that this village had the largest population (of more than 800 people) and was in some ways the most influential throughout the extreme northern Pimería Alta. With regard to San Xavier del Bac, Bernal commented in 1697 that "at this very large ranchería, the largest which Pimería has . . . the Governor is called Eusebio, an old man, a good administrator and well liked. In the rest of the rancherías they obey him promptly" (in F. Smith et al. 1966:45, also see 40). Thus, Carrasco's statement supports the notion that Kino also meant that San Xavier was the primary great ranchería or geographically the *first great* village, not the *first* Sobaipuri village that was also great. This again is supported in many other passages, such as when Kino states: "I found the natives very affable and friendly, and particularly so in the principal ranchería of San Xavier del Bac, which contains more than eight hundred souls" (Bolton 1948:I:122).

Archaeological Resolution

These passages have spatial implications for the distribution of Sobaipuri versus Piman material culture that can be examined in the archaeological record. It is therefore possible to assess the validity of my inferences in comparison to those originating with Bolton through an exploration of Sobaipuri settlement patterns, site types and sizes, and excavated feature and artifact assemblages.

Comparatively little work has been conducted on Piman residential sites in Sonora, and therefore efforts at cross-border archaeological comparisons would be sketchy (but see McGuire and Villalpando 1993). Moreover, little is known of early Piman and potential Sobaipuri sites on the Gila or on the upper San Pedro from this period.[3] It is possible, however, to compare site and artifact characteristics between the upper and middle Santa Cruz north of the international line on sites I have documented and excavated. Bolton's interpretation of the documentary record posits that sites to the south on the Santa Cruz should be different in discernible ways from those in the San Xavier and Tucson areas and on Sobaipuri sites on the middle and lower San Pedro. These ethnic differences, it is suggested, might be conveyed in site layout, artifacts, feature attributes, and so on.

Long-term and intensive work on the Santa Cruz River that has been specifically focused on the Upper Piman/Sobaipuri occupation bears directly on this issue and suggests that differences of the sort that might be attributable to ethnic differences at this level are not apparent. As I have noted (Seymour 1992, 1993a, 1993b, 2011a), there are subtle differences between the San Pedro and Santa Cruz sites that seem most closely aligned with differences in geology (e.g., mica color in pottery), intercultural contact, and temporal factors. The pottery at Guevavi and also along Sonoita Creek exhibits some differences from that found at other Sobaipuri sites. At least some of the villages along Sonoita Creek exhibit a slightly different house arrangement that is likely related to landform size but may also be related to minor between-drainage ethnic differences among Sobaipuri groups (see chapter 6; Seymour 2015a; Seymour and Rodríguez 2020). But these differences fall within the range of what is defined as Sobaipuri. One problem is that residential sites of this affiliation and period have not been excavated in the Tucson area, and so it is not possible to directly address this issue as fully as we might like at this time. Yet, examination of surface evidence including pottery at the archaeological sites I attribute to the Kino period at San Xavier del Bac (AZ AA:16:396; AZ AA:16:432; AZ BB:13:19, ASM) and in Tucson at the site inferred to be among others, San Cosme del Tucson and San Agustin del O'ohia (AZ AA:12:788, ASM; AZ AA:16:6, ASM; and AZ AA:16:335, ASM) suggest similarities between the upper to middle Santa Cruz (see Seymour 2019a, 2022).

Another expectation of Bolton's reconstruction is that Piman sites of variable sizes (large and small) should be present to the south of San Xavier, itself representing an entire Piman settlement system. Similarly, large and small Sobaipuri sites are expected to the north. In other words, in Bolton's scenario, San Xavier is the first settlement of the Sobaipuri and it happens to be large but smaller ones are also expected north of it, as were present at one time. In presumed Piman territory to the south, there should similarly be a full complement of residential site sizes. Yet, in fact, only smaller residential sites are present to the south on the upper Santa Cruz, other than perhaps at Guevavi (once a head mission), where eight loci and hundreds of years of Sobaipuri (and pre-Sobaipuri) occupation are apparent, though each locus is quite mall. San Xavier is the *first large* site and the *first principal* village as one travels north along the Santa Cruz, but it is not the first Sobaipuri site. Thus, archaeological site distributions do not support Bolton's inference.

Similarly, the documentary record also reports only smaller villages to the south (see Seymour 2011a:table 6.1). Reportedly the largest villages to the south have populations sizes of only seventy to ninety people. Even at Guevavi, which was the most important place for the Jesuits and Franciscans and where they designated a mission headquarters, had a smaller population. On-the-ground evidence, as a result of accumulations of repeated occupations through time, shows that the settlements around Guevavi cumulatively are the largest concentration documented archaeologically. San Cayetano del Tumacácori is where the Piman occupation is said to have ended, with Sobaipuri occupation to the north, but as noted, Kino referred to residents of San Cayetano del Tumacácori as Sobaipuri. Thus, while historic Kino-period maps show an occupational break between San Cayetano del Tumacácori and San Xavier del Bac (with only one village filling the space between [e.g., San Martín on Kino's 1695–1696 *Teatro de los trabajos apostólicos de la Comp. de Jesús en la América Septentrional* map; see figures 2.6 and 3.1; see chapter 2]), and diary accounts imply this break, such occupational breaks are common on these rivers for the Sobaipuri and were not necessarily indicative of ethnic differences. As noted, in this case the break is attributed to river channel characteristics (see chapter 2). Elsewhere along the Santa Cruz, river segments lacking Sobaipuri occupation seem related to river channel characteristics as well (Seymour 2011a, 2019a, 2020a; Seymour and Rodríguez 2020). On the San Pedro in the 1690s, occupational empty spaces marked political subdivisions between the middle and lower San Pedro Sobaipuri, even though evidence is beginning to suggest that this division was a fairly recent development. It makes sense that spatially distinct groups of Sobaipuri villages would cooperate and perhaps accommodate related families, while other sociopolitical groups of related families might occupy suitable areas with reliable surface water beyond an unoccupied expanse. Thus, geographic and hydrologic characteristics likely resulted in or contributed to social and political distinctions, but these were not necessarily of the type Bolton suggested (although he never did define the implications of these distinctions) between the Pima proper and the Sobaipuri.

All evidence points to a similarity in material culture between these two areas on the Santa Cruz: the middle and lower segments from San Xavier north and San Cayetano del Tumacácori / San Martín south, suggesting that Bolton was incorrect and that my interpretation is more representative—"We could reach the Sobahjipuris [nation] and its *first great* ranchería," having passed a series of lesser Sobaipuri settlements. In this instance, archaeological data serve as an arbiter and provide a basis for seeing that there might be an alternative interpretation to the commonly viewed meaning of this text.

CONCLUDING STATEMENT

Bolton's inference was incorrect that the Sobaipuri occupation of southern Arizona began at San Xavier del Bac on the Santa Cruz. It seems that the entire upper and middle Santa Cruz was within the Sobaipuri domain.

The relevance of these ethnic distinctions will only become apparent when archaeological work on a wider range of early Piman sites is made at levels commensurate with the extensive work carried out on Sobaipuri sites (e.g., Seymour 1989, 1990, 1991, 1993a, 1993c, 1997, 2003, 2007b, 2009c, 2011a, 2014). It is immediately apparent, however, that inferences derived through the years from these interpretations of Pima versus Sobaipuri distributions must be reconsidered. This issue has relevance to more than simple academic understanding. Descendant populations recognize distinctions among themselves, some of which are related to these historical divisions. Greater understanding of the distributions and character of their ancestors will contribute to their understanding of themselves and their unique heritage.

NOTES

1. This chapter was first written in 2011 and was included in Seymour (2011b); it was subsequently modified for this book.

2. This is also a primary basis for many people assuming the San Xavier del Bac was initially a "Papago" or Tohono O'odham settlement rather than a Sobaipuri one and that it only became Sobaipuri after the 1762 exodus from the San Pedro Valley (see Seymour 2011b).

3. See chapter 3 regarding the Gila. Archaeology seems to confirm that there is a break in occupation on the San Pedro between the southernmost O'odham settlements (first shown as San Joseph, Guachuca, and perhaps Ternate) and those in the general vicinity of Fairbank and the Babocomari River, where Quiburi and Santa Cruz were located during Kino's time. Owing to insufficient archaeological work to the south, it is not known what political, ethnic, or geographic significance the upper and middle San Pedro occupational break represents. The basis for this break likely relates to surface water availability and to the characteristics of the floodplain and adjacent terraces, as is relevant to site distribution of O'odham river dwellers through time (e.g., Seymour 2011a). Until archaeological data are available from these southernmost sites, it will not be possible to comment much further on whether there were ethnic differences between the areas on the San Pedro River.

5

Ópata or O'odham

The San Pedro Headwaters, Huachuca, and Babocomari

Little is known about the fringes of Sobaipuri territory and, consequently, where ethnically different O'odham groups and other peoples, such as the Ópata, replaced Sobaipuri distributions. Questions include whether there were unsettled lands, such as between the Babocomari River and the San Pedro headwaters (figure 5.1). An absence of data has left this a question as to whether the upper San Pedro was a no-man's land between densely settled regions of Sobaipuri to the north and Ópata who pushed up from the south. Nor do we know where the latter's settlements begin. Typically, this issue is treated in a vague and generalized way, with the answer requiring in-depth analysis of the historical literature.

The Babocomari River and the headwaters of the San Pedro River are among the least-understood areas within the O'odham realm. Comparatively little work has been done in each of these areas, and for several reasons Sobaipuri history of these two geographic areas have been confused and intertwined in the literature. In the next few pages, I explore the reasons for this conflation in both Bolton's and Sauer's early reconstructions, that ultimately spilled over into Di Peso's (1953) work. Now that more data are available, we can revisit issues of ethnicity, territorial boundaries, and settlement distributions at this southeastern periphery of O'odham territory. Historical and archaeological work underway along the Babocomari River clarifies some of these questions, providing a new framework

https://doi.org/10.5876/9781646422975.c005

for discussing these Sobaipuri populations. Source materials from the 1600s provide a basis for reexamining past notions and as a way to obtain new and more complete answers.

HUACHUCA AND THE SAN PEDRO HEADWATERS

In the 1690s Padre Kino plotted three settlements at the headwaters of the San Pedro (see figure 5.1). Two of these (San Joseph and Ternate) were the namesakes of the San Pedro River (Río de San Joseph de Terrenate) in Kino's time before it became the Sobaipuri River and then the San Pedro River (Seymour and Stewart 2017; Seymour and Rodríguez 2020). Little is said about these settlements in period documents. Manje noted:

> When we founded the aforesaid Flying Company of 50 auxiliary soldiers which His Majesty gave for the guard and protection of these provinces, the said enemies had already ravaged and consumed the *estancias* of Terrinate, Patepitos, Janos, and San Bernardino. (Microfilm, author's translation)

In 1691 Francisco del Castillo Betancourt also distinguished Terrenate/Ternate from the Pima villages (Castillo Betancourt 1691), supporting the suggestion that this was a Spanish estancia (see later in this section; also see Kessell 1966). The third of these settlements plotted on Kino's maps was called Huachuca (spelled Guachuca on the map; the letters G and H can have the same sound in Spanish), and, as it turns out, Huachuca may be the most important of the three at the headwaters for solving long-standing questions about these villages and ethnicity in this portion of the San Pedro River. The question posed and addressed in the text that follows is whether these settlements noted by Kino at the headwaters of the San Pedro were Pima and, if not, if they were Ópata.

In the often-cited footnote quoted in chapter 4, Bolton (1848:1:248–249n2) comments that:

> on the San Pedro the Pimas proper, as they were then considered, ended with the village of Huachuca (on the site of Babocomari Ranch) . . . According to Kino, the Sobaipuris began with Gaybanipitea near Fairbank on the San Pedro and with Bac on the Santa Cruz.

For years I have contemplated this statement and these assumptions and wondered the source of this information and its validity. Kino never said that Santa Cruz de Gaybanipitea was the dividing line between distinct peoples, but, despite appearing only as a footnote without substantiating citations or explanations, this statement by Bolton has been one of his most influential

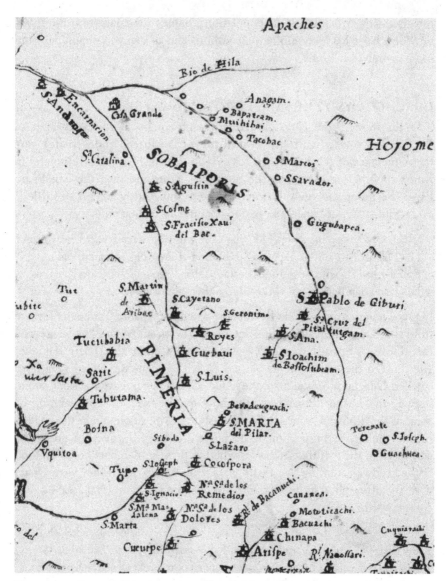

FIGURE 5.1. *Portion of Kino's 1696–1697* Saeta's Martyrdom *showing villages at the San Pedro headwaters and along the Babocomari River (rivers are not labeled on Kino's map).*

and widely cited, as discussed in chapter 4. Bolton's efforts to make his book content accessible to the general reader often rendered the content frustrating for the researcher who wishes to follow an idea to its source, examine the logic used to derive a conclusion, and to ascertain the original author of a concept in references cited. In chapter 4, I discussed the basis for Bolton's conclusion about Pima and Sobaipuri distributions on the Santa Cruz and what I perceive as the errors in logic brought to the topic by early historians. Here, I question historical distributions of the Pima (including the Sobaipuri) on the San Pedro, and I examine their implications for understanding prehistoric intercultural dynamics and culture area expansions. In short, I am questioning the authority of Bolton's statements because there are no data to support his claims and there are data to argue alternative scenarios.

If Sobaipuri villages stopped a mile or so south of the line demarcated by Bolton—a notion that remains untested—the question is raised as to whether there are in fact non-Sobaipuri Piman sites (Pima of other ethnicities or people of other ethnicities) on the upper portion of the San Pedro. This point has yet to be addressed, but by implication the assumption has become that there are no Pima settlements upriver to the south and that anything noted historically in this area is Ópata. Insufficient archaeological work has been completed to assess this issue on many counts. First, the level of focused survey I have carried out along the rest of the San Pedro north of the Fort Huachuca boundary up to the Gila River has not been accomplished south of this line. Sporadic searches through the years between Fort Huachuca and the international line have not revealed evidence of Sobaipuri and only resulted in inconclusive O'odham evidence, but these results are by no means reliable, systematic, or adequate. Consequently, our current understanding of this issue requires that we rely on documentary sources and assess the ways that they have been used to draw inferences about this issue and then consider ways in which they might be reinterpreted.

For many years, the consensus has been that the uppermost (southernmost) portions of the San Pedro were the domain of the Ópata, not the Pima, and this notion has become part of the lore among local residents and scholars. Contributing to this concept is the unspoken assumption that the San Pedro was Sobaipuri territory historically, and so since the Sobaipuri villages presumably stopped around where the Babocomari River enters the San Pedro, the area upstream to the south was either (a) a no-man's land and therefore available as a zone for the ancestral Ópata to surge north (though I have recorded Sobaipuri sites just south of this boundary) or (b) an area within the prehistoric Ópata domain ever since their formation as a distinct cultural entity. Many people, beginning with Adolph Bandelier, think that a northward and westward Ópata surge likely began with the fall of Casas Grandes in the mid-fifteenth century (see Phillips 2008). Still, the question of the ethnicity of these headwater residents in Kino's time and before remains unanswered in a methodical and direct way, largely because an important part of the area in question is south of the international border. The border itself initiates an entirely different set of permitting requirements and permissions, complicating research for American scholars, not to mention the current danger from cartels when moving around in remote areas. Nonetheless, many different sources reference this headwater area in a vague and tangential way, so as to provide a partial but noncommittal answer. For example, maps and articles discuss that Ópata distributions intrude into those of the Pima and represent a linguistic wedge in the distribution of Piman speakers (Carpenter Slavens and Sánchez 2016; Ortiz 1979:ix, map; Phillips 2008; see also Wilcox 1986). Spicer ([1962] 1981:91) notes that Ópata territory extends from the vicinity of the Huachuca Mountains in modern-day Arizona to central Sonora, but since he does not cite his sources or the basis for this conclusion, it is difficult to assess. Moreover, the vicinity of the southern end of the Huachuca Mountains incorporates a considerable amount of territory, precisely where the issue needs the most accurate geographic definition. This statement by Spicer may in fact be the origin of the incorrect assumption that the word "Babocomari" is from the Ópata language (see section "Babocomari: Its O'odham Name and Villages"). Important to this argument, Radding (1998:54) notes that the Ópata maintained contested boundaries with the Sobaipuri Pima. This may be the case, and the Ópata did seem to expand after the fall of Casas Grandes, but the question remains, where did the Ópata expand to and were the settlements at the headwaters of the San Pedro, that were noted by Kino and other early Europeans, Pima or Ópata?

All of these notions regarding the northernmost extent of the historical Ópata seem to derive initially from Carl Sauer (1934:51). Sauer, a geographer, draws inferences from a combination of cobbled-together data obtained from a couple of ethnohistoric sources that may not actually imply what he attributes to them. In this regard, Sauer says:

> The boundary of the Opatería in northeast Sonora was approximately the present international boundary. Opata names persist for streams, mountains, and valleys in this section, the Arizona mountain range of Chiricahua, for example, bearing an Opata name though it was not included in Opata territory. There is, however, sufficient evidence in seventeenth-century documents of an occupation by Opata of the San Bernardino drainage. These outposts of sedentary Indians were driven in at the end of that century by repeated attacks from nomad tribes to the north . . . The frontier Opata settlements can be deter-

mined from a deposition of the soldier Betancourt in 1691 (Provincias Internas, 30). He stated that Cabullona (south of Douglas, Arizona) lay five leagues north of Corodeguachi (the present Fronteras), that three leagues east thereof was the old pueblo of Therideguachi, then already depopulated (about the junction of the Agua Prieta and Fronteras arroyos), and three leagues beyond was the Cañada of Onodeguachi, whereas directly to the north of Cabullona lay rancherias of the Pima, namely Huachuca (Fort Huachuca, Arizona), and those of Quíburi (San Pedro Valley). The Opata, in this sector, extended therefore to the very edge of the high, dry plains of southeast Arizona, poorly suited to their type of agricultural economy and possessed by nomad Indians. (1934:51)[1]

In this it is possible to see that Sauer has incorporated some ideas from Bolton, namely, the association of Huachuca with the Pima and with the Babocomari River, which borders (is north of) Fort Huachuca. Bolton ([1936] 1960) also cites Sauer for some of his geographic information on the Pima, indicating his awareness of this source. One can imagine the two gentlemen scholars sitting in leather chairs in front of the fire, cigar smoke intermingling with the ideas materializing from their discussions. This cross-referencing demonstrates that this was fertile ground for the mutual development of ideas about Huachuca and the distribution of ethnohistorical groups. I will return to Sauer's quote later in this section after addressing some other relevant issues.

Interestingly, an important twist is introduced by early maps drafted by Kino and Gilg. On the earliest-known map, Jesuit Father Adamo Gilg's map of February 1692, two communities (San Joseph and Ternate) are illustrated at the San Pedro's headwaters (figure 5.2; Alegre 1960:mapa 2, between pages 144 and 145; Di Peso et al. 1965:plate between pages 40 and 41). Soon after, Kino's earliest map (1695–1696; the *Teatro* map drafted based on his earlier trips including this 1692 visit to the San Pedro) shows the settlement of Guachuca in this area, not on the Babocomari River as Bolton and Sauer have said, in addition to San Joseph and "Terenate" (figure 5.3; see figure 5.1). These three settlements are again shown on Kino's *Saeta* map (1696–1697), though the spatial relationship between settlements changes between maps (figure 5.4; also see figure 5.1).[2] This may reflect a better understanding of their placement or, more likely, records a shift in location of historical settlements, consistent with village drift that was a common practice for the Pima (see discussion in chapter 1). San Joseph, Guachuca, and Terenate could have been Indigenous communities, and perhaps Ternate was also or instead an estancia, as noted above by Manje, assuming the same place is being referenced in the slightly different spellings. The Castillo Betancourt account cited by Sauer clearly distinguishes

FIGURE 5.2. *Close-up of a portion of Gilg's 1692 map showing Sobaipuri villages at the San Pedro headwaters (what became the San Pedro River is not labeled on this map) and up to Quiburi near modern-day Fairbank.*

FIGURE 5.3. *Portion of Kino's 1695–1696 Teatro map showing O'odham villages at the San Pedro headwaters (river not labeled).*

Terrenate from the Pima villages. Describing distances west of Caviona, he states: "Terrenate about 26, and directly north are the villages of Pima, Bachuca some 15 leagues and those of Quiburi some twenty six" (1691). Although Kino did not comment on the ethnicity of the residents of these villages, it seems likely that at least two of these (Guachuca and San Joseph) were O'odham and possibly Sobaipuri. From an even earlier set of documents, additional evidence is available that the villages at the San Pedro headwaters, including Huachuca, along with Cananea were Piman villages, not Ópata. Still the word "Cananea" does not seem to be O'odham (Felicia Nunez, personal communication, 2020), and some Mexican nationals think the name ("Cananea"; "Carne

FIGURE 5.4. *Close-up of a portion of Kino's 1696–1697* Saeta Martyrdom *showing O'odham villages at the headwaters and along the Babocomari River (rivers not labeled).*

de Caballo") is a Chiricahua Apache one that means "horsemeat" (Ricardo Diaz and Arturo Avalos, both from Cananea, personal communication, 2020), though some sources suggest it is Spanish for "Canaanite woman." Court records from 1686 specifically mention that Guachuca was a Piman settlement, though there is also mention of a Jocome woman living among them (Zevallos 1686:151). The names of their Piman governors are also given in some instances. Huachuca was governed by a Pima named Sosoba. The Governor of Cananea was Pío Pío (Pius Pius) who was referenced as being of the Pima nation (November 13, 1686, November 24, 1686). Much later, in 1780, Rocha y Figueroa referred to the "antiguo y arruinado Pueblo de Guachuca" in this southern area (Day 25, Rocha Figueroa 1780c). Notably, Kino's maps place the Huachuca village much further south than Bolton inferred. Bolton's footnote places a village of this name on the Babocomari River, at least thirty-five miles to the north of Kino's plot (Bolton [1936] 1960:248n2, 269). Elsewhere, Bolton ([1936] 1960:543 and 635 [Index]) makes the connection between the names "Huachuca" and "San Joachín" on the Babocomari River and thereafter incorrectly assumes this connection (248n2, 269, 360, 500).

The two earliest maps for the region, Gilg's 1692 Seri map and Kino's *Teatro* map, do not show the Babocomari River; Gilg's map terminates at a more southerly latitude. Kino's *Saeta* map is the first to show the Babocomari River and two villages are illustrated: "S Ana" and "S Joachín" (figure 5.5). Bolton

FIGURE 5.5. *Close-up of Kino's 1696–1697* Saeta Martyrdom *showing villages along the Babocomari River (the river is not labeled on this map).*

places Huachuca on this drainage, connecting it with San Joachín, as noted, but Bolton seemingly errs in this assumption, and all subsequent statements, including when he says that Huachuca (which he assumes is what is now the Babocomari Ranch) was on the Babocomari River (Bolton [1936] 1960:500).[3]

Kino's *Saeta* map shows "S Joachín de Bassosubeam" (or perhaps Bassosribeam; as well as a S Ana), and "S Joachín (or S Joachim) de Bassosubeam" is clearly plotted on the modern Babocomari River, even though the river was not named on that map. Manje references this village as San Joachín de Basosuca or Baosuca (Burrus 1971:199, 359; Karns 1954:77). San Joachín de Basosuca or Baosuca sounds somewhat like Huachuca (by recognizing that [w] and [b] would be interchangeable sounds for the Spaniards), so this association must be the link by which Bolton placed Huachuca on the Babocomari, not realizing that at the same time Kino placed a village named Guachuca at the headwaters. The meaning of Basosuca or Baosuca cannot be discerned by modern Wa:k O'odham. Lieutenant Martín Bernal uses only San Joachín to reference both the valley and the ranch (e.g., village; F. Smith et al. 1966). The valley and the village have the same name, suggesting that San Joachín was the primary village in this valley at that time, thereby lending its name to the terrain, with Santa Ana being a secondary village. This also makes its leader the primary leader in the valley. Here Martín Bernal stopped to camp in 1697. He stated of this place:

> I gathered all the people into the little house which they have built for the Father (the missionary promised them). I talked to them about what they must do. Because Don Domingo Jaravilla had died I named a nephew of his

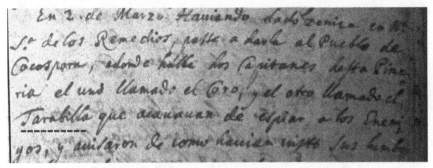

FIGURE 5.6. *Close-up of Kino's text showing the headman's name Tarabilla.*

as Governor at the request of the entire village and they were very pleased. (F. Smith et al. 1966:36)

Don Domingo Jaravilla is the leader Kino referenced (or Bolton transcribed) as Tarabilla (Bolton 1948:I:274; figure 5.6). This passage informs us that this leader was in the village of San Joachín de Bassosubeam, not Huachuca nor the nonexistent San Joachín de Huachuca, and Tarabilla's presence there indicates that this was the primary village, as just noted. The documents of this and subsequent expeditions do not mention Huachuca in this valley. These maps and texts document that San Joachín is not Huachuca as Bolton thought, but rather San Joachín is Bassosubeam, Basosuca, or Baosuca, depending on whose spelling and understanding of the Indigenous word is used. Nothing else is known about Santa Ana from the documentary record, though the name was later appended as a prefix to the village of Quiburi (see Di Peso 1953).

Huachuca was not on the Babocomari River during Kino's time, and no actual historical evidence has been found to indicate that a place called Huachuca was ever on the Babocomari. There were two villages on the San Joachín or Babocomari River during the 1690s, and neither is called Huachuca. Moreover, the Babocomari River is sufficiently far north of Huachuca's original village location at the headwaters of the San Pedro that it is not likely that the name "Guachuca" was later transferred to a settlement so far north on the Babocomari River. Huachuca and its association with the headwaters are once again noted in 1746, when Governor Don Agustín de Vildósola is cited as writing that "the Sobaipuri had their rancherías under the name of pueblos in the arroyo of Cuachuca, [at] the headwaters of the Rio de San Pedro" (Thomas 1941:203). This quote verifies that these were Sobaipuri living this far south.

Since Bolton so long ago suggested the presence of Huachuca on the Babocomari River, this notion has become established as a well-entrenched "truth." Nonetheless, there is no evidence for it that I have found, other than the similarity of the name. Regrettably, errors have been reproduced and not rechecked because the details are so few and dispersed in obscure sources (though today these sources are much more readily available than they were in Bolton's time). The result has been that one error builds on another, to the extent that even naming has become circular and self-reinforcing. For example, in his *Arizona Place Names*, Barnes ([1935] 1982:40) references Bolton's idea for the origin of the name "Huachuca," stating: "The name Huachuca was apparently first used for a Pima Indian village on what came to be the Babocomari Land grant." Because this is not the historical placement of this village, we must be cautious about other contingent assumptions as well; we especially need to examine whether this is an O'odham word, rather than, say, Ópata, Jocome, or Apache.[4] Rather than being clearly within the Sobaipuri realm as it would have been if on the Babocomari, the village of Huachuca is at the edge of O'odham territory in an area that tends to be thought of as beyond Sobaipuri territory, and within the northern extent of Ópata territory, depending on where Ópata northern reach extended to. As we just established, in the Colonial period this was Sobaipuri territory, so clearly our understanding of Sobaipuri territory needs to be revised and perhaps expanded.

In fact, some clarification is provided in that Huachuca seems to be a Hispanization of the O'odham word Waw Cuk'a, meaning "blackened cliff." Bright (2013:3) has interpreted Huachuca as "it rains here," but it is unclear which O'odham dialect was used for that interpretation, because although Tohono O'odham is mentioned, the Tohono O'odham Nation as a political entity now subsumes people of many different dialects, including those who trace their heritage to the Sobaipuri. Moreover, because words change as they are heard, transcribed, and adopted by speakers of other languages, many words are not especially clear as to their origin and original meaning. Presuming, however, that the name "Huachuca" is an O'odham word, as it clearly seems to be, then we can further assume that the village of Huachuca at the headwaters of the San Pedro is an O'odham village. This seems justified. The mountain range also has an Apache name, which is *da'dindi dzil* in Mescalero/Chiricahua and means "Thunder Mountain" (see Seymour and Rodríguez 2020:130n33).

Examination of the original 1691 Castillo Betancourt document cited above by Sauer provides further clarification for this issue. From this deposition, it is clear that the distribution of Ópata settlements is just a bit further south than Sauer suggested, not at the international line but at or south of the San Pedro headwaters. The portion of the text that referenced the

Piman settlements reads: "Y derecho al norte están las rancherías de Pimas, la de Bachuca [Huachuca] como quien se [quince] leg.s, y los de Quiburi como veinte, y seis." I would read this as: and directly north [of the presumed Ópata settlement of Cabullona],[5] are the Pima rancherías, [including] that [in the valley] of Huachuca about fifteen leagues and those of [the] Quiburi [valley] about twenty-six [leagues; e.g., another eleven leagues].[6] This construct acknowledges that the Pima rancherías include Huachuca and those of Quiburi, leaving little question as to the termination of Pima territory. From this we can discern the boundary as perceived in 1691 because we know the location of the Quiburi village at this time and the valley and the approximate location of the Huachuca village at the headwaters. Castillo Betancourt stated that Quiburi was about twenty-six leagues north of Cavuion, which in turn was five leagues north of Corodéguachi/Fronteras and three leagues west of Theridegucahi. This places Cavuion, presumably Cabullón as Sauer inferred, about seventy miles south of the crossing at modern-day Fairbank. At 2.63 leagues per mile, which was sometimes the calculation in this period, a figure of about eighty-five miles is obtained between Fronteras and the Quiburi Valley, which is just about right. This figure places the northern boundary of Ópata territory at about Cananea or just south of the extreme southern end of the San Pedro headwaters. This placement makes perfect sense given that the Pima, in this instance the Sobaipuri, were River People and farmers, and therefore would not have extended their occupation south beyond the San Pedro headwaters. It also makes sense that Ópata territory would begin at the headwaters of the Sonora River, which originates here as well and flows south. Thus, the Pima villages (San Joseph, Guachuca, and perhaps Ternate) noted on Gilg's and Kino's maps in this headwater location can be inferred to be the southernmost extent of Piman, that is, Sobaipuri, territory in 1691. Given that the Ópata were also farmers, their territory probably clung to the rivers that flowed further south into Sonora, placing them just to the south of Sobaipuri territory and the San Pedro headwaters, in the Sonoran River drainage. This interpretation is consistent with Rocha y Figueroa's 1780 map, where he shows the Ópata-Pima boundary just south of the San Pedro headwaters, suggesting the cultural boundary was pretty stable between 1691 and 1780, or at least that knowledge of it had not changed (figure 5.7).

There is another important implication of this understanding about settlements on the Babocomari River, which raises the historical importance of San Joachín. As I just noted, Taravilla was referenced as the Sobaipuri leader of San Joachín, the largest settlement on what today is known as the Babocomari

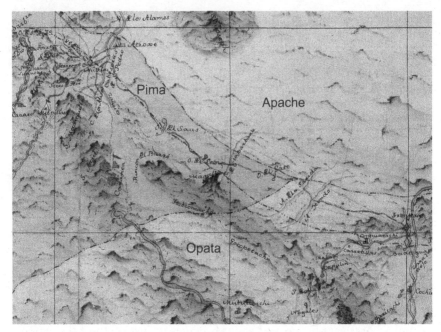

Figure 5.7. *Rocha y Figueroa's 1780 map showing the dividing line between O'odham and Ópata. © British Library Board (Shelfmark: Cartographic Items Additional MS. 17,661.b.).*

River, but otherwise a relatively unimportant village in the historical literature. Yet, Taravilla, and consequently, this place, was mentioned in 1692 when
Captain Francisco Ramírez de Salazar (1692a–d) passed through this location
on his return route from his Sobaipuri campaign. This reference to Taravilla's
ranchería makes this one of the earliest Sobaipuri villages mentioned by name
in this area.

Knowing the archaeological location of this settlement allows us to understand more about the route taken during this earliest mission period campaign.
Taravilla was said to reside twenty-five leagues from the camp and place of
their war council on the lower San Pedro (Ramírez de Salazar 1692d). This
places the location of the treaty at about sixty miles downriver on the San
Pedro, or at about Redington, acknowledging that over such a long distance,
league assessments are only approximate. This was the location of several villages visited by Kino including Cusac and Jiaspi, which were under the leadership of the Sobaipuri headman Humari (see chapter 10). As noted in chapters
7 and 10, later accounts by Manje (Karns 1954:79–80) confirm that this expedition passed the treacherous narrows in this area, Acequias Hondas Narrows

(see chapter 10; now referred to as the Redington Narrows; also see Seymour and Rodríguez 2020).

The same document that conveys the distance traveled by this campaign down the San Pedro River, tells us that the ranchería of El Taravilla was only eight leagues from the ranchería of Beradeguache (Ramírez de Salazar 1692d). Kino's first two maps (figures 3.1 and 5.1) place Beradeguache along the head-waters of the Río Santa María (modern Santa Cruz River) in the modern San Rafael Valley. This settlement, Beradeguache, was said to be two leagues from the village of Santa María (de Suamca), which is the namesake of this river in Kino's time. As Francisco Ramírez de Salazar (1692d) states, "that rancheria [Santa María] is two leagues from Beradeguache, and from that of Taravilla, about ten leagues." These league distances are appropriate, and this places Beradeguache just south of the international line and Santa María at or near modern-day Santa Cruz, consistent with current thinking about its original location. This information provides a fairly detailed understanding of the route of this early expedition through the heart of Sobaipuri territory.

The detailed and circuitous routes by which I have arrived at these conclusions demonstrate how assumptions meld within historical records to build a story that then takes on a life of its own. Opportunity to revise these initial impressions arises as more data become available. The earliest researchers laid a foundation for our current thoughts and understandings. They had many fewer data with which to work and in some instances drew the wrong inferences from what they had. In many more instances, they are to be commended for putting together a larger framework that makes our subsequent work and advances in understanding possible. Reexamination of ethnohistorical sources indicates that historically, during Kino's time and into the late 1700s, the stretch of the uppermost San Pedro near the headwaters was within the realm of the Pima, in fact, the Sobaipuri. Huachuca and another Piman settlements were situated here, and their positions will likely be revealed with archaeological survey in the area, assuming modern farming and village activity have not erased them. Still, the conclusions presented here must be considered tentative until archaeological data are presented as independent verification.

BABOCOMARI: ITS O'ODHAM NAME AND VILLAGES

The Babocomari River has been less studied than the San Pedro itself. Since Di Peso's time, little work had been carried out there owing to its status as private land. Recent and intermittent access granted to this author over the last decade has allowed survey there, providing more up-to-date information

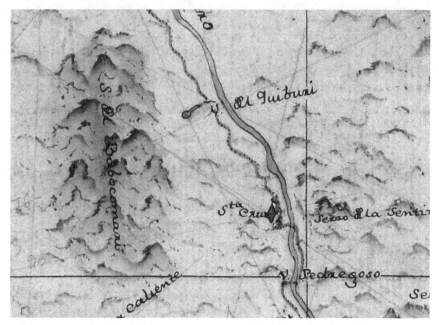

FIGURE 5.8. *Close-up of Rocha y Figueroa's 1780 map showing the Babocomari Mountains adjacent to the presidio of Santa Cruz (de Terrenate). © British Library Board (Shelfmark: Cartographic Items Additional MS. 17,661.b.).*

on the Sobaipuri presence. Intensive investigation of historical sources has accompanied this archaeological work. One area of interest relates to the origin of the name "Babocomari." While some secondary sources have said that Babocomari is an Ópata word (e.g., Forest Service 2000:5), the word is instead consistent with O'odham, and, as just discussed, the river is well within historical O'odham territory, far from that of the Ópata (see Seymour and Stewart 2017). The word in O'odham derives from *waw komali*, which means "Bedrock Flat" or "an outcrop whose shape is stretched out horizontally," referring to the thin limestone bedding visible throughout the range (Bright 2013:12; Winters 2012:306–308; compared to Barnes [1935] 1982:29).

The modern-day Whetstone and Mustang Mountains were once known together as the Babocomari Mountains (Sierra del Babocomari). In 1780 Rocha y Figueroa provided this name on his map. He did not distinguish between the Mustang and Whetstone Mountains but instead included them as a single range (Rocha y Figueroa 1780b; figure 5.8). In the late Spanish or early Mexican period, as Europeans took over the landscape, the name began to change

FIGURE 5.9. *Painting of the hacienda of San Ignacio de Babocomari by William Ahrendt. Courtesy of Tubac Presidio and used with permission of William Ahrendt.*

reflecting the new political reality. At least a portion of the range was called Mestinez, Spanish for "Mustang" (Barnes [1935] 1982:57; also see Seymour 2020b, 2022b). They were then referenced as the Whetstone Mountains by Americans because of the mineral novaculite that was mined there for use as whetstones. This designation included the entire Mustang Mountains at one time, and then later a portion of what we now know as the Mustangs was excluded from the Whetstones and became the Mustang Mountains. Gradually, the entire Mustangs, as we know them today, were differentiated as a distinct mountain range (Seymour 2020b; Seymour and Rodríguez 2020).

The San Ignacio del Babocomari Hacienda along this river was granted by the Mexican government in 1832 to Don Ignacio and Doña Eulalia Elias (Fink 1998). With fifteen-foot-high adobe walls and towers on two of the corners, it was nevertheless abandoned in 1849 owing to Apache attacks (figure 5.9). Later, between 1866 and 1869, the hacienda became Camp Wallen (AZ EE:7:1, ASM). The cavalry base used the hacienda walls as a fortification, with the lower adobe walls used as a horse corral. During the 1850s the hacienda was noted by A. B. Gray (1856:51) and was spelled Babacomeri both in the report and on the illustration (figure 5.10). The drawing/lithograph was drafted by a

FIGURE 5.10. *Artist's rendition/lithograph of the hacienda of San Ignacio de Babocomari by Carl "Charles" Schuchard in the 1850s. New Mexico State University, Archives and Special Collections, Lithograph by Carl Schuchard.*

FIGURE 5.11. *The O'odham name Babocomari changed to Babacomari and Babacomeri in the Historic period. This image shows the tile work at the modern ranch gate. Photograph by Deni Seymour.*

member of the same expedition, illustrating the building and area facing to the east. This began a change in the name that was later adopted by the current landowning family that has referenced the ranch as Babacomari for a couple of generations (figure 5.11; Ellen Brophy Williams, personal communication 2016). This also accounts for the two ways common today of saying and spelling the name ("Baba có mahrē" and "Babō cōmahrē").

The Sobaipuri presence on the Babocomari River during Kino's time was limited to the two villages noted in the preceding section, "Huachuca and the San Pedro Headwaters." These communities likely shifted along the river margin as fallowing periods, seasonal floods, or factionalism required. Both were plotted by Kino north of the river. There are only a few locations suitable for farming on the Babocomari River within the Sobaipuri worldview, and it is in these areas that archaeological evidence for Sobaipuri has been identified, both north and south of the arroyo. In some areas along this river, as on others in the region, water travels along the channel underground. In other stretches the channel margins are enclosed by bedrock, forming a narrow channel bed and rendering it unsuitable for agriculture. Yet, this attribute pushes water to the surface, making it available for use downstream. In still other locations, the surface water languishes, forming extensive swamps. One of the two most extensive swamps was in the vicinity of Camp Wallen (Fink 1998:78). The malaria problem caused much illness and many deaths, eventually resulting in the abandonment of the fort "owing to its unhealthy state" (Fink 1998:73).

This unhealthy condition may also explain why soon after Kino visited these villages, the settlements were no longer mentioned. The spread of this Old World disease may account for Sobaipuri abandonment of all their settlements along this river. A long-standing question is how quickly and when various diseases spread to this region. Malaria and other mosquito-borne diseases would have flourished in this swampy zone. It is possible that this abandonment registers the spread of this disease into this area in the late 1690s or early 1700s or the recognition of and connection of symptoms to this disease at this time (also see Roberts and Ahlstrom 1997).

The other, and likely once more extensive, marsh is called the Babocomari Cienega near the current Babacomari Ranch, upstream from a narrows that separates it from the marshy area at Camp Wallen. It is here, above the marsh that a sizable Sobaipuri village was located, which probably corresponds to the historical place called San Joachín.[7] As noted above, San Joachín was the largest and most important of the villages occupied along the Babocomari River in the 1690s. It was also the furthest west at that time. Its unusual setting above the ciénega may be a consequence of either the need for a defensive setting or to the characteristics of surface water along this portion of the river. Further investigations of the site itself are likely to provide additional answers.

Elsewhere, my reconnaissance of the Babocomari River margins has revealed a minor amount of evidence for the Sobaipuri occupation owing to subsequent disturbance. Many of the terraces overlooking the river have been bulldozed, probably to increase grass coverage and reduce mesquite for grazing, as is common in this region under the misimpression that this mimics historical conditions. Other terraces seem to have been covered with river silt, suggesting that perhaps as erosion increases through the years additional evidence may be available.

Evidence of what may be the remnants of Santa Ana were identified several years ago, further downstream, closer to the San Pedro. No follow-up work has been conducted so little more can be said about this site.

Minor evidence of a Sobaipuri occupation is visible at Camp Wallen as Whetstone Plain sherds, but this seems to represent later tradewares. Here both prehistoric and Sobaipuri evidence are visible near the hacienda foundations, an indication that in constructing this feature the earlier deposits may have been disturbed. Subsequent disturbance from the fort, sheepherders, and the railroad have all contributed to the virtual erasure of this site, if present. It is known that Whetstone Plain was sold to and used by non-Indigenous settlers in the region well into this period. The single Whetstone Plain sherd date run for this site did not produce a useable result (UW3830).

CONCLUSIONS

The Babocomari River and the San Pedro headwaters have remained a mystery. Numerous important questions have been posed in the past in part due to a lack of data. Some of the inferences drawn by earlier researchers can be questioned now that additional data are available. Among these, we must question Bolton's line that distinguishes Sobaipuri to the north of the Babocomari River and Gaybanipitea, and Pima or Ópata to the south. In fact, data show that this line is incorrectly placed. We also have a bit more information with which to evaluate the Indigenous villages at the San Pedro headwaters, and all current evidence indicates these are O'odham, and Sobaipuri specifically. A later, eighteenth-century map and this information provided by Kino provide strong evidence that Ópata territory started a bit further south and began along the Sonora River. Huachuca is an O'odham word, and the village of this name was at the San Pedro headwaters, not on the Babocomari River, which extends Piman territory to the south. Further research will undoubtedly address additional issues, including where the villages were at the headwaters and if they were all, in fact, ethnically Sobaipuri or representative of some other Piman group.

NOTES

1. In this last statement he seems to be assuming that the O'odham in this area were also nomadic, which is not the case.

2. Note that this Ternate is on the opposite side of the river and in a different location from the later Santa Cruz de Terrenate Presidio (compare figures 5.2 and 5.8).

3. Bacadéguache is shown at the headwaters of the Santa Cruz, just west of the river in the San Rafael Valley as shown in Kino's *Saeta* map (see figure 5.1).

4. From the Chiricahua Land Claims documents, we know that at least in the early nineteenth century this place, Macuka, was called *t?iscihóti*, "Cottonwood Trees Come Out" or "Four Cottonwoods" (Henderson Chiricahua Apache Land Claims field notes, 1957).

5. Here I am using Sauer's transcriptions of these village names without revisions.

6. This location has to be another eleven leagues north of Huachuca, rather than fifteen plus twenty-six leagues, because otherwise the distances are much too great.

7. There has not yet been an opportunity to obtain a sample for a chronometric date for this site.

6

Sonoita Creek is an important tributary to the Santa Cruz River and as such is in the Santa Cruz River watershed. A subset of important Sobaipuri settlements were located there in the modern-day Sonoita-Patagonia area, somewhat isolated between the Santa Cruz and San Pedro Rivers. The Hispanicized name Sonoita (Sonoitac or Sonóidag, depending on dialect) means "Spring Field" or "Field at Point Where Rocks Emerge" in O'odham (Jane Hill, personal communication, March 17, 2014). Sonoitac means Spring *Son*—also means "base," point where mountains, trees, water, and so forth emerge from ground [same as the *son* or *shon* in Tuc-son, "black base"] and Field (*oidag*, sounds like *oidak* to English speakers; see discussion in chapter 2). This name conveys the importance of the presence of surface water and arable land in the placement of Sobaipuri villages in general and those found in this location specifically. Sonoitac can also mean "base" or "where something emerges from the ground." In this case it could mean "Field where the water emerges from the ground" or even at the "field at the base or point of the mountains." Either interpretation of this name would be appropriate because the main flow of Sonoita Creek remerges near where the Sonoita village of Kino's times and later was located. This location is also very rocky and rugged, pushing the water to the surface, making it available to past and current residents. The same is true at the north end of the valley, where a fault line allows water to flow to the surface at

https://doi.org/10.5876/9781646422975.c006

Cottonwood Spring (Phil Halpenny, personal communication, 2017), which is also at a point where the bedrock pinches the channel, forcing the water to the surface.

Sonoita Creek generally hosted a much smaller Sobaipuri population than the San Pedro and Santa Cruz Rivers because it was a smaller drainage with shorter segments of irrigable land. In the upper portion of the drainage, it also had only two areas of springs within the channel during the Historic period whose flow quickly descended below the surface. On Kino's first maps just two settlements were shown and mentioned: Los Reyes del Sonoitag (also spelled Sonoydag) and San Gerónimo. Yet, the valley soon had a larger population than Guevavi when Headman Coro, with between 500 and 600 Sobaipuri from the villages of Quiburi and Santa Cruz de Gaybanipitea, moved there after the 1698 battle on the San Pedro (see Kino in 1699 in the section "Sonoita Village"). Given the size of the migrant group and their origin in two distinct San Pedro villages, these newcomers probably occupied a village of their own, or perhaps two. At this time, this valley was considered as being in the interior and was referred to as such (Kino 1698c). It had been a place away from the enemy, somewhat behind the lines protected by a shield of allied natives: the San Pedro Sobaipuri. Yet, once Coro and the populations of his two middle San Pedro villages moved here, the front line of conflict shifted. Throughout the first half of the eighteenth century, the valley continued to attract Sobaipuri populations, probably as a result of residents attempting to move farther east, away from Spanish interference, and further west from the enemy frontier. In 1741, 1742, and 1756, Francisco Xavier Pauer and Joseph de Torres Perea noted separately that they "visited the village of Sonoita and its rancherías," suggesting at least three settlements, if not more (the Mission 2000 database has conflicting entries regarding dates of these events). By this time, all or most of Coro's Sobaipuri had moved back to the San Pedro, so the occupation of these settlements must be accounted for by populations from other areas. Archaeological survey confirms a fluctuating population throughout the valley's history, with at least ten distinct Sobaipuri settlements identified.

Even so, the Sonoita-Patagonia area was surrounded closely by mountain ranges, the Patagonia Mountains to the south or east and the Santa Rita Mountains to the north or west, forming a relatively narrow valley. The rugged and mountainous terrain made the area even more dangerous for the local O'odham residents than in the major south-north river valleys. These mountains provided a direct route of attack and retreat for groups, such as the Jocome and Apache, hostile to the Spaniards and their allies. This point was acknowledged in the second half of the 1700s, after which this valley was abandoned by its O'odham residents owing to incessant and deadly attacks (Seymour and Rodríguez 2020). The mountains also, however, served as the watershed for the valley, providing reliable water that emerged through numerous springs, which of course made this valley attractive for agriculture and therefore habitation.

SONOITA VILLAGE

After extensive field investigations, only two Sobaipuri sites have been identified situated in the vicinity of the main spring with the most prolific flow. Historical maps and texts indicate that these sites represent the village of Sonoita as it shifted from one side of the river to the other through time. These village locations were used repeatedly through the centuries, as were most Sobaipuri settlements that were ideally positioned in relation to surface water and fields. Superimposed structures, and shifts in structure orientation, as well as chronometric dates indicate these villages were occupied sequentially from the late AD 1500s, if not earlier.

The village called Los Reyes del Sonoydag was initially south of Sonoita Creek in Father Kino's time (1690s) (Reies in figure 6.1a; see figure 3.1 and Reyes in 5.1). The first reference to this village on maps and texts is as Reis, Reyes, and Los Reyes (see Burrus 1965, 1971). Los Reyes was appended to the Indigenous name Sonoitag in part so that it would not be confused with an O'odham village of the same name, San Marcelo del Sonoydag, located further to the southwest in Hia C'ed territory. Fewer references to this eastern Los Reyes del Sonoydag village are available in the early period than many other places because it was off the main travel routes and also, presumably, because the populations were smaller than along the primary rivers. From the earliest records we know very little, but in 1698 Kino bestowed a cane of office or governor's staff to leaders at Guevavi and Los Reyes, because, he told us, the leaders who had received the canes before had died in the previous months (Burrus 1971:560; F. Smith et al. 1966:13). Like this one that follows, most references to the village are incidental, when Kino or Manje are discussing another place:

> On the 27th [of October 1699] at noon we arrived at Guevavi where we counted ninety souls. There are many more at the ranchería of Los Reyes to the eastward, about four leagues away. In the afternoon we passed on to San Cayetano [del Tumacácori]. (F. Smith et al. 1966:79)

In this context Kino did not state explicitly why the population was so comparatively large, but this relates to Coro and his people moving here, as noted

FIGURE 6.1. *Maps showing the location of Sonoita over time, (a) by Kino in 1695–1696 but is only called by that name in figure 6.1b and (b) depicted by Rocha y Figueroa in 1780; otherwise it is shown as Los Reyes or Reies. © British Library Board (Shelfmark: Cartographic Items Additional MS. 17,661.b.).*

above. Kino clarified in an April 24, 1700, statement that Los Reyes is, in fact, Los Reyes del Sonoydag, and he specifically referenced the 500-plus people who had fled a couple years before from the San Pedro after the 1698 battle:

> On the 24th [of April 1700] we set out for Guebavi and San Cayetano. In Guebavi, where we took a siesta, there were about two hundred souls. In Los Reyes de Sonoydag, five leagues farther eastward, Capitan Coro had gathered with all his people, who numbered more than five hundred souls. (Bolton 1948:I:233)

By 1710 some chroniclers, including Father Agustín de Campos, were referencing the village and area as Sonoitac, which is just another way of saying and spelling Sonoidag in a different O'odham dialect. This more southwestern dialect was likely from the southwest in Hia C'ed territory, where the other Sonoita, San Marcelo del Sonoydag, was located, as just noted (Ives and Ruhen 1955). Or perhaps this is the way it was said in Cucurpe, where in

1710 the first-known reference to the village as Sonoitac, one by José Agustín de Campos, is contained in the mission records (Libro de Bautismos, in Mission 2000 database).

Sonoita remained along the trail between better-known locations and consequently appeared in the mission records well into the 1700s. As Padre Felipe Segesser was discussing pitahaya wine in his 1737 *relación*, which, as he noted, "is pleasant to drink but is intoxicating," he conveyed a story about the residents of Sonoita, as follows:

> When I was in Guebavi [1733–1734] I once ordered that the Pimas of village Sonoita (which belonged to my mission) should come to Guebavi on a certain day to clear my acres and uproot thorn-bushes. The magistrate, as I call the chief among them, agreed that on this day they would first clear the acres at their village (acres which were already planted) and would then come to Guebavi.
>
> On the appointed day, accompanied only by a boy, I rode to the two hour distant village. There I found my gardner [sic] lying on the ground drunk. Only with difficulty did I learn from him that a drinking bout was in progress at the house of the magistrate. I proceeded there immediately. When I was still a bow-shot distant from the house I was discovered, and the magistrate came toward me and invited me to have a little drink.
>
> I asked him whether the field had been cleared, and whether they were going to keep their word to their father missionary. To this he answered: "Father, what do you say! Taste the wine, how sweet it is. It is certainly a fine drink." Thereupon some Indians brought a gourd dish filled with wine, to propitiate me. Since I wished to have nothing to do with the intoxicated Pimas, I sat cautiously to horse so as to be ready any instant for flight. Thereupon the magistrate called his companions to greet me, according to the custom of the region. Then one should have seen the capers they cut! Some, who could not even walk on their quaking knees, were dragged up by the others, and all shouted very tearfully: "Father, the drink is good! Get off your horse and join us, the wine is good!"
>
> I did not consider it advisable to tarry longer with those drunkards. So although I could hardly contain my laughter I turned to the magistrate and said, very earnestly, "Tomorrow, we will look into the matter." Then I returned quickly to my house. On the occasion of a similar drinking-bout these Pimas killed one of my servants who was supposed to guard some horses. It is not to be wondered at, therefore, that the bishop has threatened with excommunication those who give assent to such drinking-bouts. (Treutlein 1945:149–150; also see Kessell 1970:54–55)

FIGURE 6.2. *Photograph showing the low mound that represents the remnants of the house built for the missionary where a battle at Sonoita took place. Photograph by Deni Seymour.*

This activity recorded is very likely a rain ceremony carried out to encourage rain to fall, wherein saguaro wine plays an important seasonal role in calling down the rain.

The name change from Los Reyes to San Ignacio de Sonoitac in the 1730s or 1740s suggests that the village may have moved to the north side of the river at this time. Epidemics may have resulted in villagers shifting the village more than once. Each location both north and south of the river shows some evidence of repeated use through time. On the other hand, some people think this name change was precipitated by the construction and dedication of a church. More likely, the religious structure was an adobe house that doubled as a council house (figure 6.2; see Seymour 2014). The house that served as a church was burned in 1751 during the Pima rebellion (Kessell 1970:144). Then apparently after the rebellion, another new house, or perhaps the first more substantial church, was built at Sonoita, perhaps to the south of the river, because, as was noted:

> When the wife of Juanico, native governor of Sonoita, died in the village early in 1756, the Padre noted that she was buried "en Aquella Yglesia." . . . Three

years later, Pauer buried Sonoita's foreman of oxherds in what he termed "la Nueva Iglesia," presumably there at Sonoita. (144)

This new church was probably referencing the same church as mentioned three years before. Either way, it seems that there was likely an actual church constructed at Sonoita during Pauer's time, though even then, it may have been nothing more than the "neat little house and church" constructed at Guevavi, which was essentially a one-room adobe house (Seymour 2009c, 2011a, 2014; also see discussion in Seymour 2019a). John Kessell (1970:156) states that in the 1760s Father Miguel Gerstner succeeded in finishing Father Pauer's new church at Sonoita. The presence of a substantial church, if true, indicates that the village was once again south or east of the river, because no such sizable construction has been found in the completely undisturbed village north of the river, though the remains of a small adobe structure are present (see figure 6.2). This church was mentioned again in 1772 by Fray Antonio Reyes, when he noted that the church and the missionary's house had no ornaments or furniture (Reyes 1772). Subsequent construction in the village area south of the river during the American Territorial period may have destroyed this church, despite that an adobe outline is visible that could represent its melted walls and foundation, or perhaps a later hacienda or adobe related to later settlement (figure 6.3). Alternatively, as noted, the foundations of a small adobe structure consistent with those reported and excavated at other Sobaipuri villages is visible to the north, perhaps suggesting that the adobe-walled structure ("the house they call the Father's") mentioned during a later attack (see quotation later in this section) was already there.

Epidemics in 1749 and in 1751, preceding the revolt that destroyed the house, including smallpox that killed many people from Sonoita, may have helped precipitate the uprising or at least contributed to its popularity. The uprising began on the morning of November 21, 1751, but apparently had been planned for some time. Usually characterized as a nativistic movement, it is likely that both the disrespectful treatment of Luis Oacpicagigua (meaning: "He Cannot Be Killed"; Morning Light, personal communication, 2018) of Saric and the waves of devastating epidemics contributed to the unrest. Here at Sonoita the two epidemics contributed to the death of seventeen people, a significant portion of the population. We know the names of some of these people from Sonoita who died and who, while having taken on Spanish given names, in many cases, still retained their Indigenous names that were written down as surnames. Those who died in 1749 include Teresa Cossu (*kos*, "nest" AND *kosa-*, "cover" AND kooso, "sleep"), Woman Appears (Rosa Massiubi [masi

FIGURE 6.3. *Seasonal variations in aerial photographs reveal dried vegetation showing the outlines of what could be the historic church or a later hacienda at Kino's Sonoita. Courtesy of Google Earth.*

uvi]), We Gamble (Lucas Attimait [ati mait]), and Mockingbird or Creosote (Xuucu [Ssucu] [su:g] or [segoi]), who was wife of Governor Francisco Uburistuito (no translation), who was governor from 1746 through 1747, and again from 1749 through 1750 (Mission 2000 Database). Thirteen residents of Sonoita died during the 1751 epidemic, sometime between October and November 11. These included Woman Is Hot (María Tonnori-ubi [tonori uvi]), Hand So White (Agustín Mamsstoa [mam si s-toa]), Cheppa, They Are Dying (Teresa Paibcoo [possibly + ko'o]), Tobacco Infused Water (Xavier Vivacssutac [viva-g(a) suudag]), Mountain Stands (Francisco Toacu [possibly: do:dag ke:ka]), Pale Woman (Ana María Toossic [(s-)toa osik]), Luis Cubusso, Luis, Juana, Miguel, and two children whose names were not provided.

Some of the names seem to have conveyed their condition prior to or upon dying (Woman Is Hot, Pale Woman). Others may reflect statements, such as, "just cover her up" rather than stating the name (e.g., Teresa Cossu [kos, "nest" AND kosa-, "cover" AND kooso, "sleep"]). Although written down as names, these phrases more likely represent misunderstandings between the priest and the resident O'odham or also perhaps the traditional proclivity of some O'odham families to avoid saying the name of the deceased. It is also possible that in these records, we are seeing a new custom of renaming or nicknaming a person (as occurred throughout their lives for memorable actions or events) so as not to have to say the name of the deceased.

The first Christian burial in Sonoita's cemetery—that of Ignacia, wife of the Native governor of Sonoitac—was recorded on May 20, 1738. Padre Pauer recorded the burial as occurring "in that church." This was probably the first church and, as noted, may have been nothing more than a single-room adobe structure. Ignacia's husband, Juanico, was the next burial recorded in the new church at Sonoitac. He had been governor of Sonoitac (between 1748 to 1758). The thirteen burials recorded in the church at Sonoitac were:

1. 1756: Ignacia, wife of the Governor Juanico
2. 1759: Juanico, Governor; widower of Ignacia; husband of Manuela
3. 1760: Catalina, wife of José the ox driver
4. 1764: Lorenzo, a child
5. 1765: Santiago, the foreman
6. 1769: Eusebio Vuesa, a widower
7. 1770: Francisco Maupo
8. 1771: Juan Santos de la Cruz, a child
9. 1773: Juana Teresa, a child
10. 1773: Estevan, a single man
11. 1773: Francisco, a widower
12. 1773: Antonio, husband of Josefa
13. 1773: Francisco, a widower

O'odham, still rebellious after the 1751 revolt, surrounded Sonoita in 1759 and killed one resident (Kessell 1970:143).[1]

In 1761 Padre Ignaz Pfefferkorn included Sonoita in a census of villages under his charge. For Sonoita he recorded 34 families, 2 widowers, 2 widows, with 19 adults and children receiving instruction (Kessell 1970:160). This probably equated to about 150 people, at an average of 4.28 people per family. This total would have made Sonoita's population slightly higher than Guevavi's, which was the head mission at the time (see Kessell 1970:160).

Another census in 1766 recorded 44 married adults, 17 widowed, 34 single (95 adults), 66 of whom were considered converted (those who confess) (Kessell 1970:172). Evidently, this census was taken right before an epidemic (Kessell 1970:172). Six burials of Sonoita's residents were recorded for the year 1766 (none are recorded for the following year). Cause of death is not indicated, but each was buried in the Sonoita cemetery. Two were prominent residents, having held important positions, while the remainder were either not named or were only given names were provided. These include Gregorio Upubaga ([ep e-baga], Also Got Angry) had been mayordomo of Sonoita from 1756 through 1758. He was governor at the beginning of 1759, replacing Juanico, and continued in that office until his death in 1766. He married María on February 28, 1759, and 16.5 months later had a child by Isabel on July 13, 1760. Because both women are recorded as his wife, either María died (of which there is no record), or it was one person named María Isabel, or Padre Pauer made a mistake on one of the names. It is also possible that he had two wives, as was not uncommon among the O'odham but would not have been tolerated by the priests. At the time of his death, Padre Ximeno recorded that Also Got Angry was married to Ana María (Mission 2000 database). Juan Antonio Viquimuri ([vi'ikam meri], The One Left behind Runs) was *fiscal* (court official, attorney) of Tumacácori from 1755 to 1758 and *alcalde* (municipal officer; governor of the locale) of Tumacácori from 1758 through 1766. A widower died as well, but no name was provided, while for three people only given names were provided: Isabel, who died suddenly, Juan, and Josefa.

Sometime during this period, but certainly during an interval in the mid-1700s, the village moved to the north side of the creek. A map drafted in 1780 shows that the ruined village of Sonoita was located north of Sonoita Creek (figure 6.1b). Presumably, this would have been one of the most recent occupations with houses still standing; otherwise, Rocha y Figueroa and brigadier and military governor Don Jacobo de Ugarte y Loyola would have been drawn to another location. This seems to have been the Sonoita recognized at the time. Perhaps they or someone with them had visited this location in the not-too-distant past; if not, they might have plotted the village on the south side of the river. This northern location is far more defensible than the one to the south/east, but nonetheless, still approachable from the north/east.

A report dated March 5, 1773, by Fray Bartholomé Ximeno at Tumacácori conveyed this twenty-six-family Sonoita village was attacked by the Apache in 1770 and 1771 (figure 6.4).

> Sonoytac, that is 11 leagues from the *cabecera* Tumacácori, has 26 families. But, in all of them there are only 11 women, because of an attack made by Apaches, 2 years ago, they killed most of the women in the house they call the Father's, where they had taken refuge. Almost all of Sonoitac's plantings are done

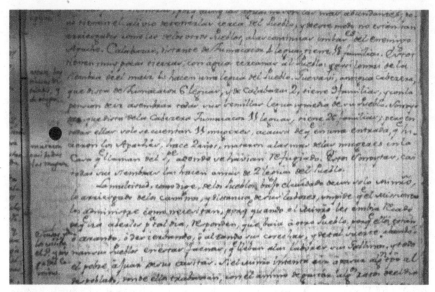

FIGURE 6.4. *Fray Bartholomé Ximeno's 1773 handwritten comment about Sonoitac being attacked by Apaches.*

more than 2 leagues from the village. (author's translation; also see Kessell and Bartholomé Ximeno 1964:307–308)[2]

The final sentence of the quotation indicates that the residents of Sonoita farmed the bottomlands more than five miles to the north or east, nearer Cottonwood Spring. As Kessell (entry 85, Tumacacori Book of Burials, page 168 of the Tumacácori Mission register; Kessell and Ximeno 1964:308n14) noted, nineteen inhabitants of Sonoita "died at the hands of the Apaches" on July 13, 1770. The names of some of these people, along with their English translations include:

> On July 13th of the present year [1770], [the following] died at the hands of
> the Apaches in the village of Sonoitac: Juan María, governor; his wife Ysabel;
> Catalina, widow; Miguel and his wife Teresa; Ines María, widow; Catalina,
> Joseph, single adults, and, of course, without sacraments. Juan Chrisostomo,
> Luis, Juana, María, Josepha, Juan María, Juanico, Joseph Antonio, Luis, Pablo,
> Lucía—all children, and they were given an ecclesiastical burial in the cemetery.
> And for the record I sign.
>   Fray Juan Chrisóstomo Gil de Bernabé,
>   Apostolic Father and Minister for His Majesty

Those listed in the Mission 2000 database who died on this date from an Apache attack match those in the above-quoted record. As in the above-referenced register, only first names are given. Eleven of these were infants who had not yet received the sacrament. Their young age indicates that the attackers were intent on wiping out the resident population, rather than taking the children and raising them as their own, as occurred later among the Apache. This event indicates a type of conflict that would result in annihilation rather than simply winning the battle. Juan María, who had been governor of Sonoita, and his wife, Isabel, both perished, also suggesting that the attackers knew who they were, killing and perhaps targeting those most important and most vulnerable in the community. The future of the settlement would certainly be placed in peril by killing leaders and children.

A second attack occurred on July 1, 1771, when three deaths occurred, two of whom were women (Rosa, wife of Antonio, and Inés, wife of Ignacio; Xavier, husband of Rosa; Burial 105, Kessell and Ximeno 1964:308n14). No O'odham surnames names were given. This event was recorded as a double attack on both Tumacácori and Sonoita.

A document resulting from Father Tomás Eixarch's visitation at Tumacácori, May 12, 1775, tells us that a few years later Sonoita's occupants moved to Calabasas:

> In addition, at a distance of four leagues, or a little more or a little less, is an outlying mission village called Calabasas in which live the Indians of Guevavi and Sonoita, depopulated because of the furious hostility of the Apaches. The number of persons at the said village is 141—that is, one hundred and forty-one. All are Indians of the Pima and Papago tribes, as are those of Tumacácori. (Kessell 1965:79)

The abandonment of the village north of the creek after the death of inhabitants is consistent with certain O'odham practices relating to death (Segesser in Treutlein 1945:158), apparently as a result of this or other Apache attacks, with the village's occupants moving to Calabasas on the Santa Cruz River. By the 1780 visit of Rocha y Figueroa, the village was in ruins, as noted, and apparently this area was not reoccupied, at least information is lacking from historical texts and maps for a reoccupation. Yet, given that archaeological investigations on other rivers continue to show occupation long after mention is made of an O'odham presence, it is possible that other European settlers had their eye on this valley and therefore made no mention of an O'odham presence, as occurred on the San Pedro, so as to have access to the land.

FIGURE 6.5. *Arrow points likely from the 1770 battle: (a) Sobaipuri, (b) Apache with base snapped off. Photographs by Deni Seymour.*

Archaeological evidence of one or both of these battles that resulted in village abandonment in the 1770s has been identified. Apache and Sobaipuri arrow points have been found, and many are clustered in one section of the site north of Sonoita Creek (figure 6.5). From past efforts at Santa Cruz de Gaybanipitea, we now know that this evidence reflects some of the hallmarks of a battlefield signature: high densities of spatially concentrated projectile points and projectile points of different groups in a village setting. Numerous quartz crystals are also present along with an arrow shaft polisher and a formalized maul (figure 6.6; see Seymour 2014, 2015b for details of this battle signature). The structure in which the residents took refuge has been identified, and it rests as a low mound of adobe at the north end of the village site (see figure 6.2). Its melted dimensions approximate those of the adobe-walled structure at Santa Cruz de Gaybanipitea, whose size when excavated was 9.5 meters by 4.24 meters (Seymour 2014:112).

These villages referenced as Sonoita have played a continued, important, and unexpected role in shaping the history and legal ownership within the

FIGURE 6.6. *(a and b) Evidence of the 1770 battle includes an arrow shaft polisher and a maul. Photographs by Deni Seymour.*

Sonoita Valley. Not understanding the O'odham custom of moving their villages, George J. Roskruge erred in his survey of the valley when establishing the boundaries of the San José de Sonoita land grant. The original land grant was surveyed in 1821 under the Spanish government. The surveyor used the 1770–1780s Sonoita village north or west of the creek as a point of reference, as well as other key landscape attributes. In fact, "the survey was commenced at a point 'on the very walls of Sonoita,' which was designated as the center point of the grant" (Bowden 2004–2018). Later, after the Gadsden Purchase, when Roskruge resurveyed the boundaries to resolve apparent discrepancies, he used the Kino-period Sonoita village south or east of the creek. This 1889 survey reshaped ownership in the valley, noting the placement of the original mission and other terrain features, while assuming that the Mexican land surveyor erred in his measurements or using this explanation to shift the boundaries.

SAN GERÓNIMO

Six previously unknown Sobaipuri O'odham villages were identified on private land along another stretch of Sonoita Creek associated with the portion of the valley that would have been fed by Cottonwood Spring. This is the section in which San Gerónimo was located when Kino visited. At least one of these is thought to correspond to the 1690s San Gerónimo recorded and plotted on Kino's maps. Another one or two might be the village(s) occupied by the Sobaipuri O'odham who relocated here from the San Pedro after the 1698 battle near Fairbank.

These six Sobaipuri settlements are situated to take advantage of water that emerged from Cottonwood Spring located near what was likely once the head of the Sonoita Creek channel. Surge from Monkey Spring, which is situated in a side drainage, may have also supplemented this flow. The river channel is currently dry to the east or upstream from Patagonia (except for water captured in a dammed area). The flow from Cottonwood Spring quickly descends underground, except that which was taken off the surface flow in canals, as was done by the late nineteenth-century American cavalry forts (Buchanan and Crittenden). These six Sobaipuri sites represent the village referenced by Kino as San Gerónimo and its various manifestations through time, perhaps some earlier villages whose names have been lost to history and, as noted, seemingly the village or villages occupied by the residents of the middle San Pedro during their exodus after the 1698 battle.

While the village named San Gerónimo was plotted on Kino's maps, upstream from Los Reyes del Sonoitag, Kino made only one mention of it in his writings:

> On the seventeenth of March, 1697, I again went in to San Pablo de Quiburi. I returned by way of San Geronimo, San Cayetano, and San Luys, looking in all places after the spiritual welfare of the natives, baptising [sic] some infants and sick persons, and consoling all with the very fatherly messages from the father visitor, and even from the Senor alcalde mayor and military commander, notifying them at the same time to be ready to go with the soldiers on the expedition against the enemies of the province, the Hocomes, the Xanos, Sumas, and Apaches. (Kino in Bolton 1948:I:165–166; also see Burrus 1971:96)

Interestingly, Manje was likely referencing the Indigenous name of San Gerónimo, when on October 27, 1699, he commented:

> We came to the settlement of Guevavi, or Gusutaqui, which gets its title from another river which runs from the east to west and joins it at this place. There

are two more settlements on this river, called Sonoyta and Auparicoso, where there are 180 people. (Karns 1954:136; also see Burrus 1971:450, 450n19)[3]

These are the only two settlements mentioned at the time, so it is likely that the name was San Gerónimo de Auparicoso. Aupa in the Wa:k O'odham dialect is a cottonwood tree, according to Felicia Nunez (personal communication, 2020), and so this may be the basis for the name. This might account for the current name of the nearby spring as well. Given the small size of the overall populations mentioned during this visit, the population count would have preceded the movement of people here who fled the San Pedro.

DISCUSSION

One interesting feature of these Sobaipuri sites along Sonoita Creek is that the spatial layout of household pairs within sites differs somewhat from that found in other valleys. On the more than 110 Sobaipuri O'odham residential sites I have recorded and mapped, structures are grouped in household pairs aligned in rows, and the pattern on these Sonoita Creek sites is no exception. The layout at these Sonoita Creek site differs, however, suggesting that perhaps ethnic or inter-drainage differences among Sobaipuri residents are being conveyed in minor variations of site structure (see figure 2.9). The first two rows in figure 2.9 show the layout of paired structures end to end or side by side observed and mapped at other sites on the San Pedro and Santa Cruz Rivers, whereas the bottom row shows the layout of paired houses in the household groups along Sonoita Creek, which exhibit a unique association.

Chronometric samples were run from each site where enough material could be collected. These chronometric dates place each of the sites in time, allowing us to distinguish those occupied during Kino's time from those earlier and later. Sobaipuri villages shifted along the river margins through time, so it is not surprising that a long sequence of use is indicated. Many more samples would need to be run from each site to ascertain the full length and true depth of occupation, but that work remains for the future with grant sponsorship. The same people and their families moved along the river margin, occupying more than one place throughout their lifetimes. For generations, their descendants continued to live along these segments of the riparian strip, taking advantages of infrastructural improvements in the valley's bottomlands. So little dating material was available on each site that only a single occupation was dated in each instance, and only four of the sites had datable material. Dates in the San Gerónimo area ranged from AD

1560 to 1640. The single optically stimulated luminescence (OSL) date run on a Whetstone Plain sherd from Kino's Sonoita (AZ EE:5:53, ASM; where considerable later [non-O'odham] occupation is apparent) produced a date of AD 1640±30 (UW3248). Two luminescence dating results from Rocha y Figueroa's Sonoita (AZ EE:5:54, ASM) were AD 1720±20 (UW3831) and AD 1770±40 (UW3792). The first result on the northern site places it during or shortly after Kino's time, reinforcing the notion that the occupants of this place moved back and forth across the river many times throughout its history, while the second date corresponds closely with the historical abandonment of the settlement. One of Kino's maps (1701, *Paso por tierra a la California*; Burrus 1965:pl. 10–13) does plot the village to the north of the creek, which is consistent with this pattern. This shifting is common for Sobaipuri O'odham sites, and many others of these along Sonoita Creek exhibit evidence of reuse. Repeated Sobaipuri O'odham reuse is evident in the reorientation of structures and by superimposed structures. Some sites, like the only possible candidate for Kino's Los Reyes del Sonoita, produced a chronometric date earlier than the Kino period, demonstrating a repeated use of this especially appropriate landform and location along the creek for settlement through time. Moreover, as noted, Sonoita shifted to opposites sides of the river, and probably back, and these movements are documented by the historic record and the single date obtained (see Seymour and Rodríguez 2020).

Most of these sites exhibit an earlier prehistoric occupation, as expected, both because this is the norm for late sites that follow thousands of years of prior occupation and because the best locations always saw previous use. Irrigation farmers tended to first choose the same locations as were occupied before because they were the best (and may have already had irrigation infrastructure) and then spread out to less-desirable locations. Therefore, those places closest to fields and water, and that had appropriate landforms for villages to be placed and expand, tended to be reused for centuries, if not millennia.

Reuse by other "protohistoric" groups is apparent on one of these Sobaipuri sites as well. Once the Sobaipuri moved, either up or down valley or out of the valley all together, other groups such as the Jocome moved in. They used the shade of abandoned structures and repurposed the especially suitable fine-grained flaked-stone material scattered nearby. This is apparent in the Canutillo complex assemblage found at AZ EE:6:106 (ASM) (figure 6.7). Here the formally prepared tools and distinctive debitage were scattered in a small area adjacent to a Sobaipuri house outline (Structure 4), suggesting that the Jocome visitor used the shelter provided by the house for a short stay. The debitage is distinctive both in the materials used (originating elsewhere) and

FIGURE 6.7. *Canutillo complex artifacts overlying a Sobaipuri component along Sonoita Creek indicating site was reused by the Jocome. Photograph by Deni Seymour.*

in the unique flaking attributes that indicate a different tool-making trajectory and technological production techniques than used by the Sobaipuri (see Seymour 2002, 2009a, 2016a).[4]

Two other Jocome, or at least Canutillo complex, sites have been identified along the Sonoita drainage. One is in a rock shelter where a light, but distinctive scatter is present, including groundstone and a flaked stone scraper (AZ EE:5:55, ASM). The second is on a terrace further downstream where projectile points and a light flaked-stone scatter are associated with roasting pits, one of which was dated to AD 1600±20 (AZ EE:9:269, ASM).

The Apache presence discussed in accounts of attacks of the Sonoita area from the mid-1700s, and so prevalent later on, are marked by side-notched Apache arrow points (Seymour 2014). These points are visible at the village referenced in 1780 by Rocha y Figueroa on the north side of the creek, indicating it was they who had attacked the village, rather than the Jocome.

CONCLUSIONS

Sonoita's history may seem complex, but it is no more so than any of the other Sobaipuri villages in any of the other valleys. The Sobaipuri practice of moving their villages every few years resulted in a complex series of occupations, as will be discussed in the final chapter and as was indicated for Quiburi in the next chapter (chapter 7). The abundance of detailed records regarding the population results in part from the closeness of this valley to that of Guevavi, which for a time was considered by the Spaniards to be the most important village in the area because as of 1701 it was the head mission. To know the names of the residents, and some of the reasons they were killed, provides an added layer of intrigue, and connects us more closely to these past residents, whose challenges mounted as they were embroiled in the conflicting interests of their time.

NOTES

1. This is not in the Mission 2000 database apparently. This is probably Juanico because this is the only burial mentioned for Sonoitac for this year, but his burial was recorded as occurring in November rather than June: He was governor of Sonoitac in 1748 and again from 1756 until the end of 1758, when he was replaced by Gregorio. He was recorded as "ex facto" governor at his death on November 19, 1759, and at his daughter's birth on March 19, 1759 (Mission 2000 database).

2. This is from Kessell and Ximeno's paper, but the original Spanish is "An unsigned letter book copy of Father Ximeno's report is among the 'Informes de los Padres de Sonora, 1772,' Documents Relating to Pimería Alta, 1767–1800, Fra Marcellino da Civezza Collection, Film 305, in the University of Arizona Library, Tucson" (Ximeno 1772).

3. It is interesting that Manje seems to be suggesting that Guevavi is on the same river as Sonoita, and he calls it the Guevavi River. This may have been a mistake, also made by later people, who assumed that Potrero Creek was the main river and the Santa Cruz, or at the time Santa María, was Sonoita Creek. Alternatively, what is today known as Guevavi Canyon goes through to Sonoita Creek and may have been perceived as the same canyon. This same mistake seems to have been made or was the perception held by John Mott in 1871 when describing the Jun-Cushing battle (see Seymour 2020b).

4. The flaked-stone assemblage that we can now associate with the Jocome was once thought to be Sobaipuri (see Seymour 2002, 2009a, 2014, 2016a).

7

San Pablo de Quiburi was described as a principal Sobaipuri O'odham ranchería when first visited by the Jesuit missionary Father Kino and military Captain Juan Mateo Manje in the 1690s (Bolton 1948:I:164–165).[1] These European visitors inducted or recognized the existing authority of Coro as governor, at which time they would have given him a cane or staff of office. Coro was the principal Sobaipuri headman and cultural attaché who occupied this settlement on the middle San Pedro River (figure 7.1).[2] Because of the richness of the associated documentary record, scholars have valued San Pablo de Quiburi as a historically referenced place, as a location where important historical figures (Kino, Manje, and Coro) visited, stayed, and conducted life's business. As a historical property, the site holds important information about the prehistory and history of the Sobaipuri. Information surrounding this settlement is also valuable as a study in the combined use of documentary sources and the archaeological record.

The documentary record refers to at least six distinct Quiburis.[3] In the 1940s and 1950s Di Peso (1953, 1956) acknowledged two of these Quiburis. Following Bolton ([1936] 1960:361), Di Peso thought he had identified the archaeological site relating to both of these Quiburis (San Pablo and Santa Ana) underlying the historic late eighteenth-century presidio of Santa Cruz de Terrenate (also see chapter 9). Although some scholars before and after Di Peso (Bolton [1936] 1960:361; Ives 1973:348; Kessell 1966) agreed that these

San Pablo de Quiburi

The Sobaipuri O'odham Ranchería of Kino's Conception

https://doi.org/10.5876/9781646422975.c007

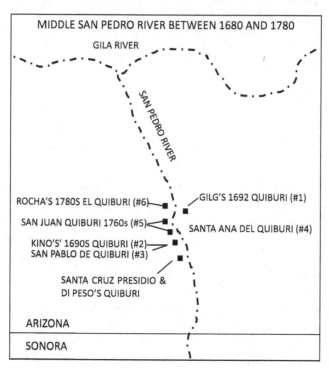

FIGURE 7.1. *Map showing the approximate locations of various villages referenced as Quiburi over time. Figure prepared by Deni Seymour.*

Quiburi settlements underlay the later presidio, well-founded opinions since then have discounted this interpretation for a number of valid reasons (Doyel 1977; Gerald 1968; Masse 1981; Seymour 1989, 1990, 2003, 2011a; also see chapters 8 and 9 in this book). Yet, until the mid-1980s, an alternative location for San Pablo de Quiburi had not been identified. In the past few years, new information has become available from my recent excavations at Santa Cruz de Terrenate Presidio and also from survey along the margins of the river and excavations at a Quiburi candidate (Seymour 1989, 1990, 1993, 2003, 2011a, 2011b). While there is a Sobaipuri site under Santa Cruz de Terrenate Presidio, it likely represents a different site, probably the successor community of Santa Cruz de Gaybanipitea, and relates to the post-1705 period, after the Sobaipuri returned from Sonoita (see Seymour 2011a, 2011b, 2012b, 2015a; see chapter 6).

I initially identified twenty-five Sobaipuri sites south of Benson as a result of archaeological inventory undertaken in the 1980s along the San Pedro River.

This research-oriented or thematic survey focused specifically on identifying Sobaipuri settlement distributions and locating these and other historically referenced places (Seymour 1987, 1989, 1990, 2003, 2011a). This count has since been increased, and new understandings have arisen as I have undertaken new investigations including mapping, excavation, and petrographic and chronometric analyses. At the time this information was originally published, I proposed a site that I thought was most likely to be the Kino-period San Pablo de Quiburi (AZ EE:4:23, ASM; Seymour 1989, 1990, 2003) owing mainly to its uniquely large size. But the addition of new archaeological data suggests that even this interpretation was in error.

There is strong evidence that the initial Kino-period San Pablo de Quiburi can be more discretely defined.[4] This present interpretation is corroborated with chronometric dates, with a site map showing approximately the reported number of houses, and by its location with respect to the correct documentary-based league distance from Santa Cruz de Gaybanipitea (AZ EE:8:283, ASM).[5] This chapter revises past interpretations of site distributions based upon more recently obtained archaeological information that is reconsidered in relation to documentary data. I also outline some of the assumptions and reasoned arguments that have led to past misinterpretations because these digressions are informative about how archaeology and ethnohistory are practiced.

QUIBURI IN HISTORY

The first mention of Quiburi is in a text from shortly before Kino arrived, when, as Bolton ([1936] 1960:247n3) said, an alliance between the Pimas and Jocomes at Quiburi was severed by Captain Francisco Pacheco Zevallos. Pacheco Zevallos (1686) provided extensive testimony during the trial of Canito (O'O'Caqui). This alliance is confirmed in 1691, wherein Blas del Castillo, alcalde mayor, accused the Sobaipuri residents of the Quiburi Valley of being united with the enemy (Forbes 1960:227). Soon after, in 1692, Captain Francisco Ramírez de Salazar descended the San Pedro, as was noted in chapter 5, passing far beyond Quiburi to the vicinity of the Redington or Acequias Hondas Narrows, and then passed back through Quiburi on the way south before turning west along the Babocomari. He referenced this as the Sobaipuri campaign, going against "those who had rebelled against the royal crown in the company of Janos, and Jocomes and other nations" (Ramírez de Salazar 1692a). At this time, Quiburi was but one of eighteen Sobaipuri settlements on the San Pedro, known at that time as the San Joseph de Terrenate River (Ramírez de Salazar 1692b).

On the way to Acequias Hondas, the Ópata auxiliaries killed a Sobaipuri woman and wounded her husband (Ramírez de Salazar 1692a). Three leagues or so further north they encountered and negotiated peace with a large group of Sobaipuri who had positioned themselves on "a peak and very rugged mountain range that you cannot climb on horseback, or even on foot with the weapons, which are required for such wars" (Ramírez de Salazar 1692a, 1692b).[6] After negotiating peace and breaking the alliance between the Sobaipuri and Jocomes and their allies, they turned back south (Ramírez de Salazar 1692b, 1692c; also see Bolton [1936] 1960:266–267, 360–361n2; Forbes 1960:244–245; Ives 1973:348; Karns 1954:79; F. Smith et al. 1966:35n5; Wyllys 1931:138). They had gotten at least as far north as the Reddington Narrows (Acequias Hondas), but it is unclear which mountain range they were referencing.

It seems the concern of an alliance noted during the Canito trial, as well as in other documents, was well founded in that archaeological survey confirms that a cluster of Jocome-Jano loci, including residential sites is situated north of Quiburi (AZ EE:4:36, AZ EE:4:169, AZ EE:4:178, AZ EE:4:179, AZ EE:4:181, all ASM). These may represent the Jocome-Jano, whom Pacheco Zevallos, Blas del Castillo, and Ramírez de Salazar and others were referencing as settling down near Quiburi.

Also sometime in this early pre-Kino-period, traders from New Mexico had visited the San Pedro villages: "We have also certain reports that before the revolt of New Mexico [e.g., pre-1680] the Spaniards of those provinces used to come by way of the Apacheria to these our most remote Pimas Sobaiporis to barter hatchets, cloth, sackcloth, blankets, chomites, knives, etc., for maize" (Kino in Bolton 1948:II:257).

Occupation at Quiburi (see figure 5.2) is then documented by Father Adamo Gilg, when he plotted Giburi on his 1692 map (Alegre 1960:mapa 2, between pages 144 and 145; Di Peso et al. 1965:pl. between pages 40 and 41). This rather late reference relates not to its founding but rather to the belated interest of missionaries and military in this portion of southern Arizona. O'odham villages of variable sizes occupied the margins of the middle San Pedro as early as the 1200s CE, demonstrating that the first historical mention of named places is not synonymous with the first appearance of Pimans in the area, despite that researchers often treat it as if this were the case. On Gilg's map this village of Giburi is plotted on the east side of the river, rather than on the west bank where it is found on Kino's first map from 1695–1696 (Burrus 1965). I have undertaken extensive but unsuccessful efforts to locate this east-side village on the ground in the late 1980s, early 1990s, and again in the 2000s. This lack of success suggests that Gilg's plot on the east side might have been based on hearsay because numerous Sobaipuri sites are present on the west side of the river with little evidence on the east. Alternatively, the settlement may have been located on low ground and has since been covered over by river sediments or destroyed by channel cutting or later occupation, such as at Drew's Station or Contention City. It may have also been much further north, though at present no evidence of it has been found immediately south of Pomerene and Tres Alamos, despite my repeated, concerted efforts to find it.[7] Any of the historic modern ranches or settlements may have destroyed evidence of this earlier village as well.

In 1692 Father Kino entered the San Pedro Valley for the first time, mentioning both Baicatcan on the lower San Pedro and perhaps Quiburi (Quiburi #2; numbers keyed to figure 7.1) on the middle. This visit was recorded in a brief statement by Kino:

> I then passed to the other Sobaipuris of the east, of the Río de San Joseph de Terrenate, or de Quiburi who are 30 leagues distant in their principal ranchería, that of San Salvador del Baicatcan. Captain Coro and the rest received me with complete hospitality. (Kino 1692 in 1698a, author's translation; also see Bolton 1948:I:123)

The meaning of this statement has long been debated. This statement suggests strongly that Coro was at his principal ranchería, that of San Salvador del Baicatcan. Coro was the head chief for this area, and thereafter Quiburi was the principal settlement on the middle San Pedro and, in 1694, with the next mention of Coro, he was at Quiburi. So, this raises the question as to whether Coro was simply visiting Baicatcan or once lived there or whether Kino went south to visit with Coro at Quiburi. Bolton ([1936] 1960:269) suggests that Kino's text was simply misleading and, instead, that Kino went to Quiburi in 1692, where Coro was living. Di Peso (1953:25–28) understood Kino's comment to mean that Coro resided at Baicatcan in 1692 and subsequently moved south to Quiburi by 1695 (Polzer and Burrus 1971:312).[8] I am in agreement with Di Peso, because Manje and Bernal later tell us that the Sobaipuri populations in this area moved south, seemingly in 1696, contracting their settlements, owing to conflicts with Humari's more northern Sobaipuri (Crockett 1918:83; Karns 1954:79; also see F. Smith et al. 1966:37; see chapter 10). Kino also noted that San Salvador del Baicatcan was thirty leagues distant, and by this he means thirty leagues from San Xavier del Bac.[9] Quiburi is much closer to Wa:k than the latter is to Baicatcan, and the distance between Baicatcan and Quiburi is substantially less.

In May 1694 Lieutenant Antonio Solis traveled to the San Pedro among the Sobaipuri (Bolton 1948:I:127n128; Karns 1954:47; Manje 1720), though it is not clear whether he passed through Quiburi. Other details of his trip are overshadowed by the ruckus he caused at San Xavier del Bac when he encountered residents with deer meat and, thinking it was horse meat, killed residents and flogged two, only later learning of his error (Manje in Karns 1954:47).

The next mention of the village is made on September 13, 1695, at which time Domingo Jironza Petris de Cruzat, Domingo Terán de los Ríos, and Juan Fernández de la Fuente and their armies of over 300 were welcomed by Coro at Quiburi just after subduing the 1695 uprising (Polzer in Polzer and Burrus 1971:312–313). The record is detailed, conveying several particulars about this settlement that are useful for archaeological inquiry. Fernández de la Fuente noted that there were *crops planted in the floodplain*, he *ordered all the soldiers and Indian allies to camp just beyond Quiburi*, and he referenced the *Quiburi fields*:

> It was noon on September 13 when the full army was greeted by Chief Coro
> of the Sobaipuri Village of Quiburi. Fuente ordered all the soldiers and Indian
> allies to camp just beyond Quiburi so the men and animals would not destroy
> the crops planted in the flood plain of the Rio Terrenate [San Pedro]. A great
> gathering was planned for the afternoon so all the Indians would pledge their
> loyalty and join in the festivities. At the banquet in the Quiburi fields that
> afternoon Coro explained to the generals that the Jocomes and Janos had
> been planning to ambush the Spaniards in the Sierra de Chiricahua. But Coro
> thought there would be very little chance of that since the Spanish forces were
> so huge. The chronicler records varying figures about the size of the army; his
> individual figures total some 352 men while his own sum is 320. But by any
> standard this was a substantial army in the isolated valley of Quiburi. (Polzer in
> Polzer and Burrus 1971:312–313)

Kino's December 15, 1696, visit to the village of Quiburi was commemorated by a detailed journal description of the settlement, referred to for the first time as *San Pablo de* Quiburi (Quiburi #3). He noted that (a) there were 400 residents, (b) an earthen enclosure fortified the settlement, (c) Quiburi was the principal ranchería on this part of the river, (d) Coro resided here, (e) an adobe-walled structure was built for the prospective missionary and this adobe-walled structure was inside the fortification enclosure, and (f) he supplied the village with a few cattle and a drove of mares:

> On the tenth of December I went to San Pablo de Quiburi, a journey of fifty
> leagues to the north, passing by Santa María and by Santa Cruz, of the Rio
> de San Joseph de Terrenate. I arrived at Quiburi on the fifteenth of December,

bearing the paternal greetings which the father visitor sent to this principal and great ranchería; for it has more than four hundred souls assembled together, and a fortification, or earthen enclosure, since it is on the frontier of the hostile Hocomes . . . We began a little house of adobe for the father, within the fortification, and immediately afterward I put in a few cattle and a small drove of mares for the beginning of a little ranch. (Bolton 1948:I:164–165; also see Polzer and Burrus 1971:95)

Kino's 1695–1696 map *Teatro de los trabajos apostólicos de la Comp. de Jesús en la América Septentrional* (Burrus 1965:43, pl. 8; Polzer and Burrus 1971:73) was probably drafted after this visit. This is the earliest mostly complete map of the northern portion of the Pimería Alta. (Gilg's map shows only the southern portion of the San Pedro and Santa Cruz Rivers, only their headwaters.) Kino may have been the source of the information on his *Teatro* and subsequent maps, but it is probable that he also consulted with Manje, Zevallos, and Solis, who had visited this river and settlement before Kino.

In 1697 Kino referenced March and April trips to San Pablo de Quiburi, and during the latter trip that he was received "with crosses and arches placed in the road" (Bolton 1948:I:166). During the third 1697 expedition to San Pablo de Quiburi in November Kino noted, quoted in part: "We found the Pima natives of Quiburi very jovial and very friendly. They were dancing over scalps and the spoils of fifteen enemies, Hocomes and Janos, whom they had killed a few days before" (Bolton 1948:I:168–169; also see Polzer and Burrus 1971:96–98).

Arriving two days later to join the expedition on November 9, 1697, Manje described the settlement of Quiburi in the following way:

At a league distance we arrived at the settlement of Quiburi, located on the banks of the river with a large valley, plains covered with pasture, and lands where corn, beans, and cotton are harvested. The Indians are dressed in cotton. All the lands are under irrigation. Captain Coro, chief Indian of the Pima nation, together with his people received us splendidly. We were lodged in an adobe and beamed house; and they gave us presents, as is their custom. We counted 100 houses and 500 persons of both sexes. The chief celebrated our arrival by giving a dance in a place arranged in circular form. Hanging from a high pole in the center were 13 scalps, bows, arrows, and other spoils taken from the many Apache enemies who they had slain. (Karns 1954:78)

From this account we learn that Quiburi was located on the *banks of the river*, overlooking *a large valley*, with *lands under irrigation*, and an *adobe-walled structure*. About *500 persons*, including Coro, dwelled in about a *hundred houses* (Karns 1954:78; Manje 1926:248; also see Bolton 1948:I:164–165, [1936] 1960:361; Polzer and Burrus 1971:200, 336, 351, 359–361). It is not known if Quiburi was adding residents or whether these differences in numbers between 1696 and 1697 represent people away on trips or differences in counting techniques between census takers. It is also likely that this settlement gained residents when an area to the north was abandoned, as Manje noted and as alluded to above, owing to conflicts between residents in the northern political zone: "We continued to the north down the river passing by some disserted settlements. Because of discord with other settlements to the north, Chief Coro had depopulated them a year before. He told us of this while traveling with us" (Crockett 1918:83; quotation in Karns 1954:79).[10] Lieutenant Cristóbal Martín Bernal supplemented this information, noting: "Asking him [Coro] how the Sobaipuris were on the river below [north of] Quiburi, he said he did not know because it had been a long time since they had communicated with him because in days past he had sent a relative of his on business and they had killed him" (F. Smith et al. 1966:37).

During this same expedition, Lt. Martín's diary provides a slightly different version but one that confirms Kino and Manje's accounts:

> Captain Coro and all his people received me. They were actually dancing with the scalps of 13 enemy Jocomes and Sumas which they had killed toward the north up among the rest of the rancherías of their own tribe . . . After having acquainted myself with everything I counted 97 houses and 486 souls at the village. (F. Smith et al. 1966:36–37)

MANY PLACES NAMED QUIBURI

San Pablo de Quiburi, the third in the series of six European-named Quiburis, was abandoned shortly after Kino's initial visits, when, following a key battle in 1698 at the neighboring village of Santa Cruz de Gaybanipitea, residents of these two (and only remaining settlements in this area) left the San Pedro to occupy a new location along Sonoita Creek (see discussion about Sonoita in chapter 6; Seymour 2010b, 2014, 2015a). The Sobaipuri had won the battle against their mobile neighbors but probably rightly assumed that the aggressors would attempt to avenge the deaths of so many (Seymour 2014). When the Sobaipuri returned to the San Pedro River in 1705 (Decorme 1941:410; Di Peso 1953:34; Spicer [1962] 1981:127) or shortly thereafter, they occupied two settlements referred to as Santa Ana del Quiburi (Quiburi #4) and Santa Cruz (the village at the later location of the presidio), though, as Di Peso (1953:34) noted, Father Keller continued to refer to the former as San Pablo.

In the 1760s the name "San Juan Quiburi" appeared in mission records (Bancroft 1886:563n23, 562–564) and was referred to as a *pueblo de visita*, or a peripheral visiting station. This reference probably dates to 1764 but certainly to the pre-1767 period, before the Jesuits were expelled. No other information is provided, but this reference shows the continued existence of the Quiburi settlement (Quiburi #5) and suggests that Santa Cruz was no longer occupied.

Most past scholars have suggested that both these settlements (Quiburi and Santa Cruz) were abandoned in 1762, when the *Rudo Ensayo* says all Sobaipuri left the San Pedro Valley (Pradeau and Rasmussen 1980:73–74; although Di Peso [1953] incorrectly said 1769). The preceding reference to San Juan Quiburi suggests otherwise, as do new documentary sources and archaeological information that have since been uncovered (Seymour 1990, 2011b; Seymour and Rodríguez 2020). A 1780 map and journal and a 1784 map prepared by Rocha y Figueroa stated that there was a small population remaining at "Quiburi" (Quiburi #6), but now the settlement was many miles to the north of the Kino-period Quiburi and Santa Cruz de Terrenate Presidio (Rocha y Figueroa 1780a, 1780b, 1784; Seymour 2011a, 2011b; Seymour and Rodríguez 2020; see chapter 8). Santa Cruz, the daughter or subsidiary settlement, was nonexistent by the time the new location for Santa Cruz de Terrenate Presidio was selected. This inference is based on a statement by Hugo O'Conor that the latter be built "at a place named Santa Cruz" (1994:63). Additionally, in his 1781 report, Teodoro de Croix noted that Santa Cruz de Terrenate Presidio had previously been moved to the abandoned pueblo of Santa Cruz (Thomas 1941:147–148).

This complex history of Quiburi means that when seeking its location, it is necessary to ask *which* Quiburi. For this chapter, only San Pablo de Quiburi is addressed, while history related to various other Quiburis is discussed elsewhere, including in chapters 8 and 9.

OLD AND NEW PERSPECTIVES

Initially, I suggested that of all the Sobaipuri sites encountered during the 1980s inventory only one (AZ EE:4:23, ASM) was large enough to qualify as the Kino-period San Pablo de Quiburi (Seymour 1989, 1990), but even so, it was too far north to match league-distance descriptions. To explain site distributions, I suggested that perhaps a number of sites were included within the bounds of a single historically referenced Quiburi. This distribution would be consistent with Spicer's (1981) model of Piman rancherías as sprawling settlements. This mile-long string of sites, I reasoned, might extend from AZ EE:4:23 (ASM), on the north, to as far south as AZ EE:4:25 (ASM), forming the expansive rambling ranchería of Kino's time. This configuration would bring the visible house count to a sufficiently high level to match historic documents, assuming, of course, that there was a correspondence between surface and subsurface evidence on these sites, which has since been shown to be the case only in situations of extensive erosion. This scenario would address historically documented league distances and explain the unexpectedly high number of Sobaipuri sites given the then-prevalent, but incorrect, assumption of a shallow time depth for Sobaipuri presence in southern Arizona (see chapter 1). Alternately, it was suggested that the southernmost agricultural field in the vicinity of AZ EE:4:25 (ASM) might define the southern edge of Quiburi, from the standpoint of the Spaniards, serving as the beginning point for league distance measurements between settlements (Seymour 2003).

I have since revised this argument based on new archaeological data and consequent reappraisal of the standard and accepted historical and ethnographic narratives about the Upper Pima. To begin, AZ EE:4:23 (ASM) is not as large as initially suggested, because it is composed of nine spatially distinct Sobaipuri loci situated on the same large landform, some of which I have dated to different periods. Occupation clusters here because of the proximity of a separate water source. The series of Sobaipuri sites to the south, including AZ EE:4:25 (ASM), are discrete settlements, not part of a single large one. This interpretation is based in part on the fact that each occupies discrete landforms, has its own internal organization and range of features, and has its own occupational sequences.

It is now my opinion that the Kino-period site of San Pablo de Quiburi (AZ EE:4:25, ASM) is in the general vicinity of Santa Cruz de Terrenate Presidio, but not at it. This change in perspective is based on several lines of evidence including better understandings about the correspondence between surface and subsurface evidence including complete surface mapping of sites, analysis of league distances and site sizes, a revised characterization of the nature of the Sobaipuri ranchería, and collection and analysis of chronometric dates. Each of these issues is discussed in the following sections, while at the same time the larger implications of these new findings are highlighted.

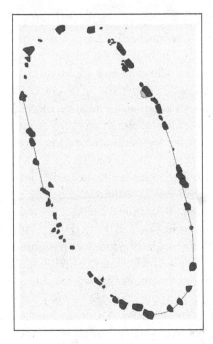

FIGURE 7.2. *Plan drawing of*
rock outline of a Sobaipuri house
at Quiburi (AZ EE:4:25, ASM).
The house is about 2×4 meters.
Figure prepared by Deni Seymour.

SURFACE DATA AND ARCHAEOLOGICAL INTERPRETATION

Past misconceptions about the nature of Sobaipuri sites arose from too-heavy reliance on surface archaeological data. Sobaipuri sites are represented by thin shallow cultural deposits, and features and the rock outlines of houses are sometimes visible on the surface (figure 7.2). These distinctive house outlines and artifact scatters, though often scant, allow the distribution of features to be mapped and a cultural affiliation assigned. The fairly recent occupation of these sites, it has been thought, meant that in some instances insufficient time has passed for sediments to cover the features, especially in the generally erosive, degrading environment that characterizes the San Pedro River Valley. In other instances, sites are shallowly buried, but, it has been reasoned, cattle grazing has resulted in devegetation and the subsequent erosion of surface sediments, exposing a representative view of cultural features. This conventional wisdom is how in the past archaeologists, including myself, have approached archaeological consideration of Sobaipuri sites (Di Peso 1953; Doyel 1977; Huckell 1984; Masse 1981; Seymour 2003).

Surface data, however, have since proven to be an imperfect window into Sobaipuri site structure and feature frequencies. Recent excavations I have conducted on Sobaipuri sites on the Santa Cruz and San Pedro Rivers reveal that despite their near-surface position, most features remain buried and are therefore not visible during survey. Vastly different perspectives of the sites arise when opening broad-scale excavations, using brushes and trowels rather than picks and shovels, and from mapping unexcavated sites where surfaces have aggraded (see Seymour 2011a). Even at Di Peso's site of Santa Cruz del Pitaitutgam (AZ EE:8:15, ASM) numerous additional structures, thermal features, and outdoor work areas are visible over those initially recorded by him, substantially increasing (more than tripling) the feature inventory and diversity over his initial counts. At the native settlement of Guevavi (AZ EE:9:132, ASM), only four houses were visible when first recorded in the early 1990s (Seymour 1990), in the eight widespread loci that constitute the Sobaipuri village through time. House counts mounted as additional broad areas were excavated. The present count is at twenty-two in Locus B, even though only a small portion of the site and only part of a single of many loci have been exposed. England Ranch Ruin (AZ DD:8:129, ASM) almost certainly had additional structures that were paired with the six houses that were visible on the surface and therefore mapped (Feature 3, Doyel 1977:113; also see Seymour 2011a:fig. 6.3). One of the Santa Rita sites (AZ EE:2:80, ASM; see Huckell 1984) has also revealed additional structures that were not originally visible but that have been exposed through erosion or noticed through application of a revised understanding of site layout (Seymour 2011a). The implication is that surface data are not as reliable as once thought for characterizing these sites as a whole, even though cultural deposits are very near the surface. These sites are also much more complex than originally conceived, with evidence of repeated and long-term use, including superimposed houses, refurbished houses, houses built adjacent to old houses as if replacing them, and subsequent occupations by other Native groups (Seymour 2007b, 2009a, 2011a, 2011b, 2015a, 2016a, 2017b).

The archaeological site I now think is the historically referenced Kino-period San Pablo de Quiburi is a case in point. More than 100 structures (as well as other features) are now visible at AZ EE:4:25 (ASM). Originally only eight houses were in evidence on the surface. The new houses have been exposed through the intervening two decades because of the gradual removal of surface sediments through sheetwash erosion related to Bureau of Land Management road maintenance and bar ditch construction. Also, recognition of the signature of partially eroded features allows still-intact mostly buried houses to be mapped. So, while initially the eight structures visible on the surface seemed nearly all that were present, the inventory now exceeds this by a substantial magnitude of nearly twelve times the original estimates.

These findings mean that currently held assumptions about the representativeness of surface data from sites of various types, including Sobaipuri residential sites, possessing thin shallow cultural deposits are in error. This misconception has several implications, including evaluating the subsurface potential and information content of shallow sites. Another of these implications relates to attempts to derive population estimates from surface data, which will be substantially unrepresentative (see also Seymour 2011a). Moreover, this lack of correspondence between surface and subsurface feature counts has relevance for recognizing historically referenced places, such as Quiburi because house counts are one of the correlates used to connect historically referenced places in the documentary record to archaeological sites. San Pablo de Quiburi was said to have about 100 houses. Although these were not originally visible at AZ EE:4:25 (ASM), they now have been mapped, providing tangible evidence that this site is in fact large enough to qualify for the Kino-referenced place (figure 7.3).[11]

IMPLICATIONS FOR LEAGUE DISTANCES

In 1697 Manje noted that after leaving Santa Cruz de Gaybanipitea, they "journeyed north through the valley and downstream. After one league," he continued, "we came to the ranchería of Quiburi" (Crockett 1918:81; also see Karns 1954:78). In 1698 Kino himself had noted that these two settlements were a league and a half apart (Bolton 1948:I:179), showing that this measurement or estimate was not exact or standard, or that alternate routes were taken. Based on these observations, Quiburi should be situated 3 miles (2.6 to 4 miles), more or less, north of Santa Cruz de Gaybanipitea.[12] This is, in fact, where AZ EE:4:25 (ASM) is located. Inferences regarding the identification of both Santa Cruz de Gaybanipitea and San Pablo de Quiburi are based upon documentary descriptions of the topographic setting and number of houses, on plots provided on Kino's maps, and now also on the basis of chronometric dates.

Previously, suggestion was made that this site (AZ EE:4:25, ASM) was in the correct position to qualify as Quiburi with regard to league distances from Santa Cruz de Gaybanipitea, but structure counts were too low for the site to qualify (Seymour 1990, 2003). At the time this was the only known Sobaipuri residential site (other than the one Di Peso suggested was under Santa Cruz de Terrenate Presidio) that fit the distance statements of these chroniclers. Now it is known that others are present. Another small Sobaipuri site is located on a nearby ridge, separated from AZ EE:4:25 (ASM) by a

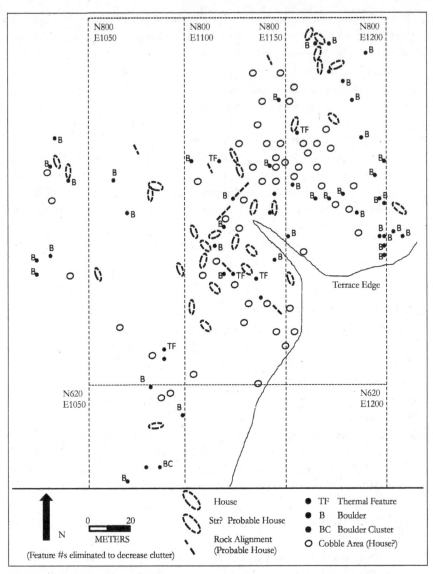

FIGURE 7.3. *Plan drawing of houses within the village thought to be Quiburi during Kino's time. Figure prepared by Deni Seymour.*

deep drainage. Also, what was initially reported as a single structure (possibly a field house; e.g., Seymour 2003) situated on the old floodplain is clearly a larger site, with two temporally distinct Sobaipuri components. The Sobaipuri components are within the newly defined bounds of AZ EE:4:5 (ASM) and are referenced as newly defined Loci C and D. These sites match the distance criteria noted by the narratives, but current evidence indicates that they are much too small and too late to qualify as the Kino-period Quiburi.[13] This leaves AZ EE:4:25 (ASM) as the only viable candidate.

THE RANCHERÍA CONCEPT

As was noted in chapter 2, my conception of the Sobaipuri ranchería has evolved considerably through the years. The initial view was based largely on historians' interpretations of the documentary record, but mapping and excavations of actual Sobaipuri sites have shown that their settlements were more properly referenced as villages or pueblos, as they were later by other Spaniards (e.g., Rocha y Figueroa; see also Seymour and Rodríguez 2020). These villages appear as spatially discrete clusters of formally arranged houses that were paired, each village usually on their separate landform. Thus, in contrast to previously held views, a house or cluster of houses situated hundreds of meters away was historically not considered part of the same village, nor has it been defined that way in current research.

At AZ EE:4:25 (ASM)—the site now inferred to be San Pablo de Quiburi—a well-organized layout is visible that is in keeping with the more widespread pattern of paired structures situated in dual rows found on Sobaipuri sites throughout their territory. Here a complex occupational sequence is suggested wherein some houses seem to be arranged in a U-shape or rectangle. At the Wa:k community at San Xavier del Bac, houses were arranged in three barrios in a triangle.[14] Data from these sites and others indicate that rather than being spread out, houses in the Sobaipuri ranchería, that is, a pueblo, were arranged in an orderly and predictable fashion, in planned and generally compact settlements, even before Kino's time.

As illustrated on the site plan (see figure 7.3), at least 100 structures have been documented at AZ EE:4:25 (ASM). As was noted, excavations often produce many more features, so it is expected that many currently unrecognized houses are present. In fact, a new house was exposed between site mapping and preparing and field checking the map. Moreover, there is sufficient space on the landform and adequate open space within the site boundaries to double the house count, which would accommodate and account for the house pairing typical of the Sobaipuri household.

At a minimum, figure 7.3 shows that this site is sufficiently large to qualify as the Kino-period Quiburi as described by Manje, for, they "counted 100 houses and 500 persons of both sexes" (Burrus 1971:336; Crockett 1918:81; quotation in Karns 1954:78). This figure also demonstrates that the main portion of the settlement is not spread out for a half or full mile, but, in fact, it is quite compact (about 250 meters by 200 meters) falling on a single topographic feature, like many others preceding and postdating Kino's era. The site just to its south may be a specialize locus of use related to this village.

CHRONOMETRIC DATES

The data presented here so far reveal that AZ EE:4:25 (ASM) has a structure count in the range of the number indicated in documentary sources. This site matches the distance from another known and agreed-upon Kino-period site, Santa Cruz de Gaybanipitea (AZ EE:8:283, ASM). No other sizable Sobaipuri sites are present at this league distance from the latter. These findings point to this site being the historically referenced San Pablo de Quiburi that was visited by Kino. But the question remains as to whether the site dates to the correct period.

Two lines of evidence can be used to address this issue: (a) European artifacts and features and (b) chronometric dates. This site and many others along this portion of the river contain historic European artifacts. Given this fact, the sites can be dated to the sixteenth century or later, but the value of these artifacts for distinguishing specific historically referenced places simply by their presence is diminished by their widespread occurrence and long date ranges of use. Here at AZ EE:4:25 (ASM) one of the most unique items found was a large metal awl.

The Sobaipuri on this river were receiving European goods long before sustained contact in the Kino period. This likely occurred as a result of the earliest recorded expeditions into the region, including Coronado (Seymour 2007c, 2009b), and also owing to contact with the New Mexico colony as noted in the section "Quiburi in History" (Bolton 1948:II:257) and northern Sonoran settlements. Moreover, later historic activity has inadvertently contributed artifacts to the assemblages of many of these sites. Unfortunately, most beads and metal found lack sufficiently narrow manufacture and use ranges, and so they are not helpful in assignment of sites to the Kino period specifically.

Chronometric dates, however, can be helpful, especially if they are precise enough to target this specific period, though repeated or continued use of sites complicates interpretations tremendously. A single date only captures a single moment of the potentially long and repeated uses of these sites. Regrettably, radiocarbon dating is generally not effective for addressing this type of issue owing to too-long confidence intervals and also to the tendency for this technique to produce multiple intercepts for much of the Historic period. Instead, OSL (introduced earlier in the chapter) and thermoluminescence (TL) have proven useful for dating other Sobaipuri sites and also Apache and Canutillo complex (inferred to be Jano or Jocome) sites occupied during this period. To this end, distinctly Sobaipuri sherds (Whetstone Plain) were collected from house interiors at AZ EE:4:25 (ASM), and two sherds were submitted for luminescence dating.

These luminescence dates from this site are consistent with the identification of AZ EE:4:25 (ASM) as San Pablo de Quiburi in showing that it was occupied during the correct time period. One date from Structure 1 produced a result of 1683±25 (AD 1658–1708; Oxford # X2962) that overlaps cleanly with the Kino period (AD 1691–1711) and Kino's initial contact with the Sobaipuri prior to their temporary exodus to Sonoita (AD 1698–1704). A second date of 1633±25 (AD 1608–1658; Oxford # X2970; Feature 77) suggests that the site was occupied over an extended period or repeatedly for short intervals. This deeper occupation is expected for a site of this importance, of this size, with this higher degree of material accumulation, and with a seemingly complex sequence of house construction that is located in such a choice place. In fact, most Sobaipuri sites along this segment of the river show evidence of repeated periods of reuse. This location was especially favorable with respect to its premier position near the canal heads. Thus, the site dates to the correct period and was likely occupied repeatedly for a long duration prior to the missionary period as well. Because later dates were not evident, these results also suggest that when the Sobaipuri returned from Sonoita after 1705, a different location may have been selected for the new Quiburi, as the name change to "Santa Ana del Quiburi" implies and chronometric dates from other sites farther north suggest.[15] Nonetheless, too few samples have been dated to understand the full complex occupational sequence of this site.

DISCUSSION

Strong new evidence supports the notion that San Pablo de Quiburi can be discretely defined. All lines of data point to AZ EE:4:25 (ASM) being the historically referenced site of San Pablo de Quiburi visited by Father Kino in the 1690s. This present interpretation seems corroborated by chronometric dates. These dates place the site in the Kino period and before. This long duration of use indicated by these dates is expected for a large and important site such as Quiburi, especially given its premier location along a broad portion of the floodplain. Moreover, these dating results also fit with the pattern that riverside locations were reused through time, after a short occupation elsewhere.

The site is compact and spatially separated from other sites, reinforcing its discreteness as a settlement. House numbers within this site are consistent with the documentary record. Not many of the other sites along this segment of the river are this large, judging from the number of houses visible and based on assumptions of additional houses that rely on knowledge of site structure. This assumption is also based on the size of the landform on which these other sites are situated, many of which would limit the number of houses that could be built. This greatly restricts the possible Quiburi candidates that might have seen the initiation of the missionary period. The site plan for AZ EE:4:25 (ASM) suggests that additional structures are probably still buried below the surface, that space is available for the paired household units typical of the Sobaipuri. Clearly, a more complex occupational sequence is evident than the documentary record indicates.

The identification of this site as the San Pablo de Quiburi visited by Father Kino seems also supported by its location with respect to the reported league distance from Santa Cruz de Gaybanipitea. This is one of only four Sobaipuri sites that are the appropriate league distance from Santa Cruz de Gaybanipitea. One reason for this absence of sites in the intervening stretch is that the series of landforms are inappropriate for Sobaipuri occupation and farming. AZ EE:4:25 (ASM) is sufficiently large to match the historical description of San Pablo de Quiburi, while the other three are too small or too late-dating to qualify.

The site also contains evidence of European contact, including historic European artifacts. This evidence for AZ EE:4:25 (ASM) being San Pablo de Quiburi is much stronger and more in line with the documentary record as compared to previous candidates for this historically referenced place: AZ EE:4:23 (ASM) or Santa Cruz de Terrenate Presidio. AZ EE:4:23 (ASM) is actually composed of nine discrete loci that date to different periods. It is too far north according to Kino-period league distances. Although it had numerous houses on an expansive landform, historic glass beads and iron, and a possible adobe-walled structure built for the missionary (Seymour 1987, 1989, 1990, 2003), several other sites have also produced similar evidence of historic contact. Given these new data, interpretations, and dates, it is reasonable to question whether instead the loci at AZ EE:4:23 (ASM) might be (1) the Santa Ana del Quiburi occupied when Coro and his people returned from Los Reyes after the 1698 to 1705 hiatus or (2) San Juan [de] Quiburi, which was occupied at the end of the Jesuit period (Seymour 2011b, 2011c). There are many other sites along this river segment as well, so until all chronometric dates are analyzed and a more expansive and systematic dating effort is undertaken these issues will remain unanswered, especially given the evidence for the shifting nature of Sobaipuri settlements.

I am now arguing that AZ EE:4:25 (ASM) is San Pablo de Quiburi, rather than the latter being situated under Santa Cruz de Terrenate Presidio, as Di Peso suggested or to the north, as I initially suggested. Many historians and archaeologists were under the impression that Quiburi underlay the late eighteenth-century presidio (AZ EE:4:11, ASM), but in recent years this inference has been dismissed. Sobaipuri material culture has now been confirmed at the presidio as a result of my recent excavations, but an alternate explanation for this evidence is being offered elsewhere (see chapter 1).

Reinterpretation of San Pablo de Quiburi is based upon newly gathered archaeological information. This understanding conveys a cautionary message with regard to the sole use of documentary and ethnographic sources and the inferences that can be built upon them using independent evidentiary sources. As new data become available, entirely new reconstructions of the historic past become possible. Ethnographic and historical sources provide a way to interpret archaeological data that might otherwise remain unclear or subject to many alternative interpretations. Similarly, the archaeological record provides a basis to question our long-held document-based assumptions and provides new insights into when and how apparently clear passages or customary understandings should be reconsidered. Moreover, the archaeological record conveys rather clearly that an overreliance on documentary and ethnographic records has led to a series of misguided assumptions that contributed initially to the wrong site being designated San Pablo de Quiburi. Yet, persistent collection of fresh data seems to have provided a remedy and a more accurate representation of the past.

NOTES

1. This chapter was first written in 2010 and was included in Seymour (2011b) and was subsequently modified for this book.

2. Coro was said by Di Peso (1953) to have previously lived on the lower San Pedro to the north, at San Salvador del Baicatcan. There is really no evidence for this information, based on a vague statement by Kino in 1692. Adherence to this assumption is based also on the thought that there was only a shallow temporal depth of occupation by the Sobaipuri on the San Pedro. Recent dates I have obtained from a number of

sites on the San Pedro and Santa Cruz show that the Sobaipuri were present from at least as early as the 1280s (among others, see Harlan and Seymour 2017; Seymour 2011a, 2011d). Settlements on the middle San Pedro, where San Pablo de Quiburi is located, show this time depth as well, suggesting that Coro's residence at Baicatcan is not needed to explain settlement distributions.

3. The five distinct Quiburis can be identified in the documentary record, but it is possible that the settlement moved more frequently and had a longer history. Quiburi is an O'odham word meaning "many houses," so this Indigenous name may have had a much longer history. There may be many more archaeological Quiburis, but the ability to attach the documentary record to a place is what gives this settlement, in its many manifestations, its historical significance. The same social groups seemingly occupied the various Quiburis through time, though additional lineages were likely added and subtracted. While each of these dimensions of Quiburi is of interest, this chapter is concerned with the ways in which the documentary record can be connected to these archaeological places and is focused on the Kino period San Pablo de Quiburi.

4. Locational information for these sites is not subject to the Freedom of Information Act and are being safeguarded but can be obtained by qualified researchers.

5. The reader will note that I have argued that the site Di Peso (1953) excavated was Santa Cruz del Pitaitutgam and that another site (AZ EE:8:283, ASM) that I documented south of that is the actual historically referenced Santa Cruz de Gaybanipitea (Seymour 1989, 1990, 2014). This interpretation is now widely accepted.

6. This type of mountain and peak describe mountain ranges on either side of the river, either the Santa Catalina or Galiuro Mountains, both of which are set back from the river's edge and are far from the *embudos*, or narrows, that occur downriver from the settlements.

7. Nonetheless, there are places I have not looked, including in the settlements of Benson and Saint David.

8. A comment by Kino in 1706 also has this sentence construction, wherein he notes: "The eighth [missionary could come] for Santa Ana del Quiburi, San Juachin, and Santa Cruz, where lives the famous Captain Coro" (Bolton 1948:II:182). Kino is referring to Coro living at Quiburi and living in the area of these three settlements, but the way this sentence is structured makes it sound as if Coro might be living at Santa Cruz.

9. A typo in *Where the Earth and Sky Are Sewn Together* indicates thirteen leagues rather than thirty (Seymour 2011a:66).

10. Although Manje is referencing settlements north of Benson and Pomerene (e.g., between Tres Alamos and the Redington Narrows), some of the settlements further south may also have been disserted at this time, with populations collapsing into fewer larger settlements, such as Quiburi. This occupational scenario would explain the accretional nature of house distributions at AZ EE:4:25 (ASM).

11. Of course, evidence for an earlier occupation means that house counts cannot be used directly to identify historically referenced places; this time depth and occupational complexity must be considered. Unless excavated in entirety, which is impractical and unadvised, exact house counts are not possible.

12. The league during this time is interpreted to be anywhere from 2.63 to 3 English miles. Distance might vary on the ground, depending on the specific path taken. Distance was sometimes recorded differently by different chroniclers as well (Seymour 2003:163).

13. Until chronometric dates are obtained from these sites and further erosion or excavations expose the limits of this site, it will not be possible to rule them out entirely.

14. Until recently, this large and important Sobaípuri settlement at San Xavier del Bac had not been located on the ground. Recent work has identified the location for at least one neighborhood of this settlement (Seymour 2019a).

15. Of course, many more dates would need to be run from different contexts on this site to be more confident that there is not also a later occupation. Dating samples extracted from different house rows might reveal temporal differences, but finding sherds suitable for analysis inside houses can be challenging.

8

The Waning Days of
Quiburi in 1780

The previous chapter discussed Quiburi as one of the first two Sobaipuri villages on the San Pedro to be noted by Padre Kino in the missionary period.[1] Quiburi's occupants were also apparently the last Sobaipuri to occupy the San Pedro River Valley during the Spanish Colonial period, except for those who in 1780 went with the Spaniards south to or were already settled around Las Nutrias. When in 1780 Rocha y Figueroa traveled with brigadier and military governor Don Jacobo de Ugarte y Loyola the length of the San Pedro River during a reconnaissance of the northern Sonoran frontier, the soldiers encountered some depopulated settlements, including the recently abandoned Santa Cruz de Terrenate Presidio (Rocha y Figueroa 1780a, 1780b; Seymour and Rodríguez 2020). Only one Native settlement was still occupied, and this was referred to as El Quiburi or El Guiburi, and its crossing was called Vado del Quiburi. Thus, Quiburi outlasted even the Spanish presidio occupation in the face of escalating frontier violence.[2] The occupants of all other Sobaipuri settlements had left to reside in the missionized communities further west and south, including San Xavier del Bac (Wa:k) and San José del Tucsón (seemingly established just for them; see Seymour 2022a), or they chose a dissentient lifeway that positioned them beyond the view of chroniclers. In 1780 missionaries did not venture into this area beyond the presidio line, especially since the protective population of the failed Santa Cruz de Terrenate Presidio had just been moved

https://doi.org/10.5876/9781646422975.c008

south to Las Nutrias in the face of incessant Apache attacks that cut supply lines, devastated crops, scattered settlers, and violently decreased the presidio ranks. Moreover, there were few Natives to minister to, and the official Spanish position was that the valley had been depopulated. Anyone remaining would be an embarrassment and a symbol of resistance to the direct order to relocate.

Although Di Peso (1953:40–42) suggested that the Sobaipuri had completely abandoned the San Pedro Valley by 1769, in reference to the 1762 removal, these more recently examined documents by Rocha y Figueroa show that this is not the case (see Seymour 2011b, 2011c; Seymour and Rodríguez 2020). Di Peso suggested an absence of Sobaipuri occupation because extant documentary sources suggested this scenario and there were no data to contradict or modify seemingly clear and definitive statements, such as the following from the *Rudo Ensayo*:[3]

> Among the Pimas, the most inured to war are the Sobahipuris who have been reared on the Apache frontier and are used to almost constant fighting. However, in 1762, being tired of frequent battles, they abandoned their pleasant and fertile valley. Some migrated south to Santa María Suamca while others went farther southwest to Guevavi and Sonoitac, and still others traveled west to San Xavier del Bac and Tucson, thus leaving free ingress to the whole Upper Pimería to the Apache enemy.
>
> Were it not for fear of the Apaches, two or three missions might have been established in the Sobahipuris Valley [San Pedro] which in time would have brought about communication with the rancherías on the north bank of the Gila River. We have already hinted that if we wished to populate the western side of the San Pedro River, we would have to do so with the little-to-be-trusted Papagos who cannot easily be induced to settle in villages. (Pradeau and Rasmussen 1980:73–74)

Juan Nentvig's (1764, 1863) rough descriptive essay (*Rudo Ensayo*) implied that all of the Sobaipuri had left the San Pedro River, but from Rocha y Figueroa's documents it is reasonable to conclude that while the majority of the San Pedro Sobaipuri may have left the valley, a small population remained behind, a population that was too small to warrant much outside attention (see especially "Population" section). Documents tell us that not all left, as will be discussed in this chapter, especially in the section "Ground-Truthing with Archaeological Data." Regardless, the community of Quiburi persisted at least until the 1780s, but without missionary interference that would have brought the village more mention. The absence of missionaries along with the official position of abandonment likely also explain why the Quiburi of 1780 was referenced only by its O'odham name, whereas earlier Quiburi settlements had Christian modifiers (saint's prefixes) appended to them. The persistence of Sobaipuri occupation in this portion of the San Pedro Valley is pertinent because a number of scholars have argued that the increased Apache raiding in Sonora was related to the complete abandonment of this valley by the Sobaipuri (Dobyns 1976:23; Stern and Jackson 1988:471; Winter 1973:72; but for discussion see Seymour 2011b, 2011c). The continued presence of this group, at least at this one settlement, requires a somewhat-modified perspective on this scenario, including explanations for the upswing in raiding, and a more critical review of Nentvig's work (also see Hastings 1961 regarding Bishop Pedro Tamarón y Romeral's contrastive account of the 1760s).

The documentary record for the period 1692 to 1784 suggests that Quiburi was in more than one location and that its position shifted through time. I have argued that the name "Quiburi" was retained to reference this community, while the on-the-ground position of the settlement changed along with the Christian prefix (Seymour 1989, 1990, 2004, 2011a, 2011b). As such, I have argued that this village was positioned in at least six distinct locations (Seymour 1989, 1990, 2003, chapter 7), both because (1) the name changed from San Quiburi, to Pablo de Quiburi, to Santa Ana del Quiburi, to San Juan Quiburi, and then to simply Quiburi or El Quiburi,[4] and (2) other types of documentary data suggest the location changed as well. In fact, chronometric dates, superimposed houses, and shifts in house orientation also suggest multiple discrete occupations at the suggested locations where each of the Quiburis was located. As previously noted (see chapters 1 and 7), this position is in contrast to Di Peso (1953), who suggested that Quiburi was at (under) Santa Cruz de Terrenate Presidio both before (then called San Pablo de Quiburi) the Sobaipuri's 1698 exodus from the San Pedro and after (then called Santa Ana del Quiburi) their 1704/1705 return.[5] Di Peso did not consider the sixth and latest occupied location because important documentary data were not yet known. The 1780s location of this much-sought-after archaeological site of Quiburi was far to the north of its Jesuit and earlier Franciscan period positions. I suggest this because the above-cited maps and journal (Edwards 2004; Navarro García 1964; Rocha y Figueroa 1780a, 1780b, 1784; Seymour and Rodríguez 2020) indicate that by 1780 Quiburi was at a considerable distance to the north of Santa Cruz de Terrenate Presidio, which is in a known location.

These more recently uncovered documentary data (e.g., Rocha y Figueroa's maps, journal, and summary reports), along with current archaeological results from the 1980s to the present (Seymour 1989, 1990, 2004, 2011b), were combined to identify the location of this important Sobaipuri site noted in 1780. A series of Sobaipuri sites is known along the river (Seymour 1989, 1990, 2003, 2011b, 2011c), but only one matches all of the specified criteria and is therefore the most likely candidate for the late eighteenth-century and early nineteenth-century Quiburi referenced by Rocha y Figueroa. This evidence for this site and the implications of its identification are discussed here.

DOCUMENTARY SOURCES

The presidio of Santa Cruz de Terrenate, located just north of Fairbank along the San Pedro River, was officially occupied between 1776 and 1780, though it was established in August 1775 when Hugo O'Conor selected its location. The residents and soldiers began their trek there in December 1775.[6] They left under the escort of Rocha y Figueroa in March of 1780. A month after its abandonment and movement of the garrison south to Las Nutrias, Rocha y Figueroa participated in an expedition and prepared a map and journal that showed this presidio in relation to the Sobaipuri settlement of Guiburi, or Quiburi (Rocha y Figueroa 1780a, 1780b, 1780c; also see Edwards 2004; Navarro García 1964:pl. 123; Seymour and Rodríguez 2020). The portion of this 1780 map with Quiburi and the presidio (Santa Cruz) is shown in figure 8.1a. Rocha y Figueroa prepared a second map in 1784 relating to a proposed campaign against the Gila Apaches, which also shows the crossing of Quiburi in the same or similar position relative to the abandoned Santa Cruz Presidio (figure 8.1b; Navarro García 1964:pl. 113; Thomas 1932:252–253; Williams 1986:130). From these sources, it is possible to see that the Sobaipuri settlement of Quiburi is located miles north of the presidio of Santa Cruz de Terrenate. This spatial relationship is one of the most important lines of evidence in placing this late Quiburi on the landscape.

Rocha y Figueroa's 1780 journal also notes that on June 5:

> We continued to the south-southeast one league to the Tres Alamos Ford, eight to the El Guiburi, and after resting, three to the south quarter southeast until the Santa Cruz Presidio . . . El Guiburi permits a small population for it is unobstructed [being clear], and with enough water, it has some springs independent of the river. (Rocha y Figueroa 1780b:209; Seymour and Rodríguez 2020:111)

This statement is consistent with the map plot and clarifies that the Quiburi settlement was three leagues to the north/northwest of the presidio of Santa Cruz de Terrenate. No Sobaipuri settlements are mentioned or plotted

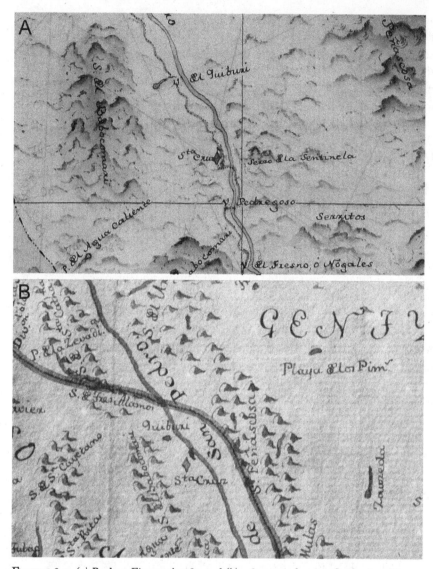

FIGURE 8.1. *(a) Rocha y Figueroa's 1780 and (b) 1784 maps showing Quiburi and its spring and crossing. © British Library Board (Shelfmark: Cartographic Items Additional MS. 17,661.b.).*

in the intervening area or otherwise shown or discussed in this area or along the San Pedro River in the documents from this expedition. Based upon this documentary data, it is reasonable to suggest that the Quiburi settlement of

1780 was positioned many miles north of the Kino-period Quiburi, which was discussed in the preceding chapter. It is also reasonable to infer on the basis of Rocha y Figueroa's documents that Quiburi was the only Sobaipuri settlement occupied in 1780 in the area or on the San Pedro (other than a few Pima at and near the settlement of San Pedro itself; see Rocha y Figueroa 1980c) and that the population in an earlier-mentioned subsidiary settlement (Santa Cruz) had moved to Quiburi or left the valley (perhaps the population shift mentioned during the *Rudo Ensayo*).[7]

EXPECTATIONS ESTABLISHED BY DOCUMENTARY SOURCES

Several expectations can be drawn from this limited-though-rich documentary data and these have important spatial, physical, material, and geographic implications. Among these are distance from a known place (e.g., Santa Cruz Presidio and northern San Juan de las Boquillas y Nogales land grant boundaries), presence of a water source independent of the river, and village size. These elements will be discussed in the following sections in detail in relation to finding the on-the-ground site. Yet, another indirect implication is that no other named or referenced settlements of any kind were present along this river at this time, except for at or near Las Nutrias and the (San Pedro fields) near the headwaters, where the Santa Cruz garrison retreated in 1780, as well as any number of enemy (Apache, Jocome, and Jano) encampments within the length of the valley. Discussion of the spatial, physical, material, and geographic implications of the documentary evidence simultaneously makes explicit the assumptions drawn from the data and illustrates how I have used these assumptions to identify and verify an on-the-ground location.

League Distance

The text of the Rocha y Figueroa's journal indicates that Quiburi was three leagues north of the presidio and adjacent to the river. This is about 7.8 to 10 straight-line miles to the north, depending upon the conversion used and several other factors.[8] One question relates to how they traveled the route along where the league measurement was made. It is especially important to know whether progress was made in a straight line or by following all the curves and turns of the river. If they followed along the river's edge, the distance would have been much longer than if they followed a straight line with the river at a distance but within view. There is a substantial difference in distance between these two approaches.

This very specific route-related question is seemingly addressed by a dotted line along the west bank of the river on Rocha y Figueroa's 1780 map that indicates the probable generalized route taken or the recognized trail from the presidio (figure 8.1a). Initially this trail likely followed the terrace overlooking the floodplain and seems to have curved in and out with the terrace edge at least four times. These demarcated bows, both outward from the terrace edge and back inward, correspond to deep washes, bends in the river, and other terrain features and obstructions that can be mapped today. In fact, many-meters-deep arroyos begin about 2.25 miles north of the presidio, which would have obstructed travel in this area, assuming of course that the arroyos were obstacles historically (figure 8.2; see Seymour and Rodríguez 2020). One reason to believe that these erosion channels or side arroyos were present at the time is that these locations are the appropriate league distances north of Santa Cruz de Terrenate in relation to where the trail is first shown to diverge from the river. Moreover, a large circular historic cairn is present at the head of one of these washes, suggesting that this feature marked the route around these impediments as the trail diverged from the river (see figure 8.2). This meandering would increase the distance traveled over the estimates that are based on distance as the crow flies.

Given this and investigational route plots on Google Earth, it is reasonable to infer that the site is situated in the six-to-eight-straight-line-mile range north of the presidio. The estimated distance traveled via the more circuitous route that avoided the arroyos would be closer to eight or nine miles.

Latitude ticks (using the Tenerife meridian) at the map margin indicate that 6.5 to 8 miles is about the proper placement for the Sobaipuri site relative to the latitude of Santa Cruz de Terrenate Presidio. Distortion of map images, enlarged place symbols, and exceeding large map-scale size contribute to some uncertainty, as does the approximate nature of the minute-to-mile (and league to mile) conversion and the fact that Rocha y Figueroa complained that league distances provided were not as accurate as he would like. Yet, on this map Quiburi is shown to be about a third of the distance between the presidio and Tres Alamos, which is where an appropriate candidate site is located on the ground.

Spring Independent of River

The diary text also noted that this settlement had "springs independent of the river." This statement corresponds to the water source shown on Rocha y Figueroa's map. The water source is illustrated on Rocha y Figueroa's map to the immediate west of El Guiburi Vado (crossing) by the tadpole-looking

FIGURE 8.2. *Photograph of the end of a deep arroyo where erosion has stopped owing to bedrock and with a historic stone cairn marking the end of the up-arroyo erosion. Photograph by Deni Seymour.*

symbol (figure 8.1a). This source is shown on many historic maps of the era, probably owing to its reliability. During the early 1800s this area was known as the Quiburi Cienega, as illustrated on the San Juan de las Boquillas y Nogales land grant map (Documents 1833–1901). This more recent reference adds another data point by which to peg this water source and village to specific geographic attributes and documented cultural boundaries.

Notably, there are only so many springs present along this portion of the San Pedro. Some springs have dried up as a result of modification of the springheads, the 1887 earthquake, and lowering of the groundwater table from pumping and overuse. Yet the geological evidence of these springs is visible even for those which are no longer active. In some cases, there is abundant corroborative evidence, including late historic irrigation canals that headed at these places. The one spring that lies within the bracketed distance north of the Santa Cruz Presidio, within the vicinity of a Sobaipuri site, is at the north end of the land grant where the Quiburi Cienega is later shown. These cumulative assumptions and their corresponding data, including negative site location evidence, suggest that El Quiburi, the settlement and the spring of the 1780s, was located at the north end of the land grant, which is less than six straight-line miles north of Santa Cruz Presidio.

The San Pedro River is located to the east of the spring and settlement, as indicated by the green (gray in figure 8.1a) ribbon running southeast to northwest in the center of this figure. Careful inspection of this green/gray band that depicts the San Pedro reveals that it is not consistently darkened. Along the entire length of the San Pedro the band cuts off abruptly, so that intermittent but distinctive segments are light, and then they are darkened. The change is clear, indicating this coloration change is intentional, rather than a copying error or careless representation. This difference depicts where the river flows reliably on the surface and where it disappears underground. This banding is also consistent with statements in the text that note some of the locations where the streambed was dry versus where there was water on the surface (Seymour and Rodríguez 2020). As Rocha y Figueroa (1780b:249) noted, a feature of the San Pedro, probably exacerbated by the ongoing drought, was that it was dry in many parts. This is a widely known characteristic of this southern Arizona river, and the surface and subsurface flow areas are consistent with what I have observed about the modern flow characteristics of this river.

This river characteristic explains why there is a break in occupation north of the 1780 Quiburi, because the river sinks beneath the surface after a large marsh, making the water unavailable much of the year. Sobaipuri settlements do not occur again until north of or downstream from the Tres Alamos Narrows, where once again the water is reliably available on the surface. Even today, and as noted in chapter 2, the emergence of water in this river tends to correspond with the constriction of the channel and presence of bedrock that forces water to the surface, making it available to residents, and attracting permanent settlement where irrigation features can be constructed (see Seymour 1989, 2003, 2020a; Seymour and Rodríguez 2020). The consistency of this attribute of the river through time means that generally where the river flow disappears today is where it would have disappeared in the past, if only seasonally. This general location, therefore, provides another data point for assessing where the Quiburi village and spring were located.

Population

Quiburi was also said to have retained or had a small population. From this assumption, we must assess what would have been considered a small population by this Spaniard. One way to evaluate this problem is contrast to the population of Santa Cruz de Terrenate Presidio and to other Sobaipuri settlements occupied at the time. Many settlements hosted considerable populations at their height, and toward the end of their occupations, populations increased at a few villages as people aggregated to address attacks by Apache and rebellious O'odham. The unanswered question is whether this presidio population, now temporarily stationed at Las Nutrias, was viewed by Rocha y Figueroa as a small population. This will be discussed again in the following section, "Ground-Truthing with Archaeological Data."

The location of Quiburi allowed a small population because it was situated in an area that was unobstructed, and so they did not need a large population to protect themselves. Otherwise the enemy could sneak up on them, as had proven the case at the Santa Cruz Presidio (despite efforts to situate it otherwise). This advantage suggests that it was either on a broad flat plain or terrace or that it was on a raised topographic feature.

GROUND-TRUTHING WITH ARCHAEOLOGICAL DATA

Using these data and their attendant assumptions, it is possible to assess where the site is located that was referred to as Guiburi by Rocha y Figueroa in 1780. Comparison of these documentary sources to those of the missionary period makes it very clear that the Quiburi of 1780 is much farther north than the Kino-period Quiburi, but this still leaves a lot of terrain and many potentially qualifying sites. Each of the data points provided by documentary sources can be independently evaluated using previously gathered and newly obtained archaeological data.

A zone of probability as to where this site should be located may be delineated on the basis of league distance from a known place, generalized and more or less imprecise latitude readings, a route as indicated by a dotted line depicting the trail, and placement relative to known geographic features depicted in relation to mapped ownership boundaries (e.g., land grant boundaries). Investigation of appropriate topographic features in this zone of probability produced only a single Sobaipuri site. AZ EE:4:38 (ASM) is positioned at the southernmost point at which the 1780 Quiburi could be located to conform to the league distance indicated (figure 8.3). No other Sobaipuri sites are known to be present for many miles to the north. The areas immediately south of this site are devoid of Sobaipuri occupation because the landforms or river characteristics are inappropriate. Thus, the location of AZ EE:4:38 (ASM) is the only candidate site found and is generally consistent with the map and journal sources for Quiburi.

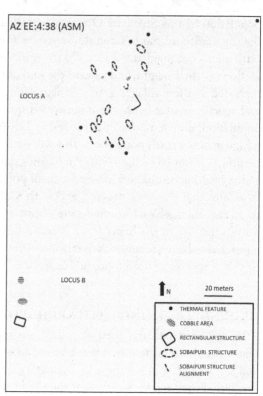

FIGURE 8.3. *Plan of the 1780 Quiburi. Figure prepared by Deni Seymour.*

The sources of water, or springs, independent from the river itself, are indicated by both Rocha y Figueroa's journal and map. These likely reference the spring and swampy area now visible near AZ EE:4:38 (ASM). These independent water sources are an important marker for the location of this site because, as noted, there are not many springs in this vicinity, on this side of the river, and the others in the general area do not have nearby Sobaipuri sites. While changes in groundwater conditions have altered the number of active springs, seeps, and cienegas, evidence of these can still be seen on the ground. There are only three known springs or seeps (on maps or identified on the ground by the author) on this side of the river in this general area. The next nearest spring of these three is the only other spring identified on the west side of the river between this location and the presidio. It does not conform in any way to league distances from Santa Cruz Presidio because it is only a couple of miles north of the presidio, far too close to the presidio to qualify as the 1780 Quiburi spring. The other is in an area that has not produced evidence of Sobaipuri settlement because the nearby landform is unsuitable. That leaves a single spring and marsh in an area with a Sobaipuri site along this stretch of the San Pedro. There are also only so many topographic features in this stretch that are appropriate for Sobaipuri settlement, and only this one is situated near its own supply of water.

Population size at AZ EE:4:38 (ASM) may be calculated based upon information from the documentary record and also upon the number of houses visible on the surface of AZ EE:4:38 (ASM). Textual sources indicate that as a result of the forced relocation of Quiburi's population to Tucson in 1762, only a portion of the population left. As Captain Francisco Elías González de Zayas, noted after the relocation:

> In regard to what Your Lordship wrote to me of the Sobaipuris, I notify Your Lordship that I have just arrived from settling them in the town of Tucson. Their number reaches 250, although the missionary and justices informed me that they numbered 400 souls. (Dobyns 1976:20)

This information seems to inform us of a discrepancy, a difference of about 150 people. From this we can subtract the twenty people who seem to have moved to Santa María Suamca mission (Dobyns 1976:21). The resulting figure suggests that perhaps 100, or a quarter of the population, remained behind.

From an archaeological standpoint, we know that households consisted of paired structures, and I have determined from comparisons of house counts and number of houses in the documentary record (as well as from archaeological evidence) that one household (or two houses) was occupied by 4.5 people, or 5 to round it off (Seymour 2009a, 2011a:147–151). As shown on the AZ EE:4:38 (ASM) site map, there are ten houses visible, but given their spacing and that some of those that are paired are not visible, and also taking into account the shape and size of the landform, it is estimated that there are perhaps twenty households at this site. This number suggests that there were perhaps 100 people living here.

This estimate would make this settlement about the size of the Kino-period Santa Cruz de Gaybanipitea. This is a smaller population given the 500 people who once occupied the Kino-period Quiburi. Yet, population sizes were decreasing during this era. In 1775 Tumacácori was a head mission and only had a population of 91, whereas Calabasas had 141, having absorbed the populations of Sonoita and Guevavi (Kessell 1965:79). The population is smaller than the estimated 160 to 200 who likely occupied Santa Cruz de Terrenate Presidio (or according to Croix, 193 men [not including their families]; Thomas 1941:226). This population at Quiburi might have been large enough to withstand Apache attacks, which, given the history of the Santa Cruz Presidio, were seemingly prevalent at the time. It is reasonable to conclude that Rocha y Figueroa might have viewed this as a small population.

These findings leave us to contextualize what Rocha y Figueroa meant by the place being "unobstructed." The landform on which this site is situated is excessively steep and well protected, about fifty meters high with thick vegetation, water, and sticky and deep mud protecting most of three sides, and the steep arroyo walls of the San Pedro shielding another. This defensive landform and its placement within a marshy area rendered Quiburi better protected than the fortified San Xavier and Tumacácori, places he had also visited, likely accounting for the inattention to a defensive layout for the houses themselves at Quiburi. Evidence of Sobaipuri occupation was restricted to this site and was not found on any of the surrounding landforms, though some are disturbed. Placement on this elevated landform seems to be what was being referenced by Rocha y Figueroa when he noted that a small population was permitted because it was unobstructed. It was high enough that it had views in all directions.

CONCLUDING STATEMENT

Situated in a protected setting overlooking independent water sources and the San Pedro River, AZ EE:4:38 (ASM) seems to conform to all the descriptive indices presented by the documentary record. Modern fields located nearby illustrate the continued fertility of the adjacent land, making this an ideal location for a habitation site and the only existing area along this river segment with reliably accessible surface water independent of the San Pedro (excepting, of course, the abundant water a bit further north).

Of all the known Sobaipuri sites along the San Pedro, only this one matches all of the specified criteria and is therefore the most likely candidate for the Quiburi referenced by Rocha y Figueroa. The 1780s Quiburi referenced by Rocha y Figueroa is likely AZ EE:4:38 (ASM) because this site is the farthest north of all known Sobaipuri sites along this stretch. The site is small, as expected for this period (or at least smaller than the occupation at the Kino-period Quiburi and many other sites along the river), and smaller than the population of the presidio of Santa Cruz de Terrenate had been, smaller than that of Calabasas, and not much larger than Tumacácori. Its size is therefore consistent with the documentation of a small population. Its hilltop location is consistent with the need for defense, and its placement near known springs supports the documentary descriptions of this place.

There were probably several reasons the residents of Quiburi moved this settlement so far north compared to its originally documented position. Rocha

Figueroa's journal indicates that an area to the south had experienced a great flood in 1770 that, had it effected the middle San Pedro, may have washed out fields and canals. With such improvements destroyed, movement to a more protected location may have seemed sensible. Rocha y Figueroa (1780b:136) also noted that 1780 was experiencing an extreme drought, so the positioning of the last-remaining settlement on a hill amidst the most reliable water source along this portion of the river is not so difficult to understand, though usually marshy areas were viewed by the Sobaipuri as unhealthy. The desire of Quiburi's residents to avoid being used in the service of the presidio, and as agricultural and mining labor, may have also been a factor, as it was a common concern in Sonora at the time (Hastings 1961:334). Quiburi's placement was sufficiently distant from Santa Cruz de Terrenate Presidio to maintain independence, while appropriately close to take advantage of the presidio for defense, at least until the presidio was abandoned and moved south in the first third of 1780.

Without the documentary record, there would be no way to know that this was the latest manifestation of this once sizable and important settlement. AZ EE:4:38 (ASM) would be but one of many Sobaipuri sites strung along the riverside, though it would be fairly indistinguishable despite its importance in the political history of the area. Chronometric-dating methods cannot distinguish this time period with such specificity, especially if the occupation was short, so in the absence of corroborative data we would be hard pressed to argue that the Sobaipuri persisted here even after the Spanish presidio attempt failed. A second map for a planned expedition dating to 1784 by Rocha y Figueroa suggests that Quiburi may have persisted, for at least a few more years.[9]

These specific documentary records provide evidence of a Sobaipuri presence on this river even after the Spanish gave up hope of taming this land. Since the *Rudo Ensayo*, and later reiterated by Di Peso (1953), it has been thought that the O'odham had completely abandoned this river many years before. It turns out, however, that this inference was incorrect. The location and translation of these undercited documents provide a refreshed view of this important period that extends the end point to the close of an era on the San Pedro. The actual fate of Quiburi's residents is not known beyond this period because the Spanish either operated as if the Sobaipuri were not there, did not visit them, or did not remark on their exodus, gradual attrition, or massacre. Lieutenant-colonel José de Zúñiga set out from the abandoned presidio of Santa Cruz in April 1795, moving north along the San Pedro, and did not mention encountering Quiburi (Hammond 1931:53), suggesting that perhaps by this date the settlement was no longer occupied, or perhaps they veered northeast before reaching this village.

Quiburi's persistence at this late date may mark efforts by its isolated residents to avoid missionization, especially in light of the epidemics that were raging through the missions in the 1770s (Di Peso 1953:42). Such incidents may have led to a reassertion of traditional lifeways and isolation from mission influences. Sobaipuri residents on the Santa Cruz River and many from the San Pedro had long since congregated into the mission settlements of San José de Tumacácori, San José del Tucsón and San Agustín del Tuquison (Tucson), and San Xavier del Bac that had adopted defensive layouts, while other missions and visitas, such as Guevavi, Sonoita, and Santa María Suamca, that had at one time received refugees, had been recently abandoned. Reference to this site as Quiburi without a religious prefix supports this notion that the residents of this late community were not inclined toward missionary interference or assimilation into European society. Persistent efforts to maintain residence in this section of the eastern O'odham frontier overrun by those peoples hostile to the Spanish presence tells of an intractable optimism in the face of inevitable defeat. Ultimately, attempts to maintain the traditional lifeway in this remote area seem to have been thwarted by the brutal and ever-more-powerful assaults by the Apache. Yet, one wonders how Quiburi managed to sustain a smaller population in the face of such hostility. Although in a well-fortified setting and set behind the protective shield of the marsh, it is impressive that its residents managed to grow their crops and carry out daily tasks, especially when the presidio residents had already folded under pressure from crops being burned and supply lines truncated. Perhaps the pressure of increased Spanish campaigns against the Apache or enemy focus on the presidio bought Quiburi's residents additional time. It has been presumed that these last Sobaipuri holdouts eventually moved west to Tucson and San Xavier del Bac, but it is equally plausible that they maintained a special relationship with the Apache and were ultimately recruited into the Apache lifeway. The archaeology is silent on this issue, and to date no pertinent documentary records have been identified, though by 1786, Brinckerhoff (1967) argues, the Apache problem had begun to subside, perhaps extending the occupation of Quiburi a few more years. In this presumably Brinkerhoff is referencing the policy shift that Viceroy Bernardo de Gálvez had instituted on the northern frontier of New Spain in 1786. This caused some Chiricahua Apache bands to sue for peace, ultimately leading to many coming in to reside at peace camps. We are to presume, perhaps intentionally but maybe inaccurately, that Quiburi's residents were gone by the time the Boquillas y Nogales land grant was issued in 1827, a few short years after Mexican independence, because the boundaries of this land grant encompass this final Sobaipuri settlement, seemingly showing a disregard for or lack of knowledge of this formerly influential settlement and its residents.

NOTES

1. This chapter was first written in 2009 and was included in Seymour (2011b) and was subsequently modified for this book. There are actually three villages mentioned by name when Santa Domingo is included from the 1692 Ramírez de Salazar expedition.

2. Technically, since the Santa Cruz de Terrenate Presidio population had moved south to Las Nutrias and temporarily resided in a location that was not along the San Pedro River, it could be argued that these Quiburi Sobaipuri were the last settled occupants along this river.

3. In noting that "Arricivita, in his chronicle, claims that Santa Ana del Quiburi and the rest of the valley were completely abandoned in the year 1769" and that "the Spanish reportedly [were] very much against this withdrawal of the Sobaipuri from the frontier valley and took measures to stop it, but without success," Di Peso (1953:41) cites Bancroft 1886:562, but search of this source mentions nothing of any of these topics, including the Sobaipuri, and his subsequent citations about Santa María de Suamca are not supported either. Consideration of Bancroft's (1889) *History of Arizona and New Mexico* suggests that as of 1767 Quiburi was referenced as San Juan Quiburi, which was now a visita of Santa María Suamca, but there is no mention of its abandonment, only that Quiburi was north of the presidio line, at which time Terrenate presidio (Terrenate Viejo) *was* south of the modern international line (prior to its movement to the north).

4. If Bancroft (1989:371n24) is correct, another reference to this settlement was made as San Juan Quiburi, perhaps indicating another locational shift.

5. Decorme (1941:410–411) says 1704; see Di Peso (1953:34–35) for his dates; Spicer ([1962] 1981:127, 542–543) says 1705; and Bolton (1948:I:178–183) says 1706.

6. The soldiers may have moved there in December 1775, but it is not known how long it took them to reach Santa Cruz de Terrenate, and so many sources say the presidio's occupation was initiated in 1776.

7. Also see Hammond (1929:229) for a reference to the place of Santa Cruz de Dequibuiri.

8. While the league varied, it tends to correspond to about 2.6 miles or 4.2 kilometers per league for this period. During the missionary period (1690s), Kino and his military escort sometimes presented different league distances between the same two closely spaced settlements, suggesting differences in measurement techniques, distance equations, and also perhaps slightly different routes taken.

9. The persistence of a named location on a map does not guarantee that a place remained occupied. Santa Cruz Presidio continued to be plotted on Rocha's maps even

after it was abandoned, probably because it was a known location and it seems to have been used as a stopover point for later campaigns, including the Zúñiga campaign of 1795. The continued notation of Quiburi may have been nothing more than a referent to a reliable spring along the trail and a good crossing, even after the settlement was abandoned. On the other hand, there is no reason to believe that this settlement would not have persisted through 1784.

9

A long-standing question is whether there was ever a Jesuit mission founded on the San Pedro River.[1] Charles Di Peso, who excavated the presidio of Santa Cruz de Terrenate in the 1940s and 1950s, thought that he had uncovered evidence of this Jesuit mission. As noted in chapters 1, 7, and 8, he also thought that the Sobaipuri village of Quiburi underlay the presidio. Each of these questions will be addressed in this chapter, with priority given to the issue of the Jesuit mission.

As a little background, Santa Cruz Presidio was occupied by the Spanish between December 1775 and March 1780. Di Peso thought that the 1757 Jesuit mission was part of one of two earlier Sobaipuri components referenced in the historical record that were associated with the name "Quiburi" (see previous two chapters). As will be discussed later in this chapter (see, e.g., the section "Capturing an Earlier Occupation"), the Sobaipuri component underlying and predating the presidio was called Santa Cruz and was distinct from the contemporaneous village of Quiburi. Di Peso arrived at the interpretation that this place was Quiburi, based in part upon conclusions drawn by Bolton ([1936]1960:361) who years earlier had made this erroneous association between Quiburi and the presidio, probably because the village was sometimes referenced as Santa Cruz de or of Quiburi.[2] Here at the presidio location, Di Peso thought he had identified the additional mid-eighteenth-century Sobaipuri O'odham occupation representing Santa Ana del Quiburi, sandwiched

https://doi.org/10.5876/9781646422975.c009

157

temporally between Kino's San Pablo de Quiburi of the 1690s and the construction of the presidio in the mid-1770s. Of specific relevance to this chapter, Di Peso (1953:40, 58–59, 88, 108) said there was a 1757 Jesuit mission at the site, associated with the Sobaipuri settlement of Santa Ana del Quiburi, which he attributed to the period of 1705 and 1762. This, of course, is the period of occupation postdating the return of the Sobaipuri from Sonoita after the temporary hiatus following the 1698 victory (see chapter 6). If this were in fact a Jesuit mission, this would have been the only Jesuit mission constructed on the San Pedro, because all other settlements were visiting stations with small chapels, at best. These were adobe-walled structures "built for the missionary they hoped to receive," though sometimes they were called churches, despite their small size, and usually represented or doubled as Indigenous communal or council houses. Yet, this remote Valley of the Sobaipuris (San Pedro) seemingly never did see the installation of a resident priest, the development of a mission, or the construction of a Jesuit mission church. Newly collected data from my multiyear excavations at Santa Cruz de Terrenate Presidio, with special attention to the features that Di Peso connected to the 1757 Jesuit mission, provide the basis for this view as does the fact that Quiburi was not in this location. Specifically, reexposure of some of the walls, floors, and hearths and chronometric dating of wall adobes provide a revised perspective. Supplemented with fresh documentary data, new interpretations are in order.

DI PESO'S POSITION ON THE JESUIT MISSION

Regarding the establishment of the 1757 Jesuit mission at Santa Ana del Quiburi, Di Peso stated with respect to his evidence at Santa Cruz de Terrenate Presidio:

> German Jesuits arrived in 1757 [at Quiburi] . . . during their short stay they did manage to build a crude mission house and several outlying buildings, and they prevailed upon the natives to repair and rebuild their village. This is indicated by the presence of adobe brick native dwellings, and by the adobe brick walls which replaced certain of the jacal wall rooms . . . The priest prevailed upon the Indians to construct native type stone houses as lookouts at strategic positions along the eastern face of the cliff. (Di Peso 1953:108, also see 59)

It is not clear where Di Peso obtained such detailed information about the urgings of the priests and the building activities of the Indigenous people. This reconstruction seems to be based on the arrival of the German Jesuits and bits

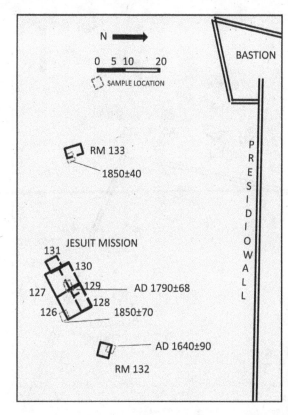

FIGURE 9.1. *Redraft of a portion of Di Peso's map of Santa Cruz de Terrenate Presidio showing houses outside and to the south and east of the perimeter wall including the so-called Jesuit Mission. Figure prepared by Deni Seymour.*

of documentary data that are far from clear (see the section "Documentary Evidence").

Di Peso attributed several structures, including a large one, on south side of the presidio (figure 9.1), to this Jesuit Mission of 1757. He suggested:

> Upon inspecting Figure 34 [e.g., herein figure 9.1], the reader will note a group of buildings located some 70 m. south of the compound village . . . marked "Jesuit Mission, 1757." This group of buildings, which included Rooms 126–133, was constructed by several German Jesuit priests in 1757. These tumbled-down adobe rooms marked the final, but unsuccessful, attempt of the Jesuit Order to set up a mission at the Sobaipuri village of Santa Ana.

The rooms represent three spatially distinct structures. Rooms 132 and 133 are single-room freestanding structures located east and west, respectively, of a larger eight-room structure that consists of Rooms 126–131 (see figure 9.1). The latter is the structure Di Peso inferred to be the church itself or "crude mis-

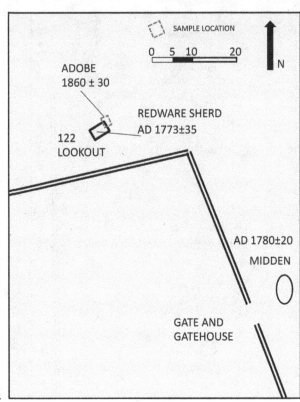

FIGURE 9.2. *Redraft of a portion of Di Peso's map of Santa Cruz de Terrenate Presidio showing a house outside and northwest of the perimeter wall including Room 122. Figure prepared by Deni Seymour.*

sion house," whereas Rooms 132 and 133 were subsumed in what he referred to as "several outlying buildings." Other buildings associated with this phase of occupation, according to Di Peso (153:93–94), were the many stone structures, actually stone and mortar, referred to as "lookout houses." These included Rooms 122, 123, 124, and 125 (not shown on figure 9.1, but located to the east of structures shown, and on the east side of the presidio; figure 9.2). This chapter focuses largely on Rooms 126–131 because this was the core of Di Peso's "crude mission house," though findings related to Rooms 122 and 132 are also discussed briefly.

ALTERNATIVE VIEWS

Rex Gerald (1968:16–21), who had worked with Di Peso during the presidio excavation, had his own ideas about this mission house and these outlying buildings, suggesting their construction and use by presidio soldiers and their families instead of as a Jesuit missionary:

> It seems entirely probable to me that some, if not all, of the stone houses located within and without the perimeter wall of the presidio was [*sic*] designated by Di Peso (1953:fig. 34) as belonging to the pre-presidio Santa Ana de Quiburi Phase must have been constructed and occupied by presidials . . . It seems probable also that the *jacal* structures of the San Pablo de Quiburi Phase may have been constructed and occupied as temporary quarters during, and perhaps after, the construction of the few permanent presidial quarters. (19–20)

I have also suggested that the outlying buildings were settlers' structures associated with the presidio, potentially used by civilians, both related and unrelated to presidials (Seymour 2011a, 2011b). Those inside I thought might be those constructed for soldiers and perhaps later for residents, as hostilities increased and residents were burned out of their outlying homes. Each of these scenarios seemed more reasonable than Di Peso's suggestion, but, as I will discuss, an alternative explanation now seems apparent given recently obtained dates, newly considered documentary data, and evaluation of other related evidence.

Two classes of questions arise from this debate that will be addressed in the following pages. The first is whether the structure referred to by Di Peso as the 1757 Jesuit mission (a) was constructed during the presidio occupation, (b) whether it was built earlier by the Sobaipuri and simply reused, or (c) whether it dates to some other period of use. Multiple lines of evidence have been accessed to address this issue and the preponderance of the data suggests strongly that Di Peso was wrong about the provenance of this structure. But interestingly, so were Gerald and I.

These related series of questions are especially pertinent in light of new data that affirm the presence of a Sobaipuri component at this site. Clear evidence for a Sobaipuri component preceding the presidio involves a second series of questions that pertain to and discredit Di Peso's claim that this place was Quiburi. This interpretation is based not so much on Di Peso's evidence, but, rather, the component has been defined on the basis of the most modern criteria for the Sobaipuri signature and by new investigations I undertook at the site and subsequent analyses. Evidence for this earlier seventeenth-century Sobaipuri occupation and the facts surrounding Room 132 both raise the possibility that this structure was initially used by the Sobaipuri as a council house or adobe built for the visiting missionary at a place later called Santa Cruz and then was reused during presidio times. This is consistent with part of Di Peso's original notion. Evidence from Room 132 will be presented that may support this idea. This evidence and argument, however, should not be confused with the discussion of the purported Jesuit mission (Rooms 126–131) or the actual name of the Sobaipuri village at this location.

DOCUMENTARY EVIDENCE

There are a few vague documentary statements about a Jesuit church on the San Pedro. The first hint of building a church, or at least an important step in the desire to do so, was when in 1706 Kino noted that he had collected the money necessary to build a church and other facilities at Santa Ana del Quiburi:

> One person alone offers five thousand in suitable goods, with some silver, for the founding and for the church, house, and fortification of the settlement or great mission of Santa Ana de Quibori, where Captain Coro lives; because it is notorious that those his natives will be able to continue to pursue the neighboring avowed enemies, the Hocomes, Janos, and Apaches, for the very great and total relief, or remedy, of all this province of Sonora. (Bolton 1948:II:272)

This same year Kino also commented about the need for a missionary in this area. He listed the existing missions that were administered by missionaries and those that would benefit from them. The relevant part is later in the paragraph, when Kino comments that churches had already been built at these proposed locations:

> Thus far the father rector. In virtue of these two letters I immediately made the reports which were asked of me, one of which I despatched [*sic*] by a messenger to San Joseph de Guaimas to the father visitor, who sent it to Mexico to the father provincial. As his Reverence wrote me, he despatched [*sic*] it to Rome to our father general. This report was accompanied by the long relation of all the posts suitable for very good districts and missions in this Pimeria, with a very clear map of the nine pueblos which we three fathers who have lived in this Pimeria are actually administering. Father Agustin de Campos at San Ygnacio, Santa María Magdalena, and San Joseph de Ymires, Father Geronimo Minutuli at San Pedro y San Pablo del Tubutama, Santa Thereza, and San Anttonio del Uquitoa, and I here at Nuestra Señora de los Dolores, Nuestra Señor de los Remedios, and Nuestra Señora del Pilar y Santiago de Cocospera; an account of the other five alms which his Royal Majesty, God save him, had granted for five other new fathers and five new missions; and the opinion that therefore immediately, besides us three missionary fathers who were here in

our three already settled districts, or missions, at least five others could come for five other good districts, or new missions; and that accordingly the fourth Pima father could come for Nuestra Senora de la Consepcion del Caborca, San Diego del Pitquin, and San Valentin, the fifth for Santa María, San Lazaro, and San Luys; the sixth for San Ambrosio del Busanic, Santa Gertrudis del Saric, and San Bernardo del Aquimuri; the seventh for San Xavier del Bac, San Agustin, and Santa Rosalia, of the Sobaipuris; the eighth for Santa Ana del Quiburi, San Juachin, and Santa Cruz, where lives the famous Captain Coro. *For in all these posts or pueblos already named there are very good beginnings of Christianity, houses in which to live, churches in which to say mass,* fields and crops of wheat and maize, and the cattle, sheep, goats, and horses, which the natives for years have been tending with all fidelity for the fathers whom they ask and hope to receive. (emphasis added; Kino in Bolton 1948:II:182)

Clearly the churches mentioned as already existing could very well be the adobe-walled structures at each settlement in which Kino had stayed, something today we would call a chapel.

Despite the desire to build a church on the part of the Jesuits, and continued requests from some of the Sobaipuri for a priest, there is no unequivocal documentary evidence that a church was ever built. In fact, given events occurring recently surrounding the 1751 Pima Revolt, one wonders if there were in fact continued pleas for missionaries. Throughout the Jesuit period, there is no indication that a priest had been assigned to the purported mission. Moreover, some of Quiburi's recorded baptisms, marriages, and other sacraments that postdate this inferred construction date were performed by priests assigned to other missions and were performed at those other missions on the Santa Cruz River (Miguel Gerstner, Francisco Hlava, and Ignacio Keller), suggesting that there was no church at Quiburi. One example that this area was being ministered by a nonlocal priest is from a 1746 report by Vildósola, which was later discussed by Teodoro de Croix:

> The Sobaipuri had their rancherías . . . in various spots close to its [San Pedro River] banks called Quiburi. Tres Alamos, Naideni, Bacoachi, Santa Cruz, and La Azequia Grande, [and he said] that the father missionary of Santa María de Suanca was visiting them. (Thomas 1941:203)

The fact that Keller, one of the German Jesuits, was still ministering to all of the visitas or settlements along the San Pedro is a fairly clear indication that a church had not been built. So, while this source indicates that both Quiburi and Santa Cruz still bordered the middle San Pedro at this time, there is no hint of a church. A census at Quiburi in 1743 reported that there were forty-one men, old and young, and forty-two women, old and young, indicating that Quiburi was only a small settlement at this time (Mission 2000 Database, Quiburi census).

A single textual source raises some doubt about this position, however. In 1751 the Marqués de Altamira, Spain's auditor of war, had suggested moving Terrenate Presidio north from "its incommodious terrain in the *cañada* of San Mateo . . . establishing itself in the valley of El Quiburi to protect the frontier and the new mission of the Las Cruzes" (Thomas 1941:203). Las Cruzes probably refers to the many locations of Santa Cruz as it moved around because a portion of the area was known as Santa Cruz, first to the south of the narrows and then where Santa Cruz de Terrenate Presidio was finally positioned. Taken at face value, it is easy to see how one might interpret this as clear evidence that the church had, in fact, been built. But this passage can also be read to indicate that it was the planned mission, one of several planned. Thus, this may also be taken as a statement about the continued desire to construct a church in this location.

My interpretation is supported by another account from the same year (1751) by Jacobo Sedelmayr that refers to the San Pedro (Valley of the Sobaipuris):

The stipend for the mission of Dolores seems to have been transferred to found a mission among the Sobaipuris. It would seem that to use the alms of the Marquez there would not be in accord with the intensions of the donor. We are still short a missionary who can use the stipend of Dolores to found a mission in the valley of the Sobaipuris, who are in great need of a minister. (Sedelmayr in Matson and Fontana 1996:35)

This latter suggestion is borne out by other documents that while there was a desire, the church was never built, in part because there was no priest to minister to these Sobaipuri and to build the church. Clearly the Jesuits continued promoting the desire to build a church in the San Pedro Valley. In 1756 Miguel Gerstner, Francisco Hlava, and Ignacio Xavier Keller rode from Santa María Suamca to the San Pedro Valley with the intent of establishing a church. But upon their arrival, they were met with menacing looks, told that they did not desire the two new priests and that Padre Keller of Santa María Suamca was their priest and his church was their church and they needed no other, and the priests were told they would kill any other missionary sent to live with them (Kessell 1970:146).

In the mid-1760s a *pueblo de visita* referred to as San Juan Quiburi appears in mission records (Bancroft 1886:563n23, 562–564). This reference involving a new name of San Juan suggests that the residents of Santa Ana del Quiburi had likely moved to a new location in the preceding years, precipitating the attachment of a new saint's prefix. New names were often appended to Indigenous village names when a different location was occupied, and, as discussed in chapter 2, it seems that moves occurred every decade or two, if not more frequently, depending on political events and environmental conditions. The reference to this place as a visita indicates that Quiburi was not a mission settlement, but, rather, it was still just a visiting station. This visita mention also suggests that a Jesuit mission was not established at the old Santa Ana de Quiburi to the south because, had it been, the Quiburi residents would likely have remained at that old southern location or chroniclers would have lamented its loss. Less than a decade had passed between the date Di Peso suggests as the founding of the Jesuit mission and this reference to Quiburi by a different name and as a visita. There are no mentions of battles or other events that might precipitate the abandonment of a mission, though clearly not all-important events were known or recorded by the Europeans.

Another source supports this other evidence that a mission was not built at Quiburi. In 1763 or 1764 Governor Juan Claudio de Pineda, who had ordered an inquiry regarding the loss of residents at many mission settlements:

> concluded that it was not advisable to send any padres nor to attempt the reduction of the Sobaipuris [in the San Pedro Valley], fearing that an attempt to exercise any restraint would convert that people from friends into foes. (Bancroft 1886:562–564)

This of course would have been within a year or two of the 1762 forced relocation of some San Pedro Sobaipuris to settlements on the Santa Cruz River and the Tucson area, where elsewhere along the Santa Cruz River the missions were now being abandoned. Left behind were only the noncompliant residents of Quiburi who refused to relocate (see Seymour 2011a, 2011c; see chapter 8), suggesting that the governor was wise in his assessment. At about this same time, in 1764, a statement by Nentvig (Pradeau and Rasmussen 1980:73) supports the same idea: "Were it not for fear of the Apaches, two or three missions might have been established in the Sobahipuris Valley."

This issue of a Jesuit church is an example of how new evidence gathered gradually over time can address questions in fresh ways, leading to different resolutions. New documentary sources shed light on this issue, providing tantalizing hints, but external evidence from the archaeological record provides even more solid data needed to address the question.

FRAMING AN ARCHAEOLOGICAL QUESTION

Recent excavations at Santa Cruz de Terrenate Presidio have provided fresh data by which to reevaluate this question of the Jesuit mission. In considering how to assess this question using archaeological data, the issue became one of figuring out how to sort the complex occupational history of the presidio. Specifically, the problem was one of how to date the structures in question. During the four years of work there, several chronometric dates were obtained, including some from reexposure of outlying structures that are specifically applicable to this discussion.

Organic-Tempered Redware from Room 122

The first sample selected was analyzed to reinforce the notion that luminescence dating is a reliable technique for this period in this region and to affirm that this organic-tempered pottery first appears in the late 1700s in southern Arizona, or at least at the presidio. Fortunately, and relevant to this issue, Di Peso did not actually reach the floor in many of the structures he excavated outside the presidio walls (and in some cases he may have excavated through the floors).[3] This reality provided important opportunities for dating and a basis for new interpretations. The backdirt from the features had in most cases been piled outside the exterior walls. Because the features were not back-filled, the floors and walls in many cases were not far below the surface and were easily reached for inspection and sample collection.[4] Initially I collected an organic-tempered redware sherd from the floor of Room 122 (see figure 9.2). This structure was referred to by Di Peso as a "lookout house" and was presumed to have been used during the occupation of Santa Ana del Quiburi and presumably during the presidio occupation in lieu of a second (northwest) corner bastion. This was one of a half dozen sherds found in the west half of the room in a slight depression that had either not been previously excavated or, more likely, that had brought up artifacts from below when the floor was cut. The inference that this location did not contain artifacts washed in from the backdirt derives from the fact that the fill differed from the washed-in fill in the rest of the room and that numerous sherds and flaked-stone artifacts were present only in this restricted area. Moreover, the backdirt was separated from the room by the cobble-and-mortar wall that restricted the backdirt from eroding directly back into the room.

The organic-tempered redware sherd produced a date of AD 1773±35 (X3090). This result is very near the date of presidio occupation (1775–1780), suggesting the room was used during presidio times. The vessel from which the sherd originated could have even been made at Las Nutrias or Terrenate Viejo before being transported to this location. This result is consistent with another date from other artifacts at the site that corresponds rather closely to the historically noted period of presidio occupation. A Whetstone Plain sherd from the east presidio-related midden outside the gatehouse produced a date of AD 1780±20 (UW2028). This sample reinforces the notion that this pottery type was produced as late as this period (actually into the early 1900s) and was used at this presidio, probably having been obtained from O'odham laborers or domestic servants or from a nearby settlement. The Sobaipuri settlement of El Quiburi was occupied at this time, located three leagues north of the presidio (see chapter 8). O'Conor mentioned laborers at the presidio who came from San Xavier del Bac and San Agustín del Tuquison (O'Conor 1952:65; also see Gerald 1968:18), many of whom were likely Sobaipuri. Moreover, apparently the Spanish households had Indigenous domestic servants, some of whom might have been O'odham. This Sobaipuri-made pottery could have originated from any of these sources.

While these pottery dates illustrate the value of luminescence dating for this period, the organic-tempered redware dating result still does not solve the possibility that the room could have been built earlier but reused later, as Di Peso suggests, or some other scenario not thought of. As Gerald (1968:19) points out: "Di Peso (1953:58) admits that the presidials occupied these structures but thinks they were constructed earlier by the Sobaipuri Indians, the aboriginal, Piman-speaking occupants of the middle and lower San Pedro and Santa Cruz River valleys." This issue could not be resolved by examining artifacts found in the rooms, because reuse of older built structures would result in later artifacts being found in the rooms. Consequently, submission of another artifact for dating from other structures would not address this problem of use versus construction. Complicating this issue was the problem that the walls in each of the rooms were constructed from cultural fill deriving from earlier occupational episodes on this multiple-component site, with artifacts from all periods, even Archaic dart points and Hohokam pottery, being found embedded in adobe blocks made from earlier fill. This mixture meant that artifacts have eroded out of the walls or were brought up by rodents, and so the artifacts themselves would not provide a reliable indication of time of room use. Additional issues relate to the fact that documentary and archaeological evidence indicate that the presidio had been reused many times after its official abandonment. Some of the more expedient hearths found in these rooms may have been added during periods of later presidio reuse. Sources identify visitation during expeditions in 1780 by Rocha y Figueroa and in 1795 by Captain José de Zúñiga (Hammond 1931; Rocha y Figueroa 1780a, 1780b, also in Seymour and Rodríguez 2020). Evidence in the fills and on the floors suggests reuse of these rooms by visitors practicing various other lifeways. Consequently, archaeomagnetic dates of thermal features, such as corner hearths or burn spots on floors, might produce post-presidio dates, as, of course, might artifacts these visitors brought with them and left or lost. For this reason, it was viewed as essential to obtain information on the actual construction date of the features themselves.

The only viable way to date the construction of these features was to sample the adobe blocks and mortar. A previous study had reported on the reliability of such an approach, but for fired bricks (Bailiff 2007), and tests at various sites in this region during my own projects have analyzed the reliability and accuracy of the technique on unfired adobes (Seymour 2002, 2007c, 2011b, 2011d). These unfired adobe blocks from Santa Cruz de Terrenate present special challenges for dating. Dating was complicated by the fact just discussed that the unburned sun-dried adobe blocks were often made with prehistoric fill that included burned material that would potentially date many centuries earlier by thermoluminescence. This challenge meant that the only viable dating technique was OSL, under the assumption that some of the quartz particles were last exposed to light when they were being mixed for blocks or mortar and that the signal from particles exposed to light earlier in time did not overshadow the latest signature. This aspect of dating the adobes was discussed with the University of Washington Luminescence Laboratory prior to sample analysis.

ROOM 122 WALL

The date derived from the mortar in the stone-and-mortar wall of Room 122, the apparent lookout structure with the presidio-period organic-tempered sherd, produced a confidence interval that postdates the presidio (1860±30; UW2629). This date suggests that the building was constructed during the period when this portion of the river was a land grant (San Juan de las Boquillas y Nogales), not during use of the presidio. This might make this location and its partially ruined buildings part of the land grant headquarters. But what of the organic-tempered redware sherd found in the floor depression? This wall date indicates that the sherd did not relate to the use of the structure, but rather it seems that the sherd was incorporated fortuitously into the structure walls as contents of adobe bricks, much as artifacts from earlier periods had been. An alternative explanation is that the floor was cut in this area and the depression was a hole in the floor exposing artifacts from below. So, while the sherd accurately dates the introduction of this new pottery type into this area and the occupation of the presidio, it is misleading regarding the room construction date. This late date also explains why the building technique is so different from that of many of the other presidio structures. This is a complex occupational sequence, indeed, making one wonder how many other occupations that have been dated by a single sample present a misleading result.

The Jesuit Mission/Rooms 126–131

Adobe block samples were taken from both the interior and exterior walls of Features 126–131, but initially only the sample from the interior wall was run. The interior intersecting walls to this room block that partitioned Rooms 127, 130, 126, and 129 were exposed, revealing bricks separated by thick mortar joints (figures 9.3 and 9.4). A sample of brick was taken from the interior wall between Rooms 127 and 130. This sample was removed from a clearly defined brick that was dark from incorporating prehistoric deposits. It was hoped that the hardness of the brick would contribute to a successful dating result.

This sample produced a date of AD 1790±68 (UW2026), with a center point that is very near the expected construction date associated with the presidio. Jim Feathers of the Washington Luminescence Laboratory noted that "the error (±68) is a standard deviation, so just imagine a probability curve in the form of a normal curve centered at the midpoint. Points closer to the midpoint have higher probability than points located in the tails." (Jim Feathers, personal communication, 2011). This answer was in response to my question about whether it is any more statistically probable that the actual date is closer to this midpoint (e.g., 1790) than to, say, 1722. Or whether each year between 1722 and 1858 is equally likely as 1790 to be the correct date. Knowing the probability is especially important because the site has so many components and the relevant question pertaining to this sample relates to whether this result can differentiate between 1757 and 1775–1780 for this feature.[5] Feather's response indicates that this feature is most probably related to the presidio occupation and not the period pertaining to Di Peso's suggested Jesuit mission. The date, like other evidence to be discussed in this chapter, especially in "The Jesuit Mission: Rooms 126–131," supports the notion that the Jesuit mission is the least likely explanation for this feature.

One of the most interesting aspects about this building as a whole is that the interior adobes were made so differently than the outer ones. This is accounted for in part by the age differences as reflected in the composition of the adobes themselves and the care taken to make the adobes. Adobe quality in turn

FIGURE 9.3. *Photograph of interior walls intersecting showing adobe blocks that are similar to the outer presidio wall including one that was sampled. Photograph by Deni Seymour.*

FIGURE 9.4. *Photograph of Di Peso's Jesuit Mission. Courtesy of The Amerind Foundation, Inc., Dragoon, Arizona. Charles C. Di Peso, Photographer.*

influenced the way the walls themselves were built. This interior wall between Rooms 127 and 130 was constructed of formed blocks that were especially compact and remarkably similar in size and shape to those used in construction of the presidio's exterior wall itself. The initially dated sample was taken from this row of clearly defined blocks (see figures 9.3 and 9.4). The exterior walls exposed around Rooms 127, 128, 129, and 130 revealed adobes made of less-compact blocks seemingly shaped by forming puddled adobe into loaves, with the finished product looking distinct from those in the interior.

The interior walls in this structure are constructed differently than the exterior walls, while the interior walls are constructed in a way that looks visually and compositionally similar to the perimeter presidio wall. Dates from the outer walls of this structure and these differences in character indicate that additions were made to the existing building over time, at least one outer wall being constructed in the land grant period (AD 1850±70). Again, this date suggests that this part of the structure was added during the Terminal Spanish period or the Mexican period when this was the San Juan de las Boquillas y Nogales land grant.

Just as Barbara Voss (2008:192) notes for the San Francisco presidio, "settlers themselves were responsible for building their own residences" (Langellier and Rosen 1996:33). In agreement with her findings, responsibility for construction placed on residents would account for the differing dimensions of the structures themselves and variability in numbers of rooms. This explanation also accounts for adobe-block-forming techniques for most structures that differed from those used in presidio construction and that resulted in blocks of a different visual character and quality from those used in the presidio walls. Most residents probably enlisted the aid of Indigenous laborers to help with house construction, and as the documentary record says, O'odham came from the west for this purpose.

The archaeological evidence of the similarity of the interior walls to those of the presidio provides strong evidence that this so-called Jesuit mission was at least initially a presidio-period construction. Yet, even then the building was updated during the Mexican period with the addition of at least one new wall to form another enclosed space.

Interior Features and Construction Techniques

The nature of these structures, especially Rooms 126–131 that composed the so-called Jesuit mission, indicate that they were habitation structures rather than, as Di Peso (1953:88) suggested, a church. It is true that Di Peso's "crude mission house" is long like many Franciscan missions constructed throughout Sonora and is sufficiently large overall (14 meters long, 7.5 meters wide) to conform to expectations for a row house or mission church. Yet, as Gerald (1968:20) notes, at Santa Cruz de Terrenate, "these structures encompassed numerous Spanish architectural features such as adobe brick, corner fire hearths, and bed platforms (Di Peso 1953:111–116)." The room block (Rooms 126–131) is also internally partitioned, like a habitation structure and unlike a church, and at least some of these interior walls, the core of the building, were built no earlier than the presidio period (see figure 9.4). The six contiguous rooms are characterized by interior dividing walls. Some of the walls had breaks for entryways, and four rooms had corner hearths, one had a centrally placed one, while one room lacked a hearth suggesting its use for storage. A partition wall lacking entryway breaks divides the feature in two, suggesting this might have been a townhouse-like configuration for two families. Room 131's attachment to the outside with its own exterior entryway indicates that this might have been a special purpose room or perhaps for a domestic servant. These modifications could also represent much later additions, something that remains to be tested by running more dates (hopefully soon, before the walls completely melt away).

Both presidio-specific documentary sources and government regulations indicate that civilians were at Santa Cruz de Terrenate, so there should be evidence of their dwellings. As Max Moorhead (1975:222, 224) points out, the frontier presidio served as the nucleus for the civilian settlement and the Regulation of 1772 promoted the growth of civilian populations at these centers. Some residents, he notes, lived outside the fortress walls. Gerald (1968:18) also mentions that "it was understood that the men would have their families at their posts with them." A more diverse presidio community was shaped not only by the soldiers' families but also by domestic servants, laborers, merchants, Indigenous scouts, and so on. Referring to frontier presidios in general, Moorhead (1975:222) notes: "Eventually a number of purely civilian families came and settled at or near the presidio, drawn not only by the protection it afforded but also by the market it offered for their produce."

Several documentary sources confirm that settlers were in fact present at Santa Cruz de Terrenate. For example, in 1776 Viceroy Antonio María de Bucareli y Ursúa provided an account of an important campaign that originated from Santa Cruz de Terrenate during which the troops were ambushed and Captain Francisco Tovar and several others were killed (Bucareli y Ursúa 1776; Harlan 2009; Seymour 2016b, 2020d). In this letter Bucareli y Ursúa indicated that a merchant resident at Santa Cruz de Terrenate participated, as was consistent with the requirement for settlers to join troops on campaigns against the enemy (e.g., Moorhead 1975:225). This incidental reference provides evidence that nonmilitary residents were present early in the life of the presidio. If this merchant lived in this structure, his presence may explain the oversized character of the so-called Jesuit Church, Rooms 126–131, given the need to store goods and the likelihood that he would presumably be better off than many of the other residents.

Another source reinforces this evidence of a civilian presence. In 1777 Teodoro de Croix commented on the fact that the settlers had dispersed because their houses were burned and crops destroyed by the hostile tribes: "The captain of Santa Cruz presidio reported its crops burned, the settlers' houses fired, and the settlers scattered" (Thomas 1941:31–32).

Consistent with this account, portions of the floor exposed in Features 126–131 and 132 revealed evidence that these structures had burned. This evidence of burning contrasts with Di Peso's (1953:88) suggestion regarding the house block south of the presidio (Rooms 126–133): "This house block was not burned, as was the rest of the village, but disintegrated due to negligence and abandonment." Yet, recent exposure of these structures indicates that Di Peso did not excavate to the floor in this room and others where clear evidence of structure burning is provided by a stratum of dark ashy sediment that covers each of these floors. It seems that rather than excavating to the floor, Di Peso probably excavated to the post-presidio occupation surface after sediment had accumulated from adobe washing off the walls. These erosion layers of fine adobe often look like floors.

Indigenous Architecture at Local Mission Sites

This recently obtained information regarding these outlying adobe-walled structures supports the suggestion that at least one of these buildings was occupied by a civilian, perhaps a vender, artisan, or laborer. This interpretation recognizes the important distinction between Spanish and Sobaipuri residential structures at this time in this region. While Di Peso (1953:108) suggested that Sobaipuri persons repaired and rebuilt their pre-presidio village, resulting in adobe block native dwellings, this is not consistent with local Sobaipuri residential characteristics at this time. Di Peso's assumption was that the Sobaipuri residents would have occupied adobe-walled structures surrounding the mission, consistent with practices ascribed to Indigenous residences at later Franciscan missions in Sonora (see Pickens 1993). Yet, this inference is not supported by the evidence from dozens of other Sobaipuri sites in the region from this time, including Sobaipuri communities surrounding Jesuit missions and *visitas*, such as Guevavi, San Cayetano de Tumacácori, and San Xavier del Bac. During the Jesuit period (and presumably before), a single adobe-walled structure was built in some settlements for defensive and ceremonial purposes. But at each of these sites, my investigations reveal a Sobaipuri Jesuit-period settlement of traditional dome-shaped residential structures. In Jesuit southern Arizona (northern Pimería Alta), Sobaipuri residents occupied elongate domed barrel-shaped structures of branches, mats, and mud with rocks surrounding and defining the base. These residential structures were used from at least as early as the late 1200s. Adobe structures were adopted for defense for a short period at some villages around the 1780s that were under direct priest oversight (see Seymour 2019b), but there is no evidence for this at Santa Cruz or Quiburi during the Jesuit period. Adobe-walled residential structures were not again introduced, readopted, or adapted until the late 1800s, when they were incorporated into the residential structure repertoire. During the late 1800s both rectangular adobe-walled structures and the traditional domed residential structures were used, until the latter were replaced by modern housing. Given this information, most of the adobe-walled structures were most likely presidio-period civilian residences.

CAPTURING AN EARLIER OCCUPATION

Evidence of an earlier Sobaipuri O'odham occupation was captured in remnant outlines of traditional houses, artifacts of a variety of types that were indicative of the Sobaipuri, and a luminescence date on a Whetstone Plain sherd (AD 1691±27 or AD 1664–1718, UW1899), as well as in an OSL adobe block date from Room 132. Of significance, however, this village was not Quiburi. In brief, documentary evidence is clear that the Sobaipuri settlement of Santa Cruz, not Quiburi, was at this location and, according to O'Conor and Croix (O'Conor 1994:63; Thomas 1941:147–148; also see Seymour 1990, 2011a, 2011b, 2014), Santa Cruz donated its name to the presidio. Quiburi was never referred to as Santa Cruz and was not situated at the location of Santa Cruz de Terrenate Presidio, contrary to the claims by Bolton ([1936] 1960:361) and Di Peso (1953). Santa Cruz was sometimes referred to as Santa Cruz de Quiburi (Santa Cruz of Quiburi or Holy Cross of Many Houses) but only because it was situated in the Quiburi Valley and was a subordinate settlement to Quiburi, thereby justifying the name "Santa Cruz *of* Quiburi." Santa Cruz was likely situated here under the presidio in the post-1705 period, which was during an interval close enough to the establishment of the presidio that the Europeans would have been aware of the association of this place with the name "Santa Cruz." Whether there were other Sobaipuri settlements in this specific spot that went by other names is not addressed here, though my research indicates that most Sobaipuri settlements on the San Pedro River and elsewhere show evidence of multiple reoccupations.

The luminescence date returned on the adobe from the wall of Room 132 is highly interesting; it shows that that the wall was built much earlier than the presidio. A sample of wall material (mortar) from the north wall, west of the entryway in Room 132 returned the surprisingly early date of AD 1640±90 (AD 1570–1710; UW2027). Its standard deviation is sizable, but the center point suggests construction in the mid-1600s.[6] This valley was not yet occupied by Europeans at this time, so the most likely explanation for this structure is that it was built by the Sobaipuri occupants (perhaps as a council house) and then reused later in time by the Spaniards. Even if it was built much later, say 1710, its origin would likely be with the Sobaipuri, who were still the only stationary (nonmobile) residents on this river. The most sensible interpretation is that the Sobaipuri built this adobe-walled structure when they returned from Sonoita to occupy this area. After all, the adobe-walled structure at Santa Cruz de Gaybanipitea had saved them.

The unique construction characteristics of Room 132 as compared to the other adobe structures at the site support the possibility that this feature was built in the 1600s and that perhaps it was initially a Sobaipuri defensive or ceremonial structure or council house (Seymour 2014). If so, this would be an example of the Sobaipuri building adobe-walled structures for communal or ceremonial purposes potentially before the Kino-period missionary presence. The Sobaipuri would not have resided in this structure, as Di Peso claimed; rather, as a special-use structure, this would likely have been the only structure of its type in the settlement.

This structure's reuse as a residence in the presidio period seems evident because Room 132 contains a corner hearth, contrary to Di Peso's (1953:89) findings, and presidio-period artifacts were associated. The corner hearth was not used in earlier Sobaipuri residential or communal structures in this region (such as at Santa Cruz de Gaybanipitea, where similar wall construction characteristics are apparent), supporting the notion that the hearth was added during the presidio occupation, inferences that are consistent with understandings about corner hearth use. Di Peso's perception that there was no hearth relates to not excavating to the actual floor and is probably why he referred to this structure as an outlying building related to the mission rather than referencing it as a habitation structure. Notably, the size of this feature is consistent with both contemporary Spanish-constructed structures at Tubac presidio (Gómez house) and with some Sobaipuri-made ceremonial rooms or structures built for the missionary, for example, at Santa Cruz del Pitaitutgam.

DISCUSSION

We are now in a position to reevaluate the questions posed at the beginning of this chapter. The first was whether the structure referred to by Di Peso as the 1757 Jesuit mission church was in fact so. Was it constructed during the Jesuit period or was it was built later? All evidence suggests that this structure was not a Jesuit church. Many lines of evidence indicate that it began as a small settler's residence built during the presidio occupation. A dated adobe block provided direct evidence of when the core of this structure was built. Other characteristics of construction and the nature of intramural features point to this conclusion as well. The discovery of two types of adobe walls in the purported Jesuit church provides evidence of at least two periods of construction, and more likely accretional construction over time. A date on the interior walls of the initial construction is consistent with the fact that these adobes look very similar in hardness, color, and composition to the bricks forming the defensive wall that surrounds the presidio. This in itself is strong evidence that this room block (Rooms 126–131) is not the Jesuit church but was built during the presidio occupation. A later date on an outer wall of this structure from an adobe that was constructed differently than the interior walls is consistent with later remodeling and reuse of the building during the land grant period.

The second question is whether Quiburi was located at this site of the presidio. It has long been argued that this place was not Quiburi. Evidence has herein been presented for a Sobaipuri occupation at this place, but it was the place called Santa Cruz, not Quiburi. Even if this location had been Quiburi, the documented existence of a different Quiburi, San Juan Quiburi, a few years later in another location supports the interpretation that this location was not the focus of a key Spanish sacred edifice, the Jesuit church referenced by Di Peso. Contemporary documents specifically recognize the marginal state and volatile condition of this region and note that priests would not be sent.

Clearly a complex building sequence is represented at Santa Cruz de Terrenate Presidio. As a suitable place for occupation and defense it would have been attractive through time. Developed places on what otherwise seemed to the Spaniards, Mexicans, and Americans like an untamed landscape tended to attract subsequent occupation, and this place, called Santa Cruz, was no exception. Many of the outlying buildings were probably built and used during the land grant period, but at least one, parts of the 126–131 complex, was built when the presidio was occupied. Moreover, a date from the wall of Room 132 suggests that it was built earlier than the Jesuit period, or perhaps even in the early Jesuit period, and this date conforms to an earlier Sobaipuri occupation detected and dated by other evidence. In all likelihood, this room was built as a communal and defensive structure by the Sobaipuri of Santa Cruz but was reused during presidio times. This was probably the only substantial adobe Sobaipuri structure present, and it likely would have still been standing when in 1705 the Sobaipuri returned from Sonoita and in 1775 when O'Conor surveyed for the new presidio location. So, while there is no Jesuit church present, the record is equally interesting.

In some ways it is unfortunate that the structure referred to by Di Peso as the Jesuit mission does not date to the 1750s. This post-Kino period is so poorly known that confirmation of this as the Jesuit church would have been exciting indeed. Nonetheless, information about the Indigenous occupation of this portion of the San Pedro is available in the many Sobaipuri residential sites spread along this river, some of which date to this mid-eighteenth-century period. The Sobaipuri occupation at Santa Cruz de Terrenate Presidio is very likely the Santa Cruz village occupied during at least part of the interval between 1705 and 1762. Hopefully, this research will put the issue of Quiburi at Santa Cruz de Terrenate Presidio to rest once and for all. This was not Quiburi, and there was no Jesuit church here.

NOTES

1. This chapter was first written in 2010 and was included in Seymour (2011b) and was subsequently modified for this book. It is important to point out that the mission is different from the church, and Di Peso is using mission like we currently use church, meaning the building rather than the missionization effort.

2. This chapter focuses mainly on the Jesuit mission element of this post-1705 occupation. Elsewhere, I have addressed the issue of Kino's Quiburi and its purported relation to Santa Cruz de Terrenate Presidio (Seymour 2011a; see also chapter 8).

3. In most instances, wall melt and erosion of backfill into structures has also added strata to the interiors of structures, but in many cases this can be distinguished from original fill.

4. This position provided relatively easy access to materials for dating but is having a substantial impact on the preservation of walls, which in many cases are almost gone.

5. These adobe block samples produced weak signals, making their analysis difficult and requiring excessive machine time. Additional time reduces the error rate, which reduced the standard deviation but which should not change the date itself.

6. Future research would do well to reexpose these walls and sample another portion of the wall to be sure of the accuracy of this date. Archaeomagnetic samples were taken from the hearth but have not yet been run, owing to lack of funding. These would likely confirm a presidio-period use of the hearth (or later) but would not address the issue of initial construction.

It will also be informative to sample and date each of the structures or at least a larger sample of these structures. This work should be conducted soon, however, because most of the adobe on the walls is in the process of eroding away or have already done so.

10

The narrows located in the Tres Alamos area is considered by many to be the dividing line between the middle and lower San Pedro. For the seventeenth- and eighteenth-century Sobaipuri, the political division was farther north at the Redington Narrows. The Tres Alamos Narrows is indistinct compared to the one at Redington farther downstream. Although the latter is now referenced as the Redington Narrows, during the Spanish Colonial era it was probably most appropriately referenced as the Cusac or Acequias Hondas Narrows (hereafter referred to as Acequias Hondas Narrows). That narrows was treacherous because it was long, constricted, and brushy, making it a likely place for an ambush. Manje discussed this aspect of the route north to the Gila River when passing through this area in 1697:

> From this place Captain Francisco Ramírez (who was the one who had penetrated this region the farthest) returned, informing us that here were many *embudos* (traps) between two cliffs where the river narrows its course about half a league. We were told of this by Sergeant Juan Bautista de Escalante, who accompanied him previously and who was with us this time. (Karns 1954:79–80)

Like narrows throughout the Sobaipuri region, both of these constrictions in the river channel provided conditions suitable for water to move to the surface so that it could be used downstream by these farmers.

The Lower San Pedro

Tres Alamos to the Confluence

https://doi.org/10.5876/9781646422975.c010

One interesting aspect of the lower San Pedro is that it has overall a lower density of Sobaipuri sites than the middle San Pedro. The density within the Tres Alamos cluster is high, with eleven sites in a one-mile-long stretch, but along the remainder of the downstream portion of the river, density is on the low side, the next-highest number of known sites occurring immediately north of Acequias Hondas Narrows where water and land made the location desirable, but then there are only three in a one-mile stretch. During the initial part of sustained European contact, the lower San Pedro had more villages than were noted on the upper or middle San Pedro or on any of the other areas except the San Xavier–Tucson area. This inference derives from the number shown on Kino's maps and mentioned in his and other journals. These sites shown, in turn, are consistent with Ramírez de Salazar's 1692 account of the San Pedro, wherein he mentioned that there were eighteen Sobaipuri villages along this river, including at the headwaters, on the middle San Pedro and here on the lower San Pedro (Ramírez de Salazar 1692b). Yet, most of these were small communities. A series of small communities may have been the pattern on the middle San Pedro just prior to Kino's visits; because, as noted in chapter 7, Coro told the soldiers that the area north of Quiburi had been recently abandoned, likely causing aggregation into fewer larger settlements (see discussion in "Archaeological Evidence of Acequias Hondas Narrows and North"). Coro seemingly was referencing the area all the way north to the Redington Narrows because Baicatcan was apparently within his area of political influence, based on Kino's reference of Coro potentially being there in 1692.

TRES ALAMOS CLUSTER AND VILLAGES
SOUTH OF ACEQUIAS HONDAS

The first documented entry of the Spanish into the region near Tres Alamos and north was discussed in chapter 7. The preceding quotation indicates clearly that Ramírez de Salazar had penetrated the farthest north during Kino's time. Spanish soldiers ventured into this area in the early 1690s to break alliances between the Sobaipuri and the enemy and in search of stolen horses they never found. As was recounted, their route was soon followed by Kino, whose first visit to the San Pedro River was his 1692 trip to San Salvador del Baicatcan, a village thought to be in the modern-day Cascabel area (Seymour 2011a; also see Bolton 1948:I:123). It seems that Headman Coro, later of Quiburi, was living at, or perhaps just visiting, San Salvador del Baicatcan when Kino arrived, though Kino may have visited Quiburi as well. Not much was said about this first trip, and Tres Alamos or even Los Alamos was not mentioned. When

FIGURE 10.1. *A portion of Kino's 1701 map showing villages on the lower San Pedro (not labeled as such), including Rosario.*

next Kino traveled through this area (1697), Tres Alamos was not discussed as a village, nor were any other villages mentioned in this specific area, despite that it was ideal for settlement and irrigation. The Europeans camped at Los Alamos because of the many large and shady trees, as Manje described them, and because of the reliable surface water. It would have been a pleasant stopping place to rest up for the remainder of the journey. There were no occupied villages on this trip until downstream or north of Acequias Hondas Narrows, at Redington. This is because the population at and near Tres Alamos, and including San Salvador del Baicatcan, had withdrawn upriver to the south, as just noted. This suggestion seems supported by the changing position of settlements along the San Pedro on a series of maps that Kino produced between 1695 and 1710 (see, e.g., figures 3.1 and 5.1 of early Kino maps and figure 10.1) and also by Martín Bernal's and Manje's statements that villages south of Cusac and Jiaspi and south of the Acequias Hondas Narrows had been abandoned prior to their journey in 1697. In this reference to abandoned settlements, they were specifically referring to San Salvador del Baicatcan as well as perhaps San Marcos and presumably Tres Alamos. This area to the north of Quiburi was abandoned because of disputes between Coro's and Humari's Sobaipuri groups: "We continued to the north down the river passing by some deserted settlements. Because of discord with other settlements of the north, Chief Coro had depopulated them a year before" (Karns 1954:79).

This passage conveys that this area was within Coro's territory, as was some unspecified distance to the north. Judging from the geological character of the river, the distribution of Sobaipuri sites, and the places the Europeans passed by or camped at that were abandoned, the break between Coro's and Humari's realms was likely at or just south of the Acequias Hondas Narrows. So when these chroniclers wrote that Humari was the "chief of the tribe" or "principal captain of all the rancherías" (Karns 1954:80; F. Smith et al. 1966:40) and that Coro was "chief Indian of the Pima nation" (Karns 1954:78), they meant that they were the premier leaders over all the people and villages along their segment the river, not a leader of all O'odham/Pima everywhere or even all the Sobaipuri. This distinction explains why Quiburi came to the aid of Santa Cruz in 1698 and why the populations of both villages moved to Sonoita afterward. It also explains why so much of the valley north of Tres Alamos was for a time seemingly completely abandoned.

Lieutenant Martín Bernal also referenced this abandonment event, stating (as quoted in chapter 7):

Asking him [Coro] how the Sobaipuris were on the river below Quiburi, he said he did not know because it had been a long time since they had communicated with him because in days past he had sent a relative of his on business and they had killed him. (F. Smith et al. 1966:37)

In 1697 these officers related that the abandonment had occurred the previous year ("un año antes") or 1696 (Burrus 1971:371; Karns 1954:79). Another version of Manje's fourth expedition account states that this depopulation occurred two years previous ("dos años antes") or in 1695 (Burrus 1971:362). Regardless, the shift occurred sometime between 1692 and 1696. This short-term dispute between these two Sobaipuri political entities resulted in a major shift in settlement. As will be discussed in the final chapter, without the assistance of documentary accounts this abandonment might be missed or misinterpreted. Movement events (abandonment, establishment, reoccupation) occurred at such a tempo that they cannot necessarily be captured in archaeological analysis unless aided by parallel information sources, such as these documents.

During this 1697 expedition, Manje referred to Los Alamos as a "camp" or place ("paraje de Los Alamos"; "dormimos en el paraje de Los Alamos"; "llegamos a un paraxe despoblado que le yntitulamos Los Alamos" [Burrus 1971:201, 337, 361; Karns 1954:79]). (Also see Bolton 1948:I:170n191: "Paraje de los Álamos.") He did not mention a settlement, which again supports the notion that this area was depopulated, which is surprising given the number and density of Sobaipuri villages in this area. In this case *despoblado* is used to mean both unsettled and depopulated when he mentioned both an expedition camp that was not populated (e.g., unsettled) and also places that were once occupied but now abandoned plains (*llano despoblado*; and rancherías, *rancherías despobladas*).[1] He also used the terms *ranchería yerma*, *ranchería antigua*, and *y despoblada* to indicate that a settlement was no longer occupied (Burrus 1971:337, 362). These various usages and the term used with reference to Los Alamos suggest that Los Alamos was positioned in a location that had not recently been a Sobaipuri settlement. Eleven Sobaipuri settlements are located just to the north, and since these would have been abandoned at this time, Manje would have mentioned them by one of the terms noted, so this suggests that Los Alamos was before or upstream of the narrows and the places of settlement were perhaps at Tres Alamos, north or downstream from the narrows.

Manje's diary entries always refer to occupied residential settlements as *rancherías*.[2] His use of the term *paraje* rather than *ranchería* along this stretch suggests as well that Los Alamos was a camp along the trail rather than a residential site that had been depopulated or was uninhabited.[3] The inference that Los Alamos was not a recently abandoned or an occupied Sobaipuri settlement is reinforced by Manje's subsequent text. He described abandoned places and he otherwise described sending runners ahead (north of Los Alamos paraje) to inform the residents of occupied Sobaipuri settlements of his group's coming. Notably, Manje's diary entries after departing from Los Alamos consistently describe the number of people and houses and the greetings offered by residents as their group passed successively through several occupied settlements. This was not done at the Los Alamos paraje.

The night before reaching the first occupied villages to the north, Martín Bernal indicates that the group marched to "a place called *Baicadeat*" (e.g., Baicatcan), passing some deserted villages (Smith et al. 1966:37). Manje's diary from that night clarifies that they slept at a "plain abandoned by its inhabitants" (Burrus 1971:201, 337) or on a "deserted plain" (Karns 1954:79). The term *llano despoblado* is used, indicating that it was likely once a Sobaipuri village that had been depopulated (see Burrus 1971:337). Di Peso (1953:62) interpreted Baicadeat to be Baicatcan, but in a separate account Manje referred to this overnight spot as the abandoned settlement of San Marcos (Burrus 1971:362). San Marcos is a different place from San Salvador (del Baicatcan) according to texts and Kino's maps, which show San Salvador (del Baicatcan) south of San Marcos. So, sources do not agree as to which abandoned village they stayed at, unless the place was called San Marcos [del] Baicadeat, because it was in a different location at one time. As noted elsewhere in this book, a village was often given a different saint's reference when found in a different location, even though it retained the same Indigenous name. It is also possible that Baicadeat represents a different word from Baicatcan, despite the similarity in spelling, as in the discussion of Huachuca and Basosuca or Baosuca in chapter 5. The Baicadeat or Baicatcan would have been the O'odham name for the village and perhaps the general area. Modern O'odham language specialists do not know what it means, but Harry Winters (2012:719) suggests the first part of the name would be *vaikka*, which is "ditch" or "irrigation ditch," which in the local dialect this would be *waika*. Discussions with Wa:k O'odham elder Tony Burrell (personal communication, 2020) eventually revealed that this likely means abandoned canal (or used to be a canal) or *waikadak*, an interpretation that was confirmed by Felicia Nunez (personal communication, 2020). This explanation that the place was called San Marcos [del] Baicatcan is not likely because these two distinct places kept their names as they switched to opposite sides of the river and back again, as indicated by comparing Kino's 1695 *Teatro* map to the 1696–1697 *Saeta* map and then again to the 1701 *Paso por tierra a la California* map (see figure 10.1). On each of Kino's maps, San Marcos and San Salvador (this latter place usually associated with the name "Baicatcan") are shown as distinct villages as they move. Perhaps this phrasing suggests that the geographic location itself was referenced as Baicadeat or Baicatcan at the time, regardless of whether it had a population there, as was the case with the Quiburi segment of the larger valley.

Later documentary sources suggest that by the 1730s, the name "Tres Alamos" rather than Los Alamos had been adopted for the narrows area just north of modern-day Benson and that at that time a Sobaipuri village named Tres Alamos was occupied. It was certainly occupied in Padre Keller's time, for he and Juan Bautista de Anza went through this settlement in 1732 on their way from San Xavier del Bac to Santa María (on the far upper Santa Cruz River, then known as the Río de Santa María) as Keller was being introduced to various villagers in the Pimería Alta (Di Peso 1953:38; Hammond 1929:224, 229, 231). Tres Alamos is shown on a map of this region published preceding Padre Luís Xavier Velarde's 1716 relación, but the map by Francisco Javier Saviñon dates to 1733 (González R. 1977:26; figure 10.2) and seems to have

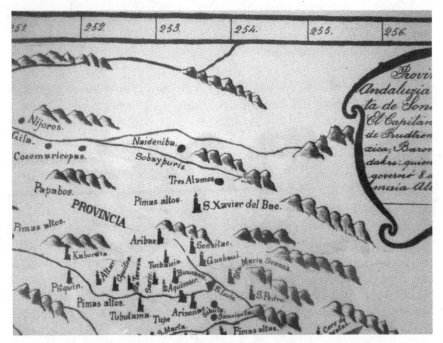

FIGURE 10.2. *Portion of 1933 map showing Tres Alamos. Provincia de la Nueva Andalucia de San Juan Baptista de Sonora, map. Manuel Orozco y Berra Map Library, Mapoteca, Mexico City, author unknown. Public Domain.*

been made as a result of or at least after this journey of Anza and Keller's. In 1746, Don Francisco Tagle y Bustamante, Captain of Fronteras presidio, listed Tres Alamos as an active village when he wrote about the San Pedro Valley (Di Peso 1953:39; Thomas 1941:203), and in 1748 Governor Don Agustín de Vildósola mentioned the visita settlement of Tres Alamos (Di Peso 1953:39; Thomas 1941:203).

The Tres Alamos area seemingly remained occupied by Sobaipuri through-out the entire period (1730s through 1750s); in 1751 existing residents were joined by O'odham from elsewhere. During the O'odham Revolt of 1751, Sobaipuri from settlements on the Santa Cruz moved to the lower San Pedro:

> Very soon after the unpropitious beginning of their own rebellion, the Indians of Tubaca [near Tubac] packed up and moved to Tres Alamos on the lower San Pedro River, where they were joined by their neighbors from Tumacacori who had departed from their homes on receiving word of the uprising from Guebavi (Phelipe Oct. 15, 1754:79). A couple of other small *rancherías* also took refuge

at Tres Alamos. There the people of Tubac seem to have remained through the winter, although they may have joined Captain-General Oacpicagigua's force in the Santa Catalina mountains. (Phelipe in Dobyns 1959:chap. 5)

It is this 1751 settlement episode that likely increased the population on this portion of the lower San Pedro River, adding settlements, perhaps one for each of the population centers on the Santa Cruz from which they fled. It is likely the remains of these villages are among those that have been encountered and recorded. One, AZ BB:15:57 (ASM), dates to this period (see the section "Archaeological Evidence of Tres Alamos Cluster and Baicatcan").

This village is not specifically mentioned during the relocation efforts of 1762, when middle San Pedro Sobaipuri were shifted to Tucson, which suggests that these villages were once again depopulated before this event. This suggestion is supported by a letter dated December 1763 by Padre Manuel Aguirrey, wherein he mentions that as of December 1761 there were no Sobaipuri at Tres Alamos and Santa Cruz because they had aggregated at other pueblos (Aguirrey 1763). Interestingly, Quiburi is not mentioned in this letter, but it seems to have remained populated during this period, as previous chapters have indicated (especially see chapter 8). By the 1770s and 1780s, the area continued to be referenced as Tres Alamos, the paraje being mentioned by O'Conor and the river crossing and mountain range (Sierra de Tres Alamos) appearing in texts and on maps by Rocha y Figueroa, absent an occupied village (O'Conor 1994:74; Rocha y Figueroa 1780a, 1780b, 1784; Seymour and Rodríguez 2020).

ACEQUIAS HONDAS NARROWS AND NORTH

When on the same 1697 expedition referenced above, Martín Bernal (Smith et al. 1966:37) asked Headman Coro at Quiburi if he would like to accompany them to the first village, which he noted was Tiaspi (Jiaspi/Rosario). But the first village was Cusac according to Manje, placing it south of Jiaspi (Burrus 1971:202; Karns 1954:80). In 1697, both villages were located north of abandoned settlements and north of the Acequias Hondas Narrows. There is no plot for Cusac on Kino's three maps, but Manje counted twenty houses and seventy people. The residents also gave them bowls of food. These details suggest that at least some of the Europeans did pass through Cusac, rather than simply noting it as a result of hearsay. Martín Bernal may have not mentioned Cusac because he may have not gone through that village. Instead, he may have gone ahead of the others in his group and bypassed Cusac as he was greeted by Jiaspi's leader and other important men, perhaps traveling on the other side of the river.

One of Kino's maps does show Rosario (compare figures 3.1 and 5.1 to figure 10.1), which was the name given to Jiaspi. Headman Humari, said to be "chief leader of all this tribe" (Karns 1954:82), heard the news of their arrival at Jiaspi and traveled south, a three days' journey to meet with the Europeans, according to Kino (Bolton 1948:I:170; Karns 1954:80). His village was at Victoria de Ojio, the last Sobaipuri settlement on the river to the north (Bolton 1948:I:170n192; Karns 1954:82), which is at most thirty-five or forty miles from Jiaspi and is not a three-day journey from the confluence. It took Kino that long because he kept stopping at all the intervening villages, but Humari might have made the trip much faster. Here at Jiaspi or Rosario, Martín Bernal counted 140 people and 23 houses (F. Smith et al. 1966:38), while Manje counted 120 people and 27 houses (or according to another version, 115 and 23; Burrus 1971:338, 364) and said that they were given lodgings in a house made of branches and mats that the residents had built for them.

Kino and his group next went to Muyva, which has long been thought to be the archaeological site of Alder Wash Ruin (AZ BB:6:9, ASM; Masse 1981b). There are no historical descriptions of the village, only that they visited it and then they provided its distance from the adjacent villages. This identification may be accurate given that no other Sobaipuri sites have been found in this intervening area, even though I have looked more than once.

After this, Manje conveyed, they passed through three more settlements before arriving at San Pantaleón de Arivavia (Karns 1954:81). Together these four settlements had a population of 500 people and 130 houses or 375 people and 75 houses or 335 souls and 75 houses (Burrus 1971:204; 365; F. Smith et al. 1966:38).

They passed through Tutoyda, with 20 houses and 100 people, and Comarsuta, with 80 people (or 12 houses and 60 people; Burrus 1971:204, 366; F. Smith et al. 1966:39), before reaching the main settlement of Nuestra Señora de la Victoria de Ojío. This is where Humari resided along with 380 other people, dwelling in 70 houses (or 315 people and 63 houses; or 315 souls and 73 houses; Burrus 1971:205, 366; F. Smith et al. 1966:39). They were lodged in a branch-and-mat structure that was so large there was room for everyone, including all the solders, the priest, and his retinue. Humari had gone south to Dolores the year before to be baptized, which likely explains why there was an altar in the center (Bolton 1948:I:169).

While Kino and his group were at this settlement, leaders from two other settlements, called Busac and Tubo, arrived with 85 men with a corresponding number of women and children (or 81 according to another version, Burrus 1971:340, 387; or 71 men and 31 women and children, F. Smith et al. 1966:39). They came from a valley referenced as Babitcoida (F. Smith et al. 1966:39).

This is thought to be Aravaipa Creek simply because today this is the largest tributary wash with the most reliable water.

The 1733 map shows only two villages in the lower San Pedro area (see figure 10.2). Tres Alamos is on the west side of the river, while Naideniba is to the north on the east side of the river. This village is referenced as Naideni in 1746: when citing a report by Vildósola, Croix commented:

> The Sobaipuri had their rancherías . . . in various spots close to its [San Pedro River] banks called Quiburi, Tres Alamos, Naideni, Bacoachi, Santa Cruz, and La Azequia Grande, [and he said] that the father missionary of Santa María de Suanca was visiting them. (Thomas 1941:203)

Some of the names given here indicate that more than just two villages were occupied on the lower San Pedro, in contrast to the map data from a few years earlier, demonstrating perhaps either the sketchy knowledge of the area or the fast-changing character of the Sobaipuri landscape. This source also indicates that both Quiburi and Santa Cruz bordered the middle San Pedro at this time. This scanty documentary evidence of additional Sobaipuri villages on the lower San Pedro is supported by chronometric dates on sites recorded in these areas (see the section "Archaeological Evidence of Tres Alamos Cluster and Baicatcan").[4] "La Azequia Grande" on the map was likely Acequias Hondas (Deep Ditch), which continues to be shown as a specific place through at least the 1780s. This large or deep acequia or canal likely references the rich farmlands and irrigation canals that surrounded Cusac.

The absence of mention of other locations, even in the 1760s when Sobaipuri in this frontier area were being removed, suggests that by then the Sobaipuri had left the lower San Pedro. This area was closest to the enemy Apache and Jocome and so may explain this migration. Rocha y Figueroa does not mention Sobaipuri settlements when he traveled through this lower San Pedro area in the 1780s (Rocha y Figueroa 1780a, 1780b, 1784; Seymour and Rodríguez 2020). Nonetheless, archaeological data suggest the area north of the Tres Alamos Narrows continued to be occupied, at least intermittently, for many years. Jocome sites are also abundant in the area around the Acequias Hondas Narrows and north to the confluence with the Gila River.

ARCHAEOLOGICAL EVIDENCE OF THE TRES ALAMOS CLUSTER AND BAICATCAN

As noted in the section "Tres Alamos Cluster and Villages South of Acequias Hondas," the documentary record indicates that Manje and Bernal encountered abandoned rancherías located to the north of Los Alamos that seemed to have been involved in the referenced abandonment episode in the mid-1690s. As they headed north members of the expedition camped at Los Alamos, in a location that was not described as an abandoned ranchería. Distances traveled indicate that some of these abandoned rancherías were a distance north of the Tres Alamos Narrows, and archaeological surveys confirm this distribution and a lack of sites to the south (upriver). These more northern populations that are represented by some of these archaeological sites retracted to the south to occupy the Kino-period villages inhabited until 1698, and those aligned with Humari likely retracted to the north (see Seymour 2011a, 2011b).

Archaeological evidence indicates that a mile-long stretch just north of the Los Alamos Narrows was occupied off and on for a substantial period of time. These seem to have been occupied both before and after Kino's visit, but, according to textual sources, probably not during Kino's time. In all, eleven Sobaipuri sites have been recorded here along this portion of the lower San Pedro: AZ BB:15:51, AZ BB:15:57, AZ BB:15:86, AZ BB:15:87, AZ BB:15:88, AZ BB:15:95, AZ BB:15:96, AZ BB:15:97, AZ BB:15:99, AZ BB:15:100, and AZ BB:15:101 (all ASM). These sites occupy a location along the river that is consistent with all other known riverine Sobaipuri sites along the San Pedro, Santa Cruz, and other rivers. The villages take advantage of floodplain and channel characteristics so that water is available for irrigation canals and a sufficiently broad floodplain is available for crops. For many miles upstream, the San Pedro floodplain is broad, and consequently much of it was likely a marshy environment, at least according to local lore.

That the archaeological sites in the Tres Alamos cluster are situated in the correct geographical location to be the historical Tres Alamos raises the likelihood that at least one of these lower San Pedro Sobaipuri sites is the historically referenced Tres Alamos from the early to mid-1700s. This finding, however, does not address the question as to which specific time period or periods this suite of Tres Alamos sites date. Knowing the often-complex occupational sequences of Sobaipuri sites, it would not be surprising to identify multiple uses of sites from as early as the late AD 1200s. This means that the 1730s and 1750s occupations likely overlie earlier occupations, and, in some instances, occupation might have continued here long after many residents returned to mission sites.

Chronometric dates were run on each of these sites where datable surface material could be found. The first sample sent in for analysis, as it turns out, come from the most likely site to have been occupied by refugees from the Santa Cruz during the 1751 O'odham Revolt. The Whetstone Plain sherd collected from the surface of a house at AZ BB:15:57 (ASM) produced an age of AD 1758–1786 (UW2521), which is consistent with a midcentury occupation related to the Pima Revolt and potentially a continued occupation of the area by recalcitrant O'odham who did not return to the mission settlements after the uprising. The largest site (AZ BB:15:88, ASM) retuned a date of AD 1690–1730 and is therefore the most likely the one occupied when Keller visited the village. Other sites returned dates from the Kino period suggesting that they were occupied slightly before or after Kino's visits, likely representing one or more whose population withdrew to the south, perhaps into the villages of Quiburi or Santa Cruz. Even earlier dates demonstrate the depth of occupation in this area, showing that at a minimum by the 1400s Sobaipuri had pushed this far north along the San Pedro (assuming they migrated into the area from the south; see Harlan and Seymour 2017). Much earlier dates have been obtained further south, or upstream, on the San Pedro. Slightly earlier dates than these for the Tres Alamos Narrows result from samples run farther north, downstream from the Acequias Hondas Narrows. It must be kept in mind, however, that usually only a single sample was run on each site, though the village locations were probably used repeatedly over time. Future researchers would encounter interesting results upon running many more samples from each known Sobaipuri site. Many samples have already been collected and curated (though it is not known how curation will influence dating results for luminescence samples).

One especially late date from the mid-1800s is another example of many that may demonstrate a continued O'odham occupation on the lower San Pedro, long after the area was said to have been forfeited and also after other parties began inhabiting this area during the American Territorial period. The continued occupation of this portion of the San Pedro is consistent with the noted ongoing occupation of Quiburi in the post-1762 period after supposed complete abandonment of the San Pedro at the order of interim governor Joseph Tienda de Cuervo to the presidio captain Francisco Elías González de Zayas in 1762 (Seymour 2011a; see chapter 8). On the other hand, this late date, associated with an adobe-walled structure, may represent the lost Butterfield Stage Station, whose occupants may have used O'odham pottery. This question deserves further investigation.

ARCHAEOLOGICAL EVIDENCE AT THE ACEQUIAS HONDAS NARROWS AND TO THE NORTH

There are about a dozen miles between this Tres Alamos cluster of sites and the next-known Sobaipuri site, near modern-day Cascabel. This break is likely accounted for by river channel characteristics as well as by historical factors; the thoroughness of archaeological coverage and access to private land are also likely factors. This portion of the river is suitable for occupation owing to conditions appropriate for agriculture and irrigation canals. Downstream and to the north, river channel characteristics change such that appropriate conditions are not present again until the river channel narrows again. In some areas the terraces are too high for occupation on one side of the river or the other. Yet there should be at least four Sobaipuri sites from the Kino period in this section, San Martín and San Salvador and settlements of the same names on the opposite site of the river, which suggests they remain to be found (see discussion in Seymour 2011a:28–30). While I cannot claim 100 percent coverage or even fair survey coverage in this area, many of the most likely locations were checked for evidence and few Sobaipuri sites were identified until north of, or downstream of, the narrows. One Sobaipuri site situated between Tres Alamos and Acequias Hondas Narrows is the Taylor site (AZ BB:11:90, ASM), thought to be Baicatcan during at least part of its long occupational history. Dates from one locus produced evidence of use around the Kino period, suggesting that this is one of at least two locations for a village of this name, consistent with the village shifting over time (see discussion in Seymour 2011a). As discussed elsewhere (Seymour 2011b), two luminescence dates on Whetstone Plain pottery obtained from AZ BB:11:90, ASM fall within the Kino period and after (AD 1764±50 or AD 1714–1814, Locus 2, Feature 41; X2077; AD 1704±50 or AD 1654–1754, Locus 3, Feature 46, X2078), confirming long-term reoccupation of the location, as also indicated by super-imposed houses, changes in housing direction, differences in mode of house layout relative to one another, multiple loci, and density and diversity of material present in some locations.

Moving north or downstream along the river, one finds many fewer Sobaipuri sites. A handful of Sobaipuri sites have been identified on the lower San Pedro in the stretch downstream from the Acequias Hondas Narrows—fewer than on the middle San Pedro for sure. This much lower density may relate to more arid conditions, many fewer suitable places along the river to irrigate, the proximity of enemy populations, and perhaps the later migration/expansion into this area. Being so close to enemy territory would have made it more dangerous to live there unless alliances were maintained. Such alliances were claimed for the northeastern-most Sobaipuri, even during Kino's time, and likely accounted for how that population under Humari was able to survive. Manje and Martín Bernal conveyed information about enemy relations, satis-fied that they found six Apache scalps and that two Apache boys had been captured (Burrus 1971:203, 363, 367). Martín Bernal commented that the leader who had come from up a side canyon to the east, mentioned above (in section "Acequias Hondas Narrows and North"), was asked what news he had about the Jocome, and he admitted they had lived together, while at other times had fought them:

> He said he has lived with them some time on the occasion an entry into their land was made; and the Spanish having made a surprise attack on them and captured the *chusma* [rabble, meaning noncombatants], five of the Jocomes escaped and came to his ranchería; and a few days after the Governor of the Jocomes died a natural death, and that after he died the others withdrew, they do not know where; that they are living at their ranchería peacefully; that they just arrived from surveying the entries of the enemy and that at that time they did not find a single trace; also they informed me how in days past they made a surprise attack on some Jocomes who had been in the vicinity of their ranchería, those and the Sobaípuris from the western part, having called them for this reason; and that they killed four Jocomes and they captured two *piezas* [noncombatant captives; piezas de chusma], whom they told us the Sobaípuris from the west [San Xavier] have; that the enemy Apaches are roaming their lands and that they are fighting them, causing deaths in one part and another. (F. Smith et al. 1966:39–40)

From this description it seems that the leader from the Babitcoida Valley was protecting the Jocome by denying knowledge of their current whereabouts, evaluating that they were peaceful and no threat at the time. This statement reflects as well something of the complexity and fast-changing nature of inter-tribal relations during this era. This passage may also provide some insight into why in some instances more than the noted number of "Sobaipuri" residents were present or why a greater number of Sobaipuri sites than named villages may be found. It seems that Martín Bernal was saying that the Sobaipuri had come out from the west and were staying, perhaps in a ranchería near theirs, when he commented: "the Sobaípuris from the western part, having called them for this reason."

Emerging from the Redington or Acequias Hondas Narrows, the valley opens in a broad lush expanse with abundant arable land. Its suitability is reflected in the numerous sizable prehistoric sites and the occurrence of four Sobaipuri sites. Only one of these is the Kino-period Cusac, but it is difficult to differentiate for sure which one relates to this specific period. One produced a date on a Whetstone Plain sherd that is much earlier than the Kino period (AZ BB:11:1; AD 1380±60). The most likely candidate for Cusac has not been dated but has the right material culture and is of the appropriate size to be the Kino-period Cusac (AZ BB:11:207, ASM). Nearby is a much smaller Sobaipuri site that may be a special-use locus, such as a purification locale, but nothing was found to date (AZ BB:11:210, ASM). Second Canyon (AZ BB:11:20, ASM), excavated in the 1969 and 1970, may have had a Sobaipuri component but produced material clearly indicative of the Canutillo complex and so likely has a Jocome component overlying the prehistoric (Franklin 1980). This may be one of the villages occupied by Jocome that Martín Bernal's informant was referencing, though many more such locations with Jocome material culture have now been identified along this portion of the river (see Seymour 2016a; Seymour and Sugnet 2016). Davis Ruin (AZ BB:11:36, ASM) is said to have had Whetstone Plain, but I have not been able to confirm an actual locus of Sobaipuri activity on the site so the pottery could be a pot break from transport or collecting activity or could have been raided from a nearby village. The site is highly disturbed because it has been previously excavated and then was later tested.

Two candidates for Jiaspi were identified based on their league distances north of the narrows and north of the various Cusac candidates. The sites dated to before and after Kino, suggesting either that (a) the actual location of Jiaspi has not been found or has been destroyed or (b) there was a longer-term and repeated use of one or both of these locations and the single sample dated at each of these sites only captured one of a series of occupations (1440±60 [UW3324] AZ BB:6:266; 1750±20 [UW3325]; AZ BB:6:265).

The next village downstream to the north, at least during 1697, was Muyva, which, as noted in the previous section, has long been thought to be Alder Wash Ruin (AZ BB:6:9, ASM) excavated by W. B. Masse (1981). Since the travelers did not describe this village in Kino's time, we can't be sure of its identity based on excavation results. Artifacts from the excavations revealed its occupation during the correct time period.

There should be additional Sobaipuri sites north of Muyva/Alder Wash Ruin, though in some instances they may have been destroyed through later activity. Others may be on private or tribal land to which I have not gained access. I have examined expansive sections of the river, including on BHP (mining company) land south of Mammoth, the area near Aravaipa Creek, and the area around Dudleyville and up to the confluence, except on tribal land. Portions of Aravaipa Creek and the Klondyke Valley were examined as well, but evidence may yet be found for Sobaipuri in this area despite that much of the land has been substantially disturbed. Some of the other previously recorded lower San Pedro sites once thought to be Sobaipuri did not produce evidence to corroborate this affiliation and so have been eliminated from my database. This elimination includes examination of sites that had been previously recorded as Sobaipuri that were field-checked and their artifacts housed at the Arizona State Museum. Most of those sites thought to be Sobaipuri are Jocome or Apache, and many of these previously recorded sites that are no longer classified as Sobaipuri were those sites recorded on the lower San Pedro.

CONCLUSION

Work my team and I have carried out along the lower San Pedro has produced twenty-one definite Sobaipuri sites and eliminated many others that have been identified as Sobaipuri in the past but are in fact Canutillo or Jocome. In other instances, there is not enough information to ascertain cultural affiliation without further, more-intrusive work. This northern section of the river provides a cautionary tale regarding use of the documentary record without input from other sources, such as archaeology. Using textual sources alone, we would conclude that Tres Alamos was not a place of Sobaipuri occupation until the first third of the eighteenth century. We might also assume that given the number of villages mentioned in the Kino-period documents, that the lower San Pedro was the most important settlement cluster on the San Pedro. With archaeology we see that many more sites are present on the middle San Pedro, reflecting a much more complex occupational history. We might also assume that the entire lower San Pedro area was abandoned by the middle of the eighteenth century, but like further upstream, there is evidence in chronometric dates and artifacts of potential use, at least intermittently, until around 1850 (at AZ BB:15:87, ASM), although, as noted, this late date may simply represent the stage station. On the other hand, without the documentary record the archaeological record would be difficult to interpret. Archaeological data alone would not capture the nuances of population shifts, including the movement of people to this area from mission settlements during the 1751 O'odham Revolt. We would not know that this entire area from Quiburi to the Acequias Hondas Narrows was abandoned before Kino's 1697 visit, nor would we know the basis for it. Without these records we would also not know for sure that at one time Jocome resided peacefully among the Sobaipuri, prior to becoming their traditional enemies, along with the Apache, and that these northern populations had successfully convinced the Spaniards that they were not aiding and abetting the enemy.

NOTES

1. Archaeology will be able to discern whether there was an earlier and therefore abandoned village in this area and so can settle this issue definitively.

2. This is Manje's practice; other chroniclers may have used terms differently.

3. This is not to say that there might not have been villages there in the distant past, as most places show considerable evidence of reuse by the Sobaipuri after periods of abandonment.

4. Bacoachi may have been a misstatement, as there is an Ópata presidio of this name ninety miles southeast of Tumacácori (see Kessell 1976:164).

11

*New Understandings
in Sobaipuri Research*

This book, like *Where the Earth and Sky Are Sewn
Together*, presents a characterization of Sobaipuri territory and landscape use that is in some cases and some
ways substantially different from past understandings.
This change results from my decades of research on
this group, studying the distribution of sites, attempting to reconcile differences between documentary and
ethnographic information on the one hand, and what
I was seeing in the archaeological record and hearing
from descendants on the other, and learning about the
nature of the people who inhabited this land before
and at the dawn of history. So much new information
has been gathered and so much has been learned that
some past interpretations based solely on documentary
sources have had to be modified. New and exciting
renditions of the Sobaipuri themselves and Sobaipuri
landscape use have resulted.

One example is while at San Xavier del Bac, Manje
wrote: "I rode on a horse and went to count the houses
of the ranchería, which is divided into three neighborhoods, in a triangular form; and I counted, in all, 166
houses" (author's translation; see Burrus 1971:378). In
this comment he did not mean that the houses were
so far apart that he had to ride between family clusters,
which would have been the default interpretation in the
past. Rather, he meant something entirely surprising
and different. He was describing a highly planned and
segmented village with closely spaced houses arrayed
in structured arrangements in each neighborhood.

https://doi.org/10.5876/9781646422975.c011

Remnants of these ancient neighborhoods can still be seen by the attuned observer in the open fields south of Valencia Road in Tucson. The house arrangements of paired structures in rows on these landforms are so predictable that houses can be consistently found in blank spaces on archaeological sites. By pacing from a visible structure, an unrecognized structure that is paired to a visible structure (or the next pair of structures) can be identified, as has been verified through mapping and excavation. The neighborhoods themselves were widely spaced, as they are today at Wa:k, though today they have begun to grow together and fill in, owing to the greater number of residents.

This unexpected interpretation had numerous other implications for the researcher as well. It has meant that the role of Kino and other missionaries in the *reducción* [reduction; relocation and aggregation of settlements] of this village and others, and of "uniting and organizing" the Sobaipuri (e.g., *Viva Kino* 2018 movie [Beltrami]), would have to be rethought. The earliest Sobaipuri villages recorded exhibit the described pattern of paired houses aligned in parallel rows, long before European contact. This attribute makes them both unique among Southwestern groups in this specific pattern and similar to the better-known Southwestern groups in the cultural practice of living in planned villages of formally arranged houses. Their villages were not chaotic scatterings of dilapidated and cobbled-together huts. Instead, these people were "united" and lived in somewhat aggregated communities long before Kino arrived. Sobaipuri sites exhibit a pattern of village planning, community organization, and population densities not previously expected. This kind of segmented village organization is seen worldwide and is usually correlated with a diverse population, which in turn, tends to increase the need for more formal oversight, involving such matters as allotting land, resolving disputes, providing for those less fortunate, and also in managing irrigation canals, water allotment, and distribution of farm produce. As was discussed in chapter 1, one of the reasons these attributes were not expected is because of small sample size, the application of inappropriate ethnographic analogies, poor execution of the direct historical approach, and an inadequate theoretical base from which to interpret these types of less visible archaeological data.

Another surprising outcome from excavation data was that superimposed houses were discovered. The assumption for decades had been that the apparent surface positioning of structures meant that, when appropriate, houses were simply rebuilt in a new location and as such were scattered across the landscape without regard to any specific landform, place, or plan. Instead, research has shown that there was considerable time depth in attachment to place. Houses were superimposed, that is, built over one another, at many Sobaipuri sites. This pattern, initially discovered at San Cayetano del Tumacácori, was not restricted to a single site, but is widespread across Sobaipuri sites in different drainages. In fact, it is the norm for larger sites, some exhibiting five periods of overlapping housing or more. Yet, even some of the smaller sites revealed this pattern. Multiple times throughout the centuries, villagers rebuilt in the same location after the spot had been vacated for some time. In fact, the important village Kino dubbed San Cayetano shows evidence of having been used not only repeatedly when it was known as Tumacácori but also later, perhaps when the name changed. It was thought that little was left of this village, because people did not know where it was and thus thought it has mostly been destroyed. Yet, a major portion of it, including what may be remains of the church, is located on private land. Enough of this site was explored that it was possible to discern that houses were paired and arranged in parallel rows. The site produced numerous chronometric dates that fit with the Kino-period textual descriptions and map plots, as no other site does, judging from extensive survey and resurvey along the river (see Seymour 1993a, 2007b, 2011a). What also seems apparent is that a portion of this site may have also been the later village of San Cayetano de Calabasas. While this is wildly unexpected, it does make sense from the standpoint of map and league distance data, which place this O'odham settlement north of the confluence with Sonoita Creek (not south, where the later rancho is positioned), and also a chronometric date on a firepit that postdates the rest of the site and contained a domesticated goat or sheep bone (see a longer discussion about Calabasas in Seymour and Rodríguez 2020:171–175). I have repeatedly surveyed through the years looking for an alternative placement, to no avail, in the areas north of Sonoita Creek along the Santa Cruz where the Calabasas village is plotted on maps from when first mentioned in the mid-1700s until 1797 (see, e.g., Matson and Fontana 1996:map 2, p. 99; Seymour and Rodríguez 2020:fig. 7.1).

Equally telling of extended occupations and planned arrangements was that site after site revealed changes in the orientation of rows of houses. As chronometric dates were obtained, this pattern suggested that villages that had once been abandoned, and or whose residents had moved, were soon reoccupied, but often the orientation of the housing was changed to utilize a fresh surface. Whereas initially the number of Sobaipuri sites encountered did not make sense based on what was known from historical documents, it now became clear that residents were moving around a lot more than expected for sedentary villagers. Yet, they maintained their close connection to certain river segments. They had an attachment to place because houses overlooked their fields and canals. Only certain river segments had reliable surface water and therefore were suitable for building canals and preparing fields. Consequently, as villages moved every few years, they moved up and down these specific river segments, staying within proximity to the existing infrastructure. They moved back and forth between a few locations along specific river segments. This segmented sedentism had not been previously described for this region. Although Ezell (1961) had described a process of village drift, its implications were not fully appreciated until archaeological data documenting this had been presented.

Guevavi serves as another example of the complexity of Sobaipuri landscape use and village organization because it was such an important place. When I began work at Guevavi, only four partial house outlines were visible on the surface (Seymour 1993a, 1993c, 1997). I initially found the site on the basis of the surface presence of Whetstone Plain. Excavations at this locus revealed not only a much larger locus but also a more densely occupied one. Prolonged use was indicated by superimposed houses, changes in house orientation, and chronometric dates (see figure 2.9). Then, as I undertook additional research, it became clear that several spatially discrete loci, not just this one, were occupied repeatedly through time. There are eight distinct loci of Sobaipuri occupation consistent with the O'odham pattern of coming and going. Additionally, there are nearby Sobaipuri village sites not included in this count and a site farther north that, given the presence of organic-tempered plainware, represents a later Sobaipuri occupation, not to mention the many other vestiges of villages between there and Tumacácori.

This more intensive and extensive use of the location is also apparent at the later end of the temporal sequence at Guevavi. The village was said to have been abandoned by 1775, an inference that is based on a single document. In fact, it does seem to have been abandoned for at least a period before being reoccupied. A document from Father Eixarch's visitation to Tumacácori, May 12, 1775, conveys that Guevavi's occupants had moved to Calabasas:

> In addition, at a distance of four leagues, or a little more or a little less, is an outlying mission village called Calabasas in which live the Indians of Guevavi and Sonoita, depopulated because of the furious hostility of the Apaches. The number of persons at the said village is 141—that is, one hundred and forty-one. All are Indians of the Pima and Papago tribes, as are those of Tumacácori. (Kessell 1965:79)

But taking into account the Sobaipuri proclivity to move from a location when water is scarce or for other reasons discussed elsewhere, this seems to have been only a temporary shift. There is evidence of continued occupation at Guevavi after this date. The continuous use of the area, the late dates, and late sites even after Guevavi was supposedly "abandoned" the final time proved to be a characteristic of sites on other drainages as well. As elsewhere, the location was left for some years only to be reoccupied when water returned to the river, enemy hostilities subsided, priests gave up on missionization efforts, or fields had sufficient time to recover. We see evidence of this in both the archaeological and documentary data.

The pattern of superimposed structures, changes in orientation, and reoccupation indicated a potentially much greater time depth for the Sobaipuri than previously conceived. This pattern explained why the sites themselves looked so short term, but the Sobaipuri presence overall seemed to encompass a much greater time depth. The problem remained, however, as to how this temporal depth would be verified, given the dating techniques available. Luminescence dating eventually provided the answer, allowing sites to be dated at precise enough confidence intervals to detect distinct components. As these dates accumulated, they quickly verified the patterns detected by other means, ultimately documenting a Sobaipuri presence at least as early as the late AD 1200s.

When this unexpected abundance of Sobaipuri sites were first discovered in the mid-1980s, there really were only two viable options for their ubiquity, given the attendant assumptions. These sites were either (a) highly differentiated and specialized sites representing different aspects of a simple settlement system, all focused on a few more or less contemporaneous residential sites with a shallow time depth, or (b) a series of smaller homesteads oriented around a central place, consistent with the ranchería model. Yet, with the ability to date each site and the potential to date each component on a site, Sobaipuri village movements up and down the river could be traced, even at a scale that would mirror some of the shifts captured by the documentary record or potentially conveyed in bead styles and pottery attributes.

Using existing archaeological theory, this Sobaipuri settlement pattern could have been interpreted in a very different way if the documentary record were not available to hint at the shifts in settlements over shorter periods of time. If this frequency of village movement is not factored into the equation, the regional population looks much larger than perhaps it was. Depending on the assumptions brought to bear on this data set, the increase in number of places occupied could look like a substantial population increase, particularly if the shortness of each village's occupation were not considered. If the shifts in and the subtleness and tempo of reuse and reoccupation were not taken into account, and the lightness of the footprint were given undue weight, the assumption would be that these sites were occupied only for a short period of time, and, in turn, this would indicate a mobile existence, as researchers thought for decades. The depth of use, the complexity of revisits, and this special type of occupational permanency had not been appreciated or understood. Without this understanding, all the preceding occupations had been missed, resulting in the misimpression of a shallow time depth to occupation by this group in this region. Yet excavations have shown that these sites are much more complex and longer term and that, along with population shifts, there was continued reuse.

The complexity of the archaeological pattern became apparent as sites were dated but also as they were rerecorded after a couple of decades of additional erosion. It also helped that a new understanding of site layout had been developed. Some sites thought initially to be special-use sites, such as a field house (e.g., Seymour 2003), turned out to be much more extensive. A single house visible thirty years before was later visible as one in a series of related houses within a formally arranged village that later became visible on the surface as a result of subsequent and continued erosion. But the presence of a larger site was not immediately obvious because, once again, it had been assumed that sites were shallow with near-surface features, most of which would be visible on the surface. Also, as erosion increased, a more diverse range of pottery types were apparent. Later pottery types were exposed, demonstrating a much longer sequence of occupation, including into the late 1800s, when the valley was supposed to have been abandoned by the Sobaipuri. Five sites are known on the middle San Pedro that date to the post-1762 period during this time, when O'odham were not recorded to have occupied the San Pedro. Moreover, accounts of O'odham interacting with settlers, being seen on the landscape, and selling pottery to Fairbank and Bisbee residents all confirm a general presence that has been glossed over in the historical record. O'odham were present, just invisible, or faintly represented in the historic record, perhaps because their continued presence was inconvenient, as land ownership depended so heavily on valleys being seen as open wilderness, overrun by Apaches, and available to the strong independent rancher who could fight for and maintain his hold. This may be why the San Juan de las Boquillas y Nogales land grant did not mention Sobaipuri, who may still have resided within the bounds of this grant in the first quarter of the nineteenth century. So, while the early end of the Sobaipuri sequence has been extended back in time into the Late Prehistoric period, so too has their continued presence on the San Pedro River been documented during a time when they were said to have abandoned the valley. The Sobaipuri remained a feature of the landscape long after they were said to have been completely removed from the San Pedro, long after the name of the river was changed, likely owing to this attempted removal, and after they were thought to have become extinct.

If nothing else, this discussion should covey the point that study of the Protohistoric period and Sobaipuri specifically is still in its infancy. So many ideas need to be reexamined and so many past conclusions reevaluated. The initial starting point, the basis for conclusions for so many years, has been so far off the mark that every statement about these people needs to be reconsidered. As new data accumulate, new directions in thought are possible. Notably, the way inferences are drawn is from the pool of existing and apparent facts. That pool has expanded exponentially over the last four decades and continues to do so at an ever-expanding rate. No doubt, inferences are built based on available information and existing thought forms.

In the past, most of the evidence was obtained from documentary sources and many of the same sources have been translated and retranslated as part of this work, in which it was hoped that new conclusions would arise without the benefit of a fresh external basis to expand possible interpretations and to contribute inspiration for the list of possible meanings. Now that archaeological data are available and an ever-widening selection of documentary sources are slowly finding their way into the pool, new ways of thinking are emerging, and new nuggets of data are surfacing that have the power to fundamentally alter perceptions. Of importance, past interpretations were based on so few data points that a single new fact could substantially alter views, a reality that continues today. This scarcity was conveyed in chapter 7 on Kino's Quiburi, where my own ideas changed with the addition of new data. As discussed in chapter 8, the long-held view that the San Pedro was completely abandoned by the Sobaipuri has also been revised on the basis of Rocha y Figueroa's diary and map, which demonstrated that Sobaipuri remained in the area long after they were said to have left. Archaeological data further corroborated the fact of the late-occupied sites mentioned above.

MISSION AND PRESIDIO LANDSCAPES

Just as Sobaipuri villages exhibit a complex series of occupations, so too do the architectural features found at the Spanish colonial missions and presidios. The mission and presidio landscapes were much more intricate and convoluted than previously considered. This fact is illustrated at Santa Cruz de Terrenate Presidio on the San Pedro River, which is one of the most contested occupational sequences in this area. As was also discussed in chapters 1 and 9, Di Peso (1953) excavated here in the late 1940s and early 1950s and laid out a sequence, which, following Bolton, had the Sobaipuri village of Quiburi preceding and underlying the presidio. The detailed discussion of this is reserved for publication elsewhere (Seymour 2023), but suffice it to say that Bolton ([1936] 1960:361) was wrong when he stated that the presidio overlay the Sobaipuri village of Quiburi, as was Di Peso (1953) when he followed suit with this interpretation. While this assertion of their incorrect interpretation has been generally understood since Gerald (1968) first raised questions, it was only in the last few decades that substantial evidence of this counterposition has been obtained. The questions about Santa Cruz (de Terrenate) Presidio relate to (a) the presence of a Sobaipuri occupation (chapters 1 and 7), (b) the establishment of a Jesuit church (chapter 9), (c) construction and occupation of the presidio itself, and (d) post-presidio use of the location.

It has already been established that the presidio site was occupied by the Sobaipuri, who at the time were identified with the village of Santa Cruz after the 1698 battle (see chapters 1, 6, 7, and 9, this volume; see also Seymour 2023). This Sobaipuri component has been identified and dated. For this treatment I would like to move beyond this issue, to, but also past, the one touched on in chapter 9 regarding the purported presence of a Jesuit church. As discussed in detail earlier, this is not the Jesuit church, and this building and its many rooms provide a hint as to the complexity of construction and occupation at this site. The adobes surrounding the presidio provide a hint of the incredibly complex use of this area. Its use through the centuries resulted because it was a known place on the landscape with certain desirable attributes, which was later perceived as especially good for defense. One reason it obtained this reputation was because it was known as "Santa Cruz." Hugo O'Conor wrote that the presidio would be built "at a place named Santa Cruz" (O'Conor 1994:63). This was the place where the valiant Santa Cruz Sobaipuri warriors lived that defeated the attacking enemy of 500 (see Seymour 2014, 2015b). Although the battle occurred elsewhere, its former residents later moved to this location and the legend was carried along with the inhabitants. In 1781, Teodoro de Croix noted that Santa Cruz de Terrenate Presidio had been moved to the abandoned pueblo of Santa Cruz (Thomas 1941:147–148). This is why it was later referenced as the "place of the holy crosses" (plural) because so many different occupations assumed this name (Santa Cruz).[1] As an existing and known place, it attracted attention, and people were drawn there. In part, this was because of its perceived value as a defensive location as it was also evaluated by O'Conor in 1775. It also had wood, water, and nearby forage, along with arable lands (Croix in Thomas 1941; Seymour 2011a, 2023).

Recognition of the value of that location for occupation began at least as early as the Archaic period, long before it was called Santa Cruz. There was also probably a Sobaipuri village there before the Europeans attached the name "Santa Cruz" to the location, in that one of the adobe-walled structures dated to AD 1640±90. This date has such a long standard deviation that while it could mean the structure was built long before Santa Cruz, it could also have been built as a defensive structure when the Santa Cruz residents returned from Sonoita in 1704 or so. The place called Santa Cruz remained attractive for occupation for centuries more. The standing walls allowed immediate protection from the Apache, as it had during previous expeditions during the Spanish period (e.g., Hammond 1931; Rocha y Figueroa 1780a, 1780b, also in Seymour and Rodríguez 2020; i.e., the Ugarte-Rocha 1780 and Zúñiga 1795 expeditions) and for Indigenous inhabitants who camped within its walls. A large part of its attraction during the nineteenth century was because of existing infrastructure that could be modified and incorporated into new plans for the location. Evidence suggests that this was the headquarters for the San Juan de las Boquillas y Nogales land grant, probably owing to the existence of still-standing structures at the presidio. It became a central place, a known place, that could be improved and adapted with less effort than beginning anew.

The continued use of this place is documented in evidence obtained from wall construction. Normally, this means the abutment and bonding of adobe walls as they are incrementally added. Here, however, I chronometrically dated adobes and mortar that formed the walls of the adobe-walled structures surrounding the presidio. The goal was to determine once and for all whether they were related to presidio use, presumably by civilians, or part of the 1757 Jesuit church and mission. Some of these results were discussed in chapter 9 (see figures 9.1 and 9.2).

In short, the so-called Jesuit mission (Rooms 126–131) produced evidence that a portion of the structure was built in the Spanish Colonial period and was contemporaneous with the presidio. The south perimeter presidio wall had not been completed to regulation height, but this structure to the south incorporated adobes into its interior walls that shared characteristics with these perimeter wall adobes and also dated to the presidio period. The size of this structure suggests that it housed a large family or perhaps was owned by the merchant known to have resided here (Seymour 2023). At least one of the outer walls of Rooms 126–131, however, dated to AD 1850±70 (UW2630). This dating result suggests that this part of the structure may have been added during the Mexican period, when this became the San Juan de las Boquillas y Nogales land grant. No other known and recorded historical events between presidio occupation and land grant designation contributed occupation and construction in this area, making this the most reasonable interpretation.

Equally important is that two other structures also date to this period. The dating result from Room 122, the apparent lookout structure, also postdates the presidio (1860±30; UW2629). The sample from Room 133 produced a similar result (1850±40; UW2631). These dates also suggest that these buildings were constructed during the land grant period, not during use of the presidio. Again, this timeframe might make this site part of the land grant headquarters. Together these new data present a much different perspective of this presidio site but one that is more consistent with the expanded documentary record and improved archaeological data set.

A similar procedure of dating the adobe walls was followed at Guevavi, wherein an effort was undertaken to isolate the various adobe-walled buildings said to have been constructed at the Sobaipuri village throughout the period it was a mission, visiting station, and then mining settlement occupied by an ethnically diverse population. Here a melted adobe building found amid one of the Sobaipuri village loci was excavated and chronometrically dated to the Kino period (Seymour 2009c, 2011a). Luminescence dates obtained from samples derived from most of the adobe-walled structures visible at Guevavi indicate a much longer and later use than previously thought. Managers and researchers have assumed that these adobe-walled structures scattered around the site related to the visible mission, but this was once again accepted lore rather than based on data-driven facts. This assumption that all were temporally related was based on the spatial association with the main church visible with still-standing walls and expectations for the complexity of Franciscan missions. But, in fact, recent excavations and testing in these outlying adobe buildings revealed that they were constructed in many different ways and date to many different periods. For example, some are *zoguete con ripio* (mortar and rock), others are adobes with mortar (but still with variation between buildings in the ways these adobes were made and their sizes), and other are flat rocks and slabs with poorly consolidated mortar. This construction evidence grows in importance when coupled with the fact that such important places with reliable water, pasture, agriculture land, and existing infrastructure tended to draw people for centuries, prehistoric occupation before and historic after. Yet, until recently there were few data to corroborate this perception, because excavations had focused on other issues and could not conceive of the range of questions that can now be raised. Now chronometric dates have been obtained on most of the buildings visible on the surface, and these demonstrate that the architectural differences between adobe buildings do have temporal relevance. Moreover, excavations are revealing an abundance of historical buildings that are not visible from the surface, which will complicate and enrich the story of this site even more.

Equally significant, these new chronometric data have greater relevance to question about which buildings relate to which occupations. I had argued that the zoguete con ripio foundation in Locus A of AZ EE:9:132 (ASM) was the building Kino referred to as the "neat little house and church" that Father San Martín completed in 1701 (Seymour 2009c; also see Bolton 1948:I:303, 307; Kessell 1970:30, 31). This argument was based in part on a date obtained from the burned daub roofing debris from within that returned a data range of AD 1686±30 (Oxford #2548). In that article I questioned where the adobe was located that was noted in 1699 and suggested that perhaps it was at another site referenced as Guevavi that was situated in another location. This argument is quoted here in full owing to its relevance to this issue:

> A related issue is whether the "neat little house and church" was the first to be constructed at Guevavi. The implication is that it was the first such building, though the documentary record provides only indirect hints. In the 1690s Manje and Kino consistently mentioned visiting Guevavi, but always traveled on instead of staying for the night there. Neither do these early visitors mention an adobe structure at Guevavi, though they do at neighboring settlements. In the next settlement north or south they stayed in an earth-roofed adobe house, suggesting that until the "neat little church" structure was built in 1701, Guevavi did not even have a place for the missionary to stay (see Crockett 1918:101, 133, 142, 179; Karns 1954:94, 126, 136, 169; Bolton 1948:I:119, 120, 204–5, 233; Burrus 1971:217).
>
> A suggestion to the contrary is provided by the translations and transliterations by Burrus (1971:115, 413) and Bolton (1948:I:204), which suggest an adobe house may have been present as early as 1699. In October 1699, when speaking of three settlements together, Kino commented, "In San Luys, where we counted forty houses, as also in the following posts or rancherías of Guebabi and San Cayetano, they received us with all kindness, with crosses and arches erected in the roads, with earth-roofed adobe houses, which they have prepared for the father whom they hope to receive" (Bolton 1948:I:204). One possibility is that the sentence structure has contributed to confusion regarding the location of adobe houses, when perhaps reference is being made to forty houses at each location or that the visitors were universally received with kindness. It is also possible in this case that the reference to an earth-roofed structure applied to only two of the three settlements, Guevavi being lumped in only for convenience or lack of specificity. One reason to believe that this interpretation might be the case is that, as in March, even after Kino records the preceding information he continues on to the next settlement to spend the night, after only a short stop at Guevavi (Bolton 1948:I:204–5).

The documentary record provides just enough information to cloud the issue of whether or not there was a structure present at this geographic location prior to 1701. Burrus (1971:115, 413) notes that earlier that year, in March 1699, Kino and Manje rested at Guevavi in an adobe-and-earth house: "y, aviendo tomado un refresco en la casa pared de adove y terrado que nos tienen hecha" (Burrus 1971:431). There are at least two difficulties with this interpretation that an adobe structure was built at Guevavi by March 1699. After this date Kino and Manje still proceed on to the next settlement before stopping for the evening (Crockett 1918:133; Karns 1954:126; Burrus 1971:247, 413)—that is, after riding fifteen miles to Guevavi they then proceeded another twenty or so miles (see Burrus 1971:247). Also the transliterated (del Castillo 1926:271) and microfilm copies of handwritten versions of Manje's (1721:155–56) journal entry for this specific visit are consistent with Crockett's and Karns' translations indicating the priests simply stopped to rest and then moved on, with no mention of an adobe structure. (Seymour 2009c:289–290)

Another possibility is that this adobe was already present in the village but was not specifically built for the missionary. Manje referenced this as an adobe-and-earth house, as would be appropriate for a council house or community structure where the Sobaipuri residents also housed visitors (see Seymour 2014).

New data suggest that perhaps this Locus A structure (thought to be the "neat little house and church") is in fact this 1699 structure used by the community and not specifically built for the missionary. In this scenario, Kino's "neat little house and church" is instead represented in the core part of the buildings on the rise at AZ EE:9:1 (ASM) that is referenced as the Franciscan church. A date on an adobe from the lower wall provided a confidence interval of 1710±30 (UW3250). This original church from 1701 may have been later incorporated into the main church complex. So, while both dates overlap the period in question during which Kino would have had this church built, the second date on the main church on AZ EE:9:1 (ASM) is more centrally and narrowly focused on the 1701 construction date. The date originally presented as the "neat little house and church" has an earlier center point and thereby can perhaps be better explained as the earlier structure mentioned vaguely by Kino, but, more directly and explicitly, by Manje, as the adobe-and-earth house, which was probably already present and being used before Kino arrived.

This scenario does not explain why the church completed in 1751 had to be built anew if the walls of the original church were still standing (but see further interpretations in the passages that follow). Once again, this uncertainty may also address the issue of whether Kino's statement references both a

1699, A non-Christian adobe (council house)?
(possibly west side of river)

1701, Kino's "Neat Little House and Church"

1722, Fathers Campos and Duran say mass
under a ramada

1731, Anza supervised the building of a structure
(for Father Grazhoffer, 1732)

1751, Last Jesuit church built

17xx?, Last Guevavi church mission complex built

1800+, Ranch- (land grant) and mining-related structures built

FIGURE 11.1. *Churches and chapels/ramadas constructed at Guevavi through time. Figure prepared by Deni Seymour.*

house and a church: "We finished a house and a church, small but neat, and we laid the foundations for a church and a large house" (Bolton 1948:I:303). Were these adobes robbed from the original church? At a minimum, this question requires further consideration. At best, now all buildings referenced though time, from the beginning of the Jesuit period, including the two mentioned by Kino himself, have seemingly been identified. Thus, like many reconstructions regarding this period and the Sobaipuri occupation, both at remote villages and those centered at missions, new data have the potential to significantly revise notions about the occupancy of a site but only as long as we are willing to question all of our assumptions and conclusions.

An alternative conclusion, given the number of churches apparently constructed at Guevavi (figures 11.1 and 11.2) and the dates obtained from those visible on the surface is that the zoguete con ripio foundation in Locus A of AZ EE:9:132 (ASM) is Kino's "neat little" house, whereas the adobe-and-mortar construction at AZ EE:9:1 (ASM) is the contemporaneous church, or vice versa. This alternative interpretation of Kino's reference to his "neat

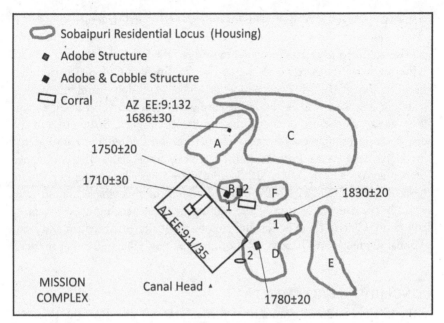

FIGURE 11.2. *Plan of the Sobaipuri village loci at Guevavi showing locus boundaries and where some of the chronometric samples were extracted. Figure prepared by Deni Seymour.*

little house and church" may mean he was referencing two structures and these dates may have isolated these two structures and, in turn, that we have yet to find the 1699 adobe-and-earth house noted by Manje, perhaps located elsewhere (even on the other side of the river, as maps may indicate). Or simply it is not as clearly visible or distinguishable from Sobaipuri house rocks on the surface.

It is more likely, however, that the adobe-and-mortar construction at AZ EE:9:1 (ASM) is the small house built under the supervision of Captain Juan Bautista de Anza in 1731 (Kessell 1970:43). This was a house, apparently, not a church, for as Kessell (1970:51) noted: "Nearby the natives built for him a sturdy, well-roofed ramada beneath which he had the altar set in place." The ramada was prepared for Father Juan Bautista Grazhoffer, who did not arrive until 1732. The advantage of this interpretation is that each structure and its date correspond to one of the historically documented construction events. If this is not the Anza structure, then Anza's building has yet to be identified and dated, which means it is not obvious on the surface or was ultimately incorporated into the convent (e.g., AZ EE:9:1 [ASM]).

The AD 1750±20 (UW3003) date for mortar-and-stone structure in Locus B relates well with the documentary evidence of a church being completed in 1751 (Kessell 1970:100). Its construction bridged the O'odham Revolt.

The final two dates relate to the end of the Spanish Colonial period and the initiation of the Mexican period 1821–1848. An adobe from the wall of Structure 1 in Locus D is the latest dating, AD 1830±20 (UW3160), and so likely postdates the use of the site as a mission complex. Structure 2 in the same locus is a much less formalized structure, and unfired and consolidated dirt clods were dated from beneath flat-lying stone slabs. The confidence interval is AD 1780±20 (UW3161). Both of these intervals seemingly postdate the traditionally held view of the abandonment of this village and so were probably constructed as part of the mining headquarters, ranch, estancia, or land grant. Clearly there is nothing simple about the construction and occupational sequences at Guevavi, or at other Sobaipuri villages for that matter.

CONCLUDING STATEMENT

The inferences drawn throughout this volume are based on the evidence currently available. As new data come to light, these interpretations may (will undoubtedly) change. After all, the point of this book and others I have written is that there is so much more to be reconceived and learned about the Sobaipuri and their neighbors, as well as the presidio and mission sites. I can only hope that you and those in the future will be gentle readers, more gentile than perhaps I have been. So many factors skew the records and prohibit us from seeing clearly back in time. First, knowledge has been lost, shredded, warped, hidden, overwritten, and even forbidden. Then, some parts of it are auspiciously uncovered, discovered, reconstructed, and shared again in the context of the present. It is critical to remember that knowledge is cumulative, and though it is not situational—I do believe facts and data do exist independent of ourselves—they are influenced by what we can see and how we see based on what we already hold in our repertoire of knowledge, assumptions, and theories while at the same time we assess what is important to know and how to present it. This assessment is nowhere truer than for historical facts. Two facts can always be connected, but when another data point is added, impressions may change entirely. The more data points connected, the more fully and accurately the historical past can be reconstructed. Given that Sobaipuri studies, protohistoric studies, and historic mission and presidio studies are so new with comparatively little uncovered, it is expected that entirely new and wonderful discoveries will become known. I only hope that

I continue to be part of the discovery process, either climbing the mountains and shoving through catclaw, laying out a few more words on paper, or being read and cited by future generations who care about the past as an insight into ourselves and as a way of contributing to the well-being of descendant communities and society at large.

NOTE

1. For a discussion of these changes and also the transfer of the name to the modern Santa Cruz River, see Seymour (2012c).

Aguirrey, Manuel. Letter to Francisco Zevallos, Decem-
ber 30, 1763. Archivo Histórico de Hacienda, Legajo 17,
Las Provincias de Pimería y Sonora, Bancroft Library,
Berkeley. Microfilm copy, Henry Dobyns Collection,
University of Arizona, Special Collections, Tucson.

Alegre, Francisco Javier. 1960. *Historia de la Provincia
de la Compañía de Jesús de Nueva España.* Vol. 4, edited
by Ernest J. Burrus, SJ, and Félix Zubillaga, SJ. New ed.
Jesuit Historical Institute, Rome.

Anza, Juan Bautista de, to Governor Juan de Pineda, Tubac,
August 2, 1769. Biblioteca National, Archivo Franciscano,
Provincias Internas, Sinaloa y Sonora, Carpeta 253/931,
México, DF.

Anza, Juan Bautista de. Carta al Sr. Coronél D. Juan
de Piñeda. Presidio de Tubac. May 19, 1770. *Documentos
para la História de México.* Ser. 4. Tom. 2.

Bailiff, I. K. 2007. Methodological Developments in the
Luminescence Dating of Brick from English Late-
Medieval and Post-Medieval Buildings. *Archaeometry* 49
(4): 827–851.

Bancroft, H. H. 1886. *History of the North Mexican States
and Texas, Vol. I, 1531–1800.* The Works of Hubert Howe
Bancroft. Vol. XV. History Company, San Francisco. Also
available as a Google Book.

Bancroft, H. H. 1889. *History of Arizona and New Mexico,
1530–1888. The Works of Hubert Howe Bancroft.* Vol. XVII.
History Company, San Francisco. Also available as a
Google Book.

https://doi.org/10.5876/9781646422975.c012

Barnes, Will C. [1935] 1982. *Arizona Place Names*. University of Arizona Press, Tucson.

Beltrami, Lia Giovanazzi. 2018. *Viva Kino*. Film. Aurora Vision.

Bolton, Herbert E. 1930a. *Font's Complete Diary of the Second Anza Expedition*. Anza's California Expeditions, vol. 4, edited by Herbert E. Bolton. University of California Press, Berkeley.

Bolton, Herbert E. 1930b. *Anza's California Expeditions*. Vol. 5, *Correspondence*. University of California Press, Berkeley.

Bolton, Herbert E. [1932] 1986. *The Padre on Horseback: A Sketch of Eusebio Francisco Kino*. S.J. Loyola University Press, Chicago.

Bolton, Herbert E. [1936] 1960. *Rim of Christendom: A Biography of Eusebio Francisco Kino Pacific Coast Pioneer*. Russell and Russell, New York.

Bolton, Herbert E. 1948. *Kino's Historical Memoir of Pimería Alta*. 2 vols. University of California Press, Berkeley.

Bowden, J. J. San José de Sonoita Grant. 2004–2018. New Mexico Office of the State Historian. https://newmexicohistory.org/2015/07/10/san-jose-de-sonoita-grant/.

Brew, Susan A., and Bruce B. Huckell. 1987. A Protohistoric Piman Burial and a Consideration of Piman Burial Practices. *Kiva* 52 (3): 163–191.

Bright, William. 2013. *Native American Placenames of the Southwest*. University of Oklahoma Press, Norman.

Brinckerhoff, Sidney B. 1967. The Last Years of Spanish Arizona 1786–1821. *Arizona and the West* 9 (1): 5–20.

Bucareli y Ursúa, Viceroy Antonio María de. 1776. Bucareli's Report. Antonio Maria Bucareli y Ursua to Jose de Galvez, September 24, 1776, AGI, Guad 515, Reel 3; Bancroft Library microfilm, Berkeley.

Burrus, Ernest J. 1965. *Kino and the Cartography of Northwestern New Spain*. Arizona Pioneers' Historical Society, Tucson.

Burrus, Ernest J. 1971. *Kino and Manje: Explorers of Sonora and Arizona*. Sources and Studies for the History of the Americas, edited by J. Burrus, vol. 10. Jesuit Historical Institute, Rome and St. Louis, MO.

Carpenter Slavens, John, and Guadalupe Sánchez. 2016. Ópatas, pimas y jesuitas: Una historia cultural preliminar de Sahuaripa y la Sierra Central de Sonora. Unpublished manuscript provided by the authors.

Carrasco, Diego. 1698. Diary of Travels along the Rio Grande [Gila River] to the Sea of California under Orders of Señor General Don Domingo Jironza Petris de Cruzat . . . [Diario fho. por el Capitan Diego Carrazco Thente. de acalde mr. y Cappn. a guerra de todos los pueblos y rancherías de la nación Pima y sus distritos y juron. por su Magd. que in Virtud de orden que va . . . del Gral. Don Domingo

Jironza Petris de Cruzat . . .], Archivo General de Indias, Seville, 67-3-28, Guadalajara 134.

Castillo Betancourt, Francisco del. 1686. Confession of Canito, July 19. "Criminal contra y Yndio llamado Canuto por haber sido traidor á la Real Corona, 1686." Archivo Histórico del Hidalgo de Parral, Chihuahua, México. Microfilm copy in the University of Arizona Main Library, film 0318, reel 1686B, fr. 758–803, Tucson.

Castillo Betancourt, Francisco del Castillo. 1691. Deposition. Provincias Internas. Tomo 30. Doc No 8.

Collier, John. 1936. Telegram from Washington, DC, January 23, to Jose X. Pablo. In NAPSR, RG 75, SIA, Folder "069.0 G&S Tribal Constitution and Indian Organization, 1935–1939." Box 58.

Cook, Edward R. 2000. *Southwestern USA Drought Index Reconstruction: International Tree-Ring Data Bank.* IGBP PAGES/World Data Center—A for Paleoclimatology Data Contribution Series #2000-053. NOAA/NGDC Paleoclimatology Program, Boulder, Colorado.

Coues, Elliot. 1900. *On the Trail of a Spanish Pioneer: The Diary and Itinerary of Francisco Garces (Missionary Priest) in His Travels through Sonora, Arizona, and California, 1775–1776.* Francis P. Harper, New York.

Crockett, Grace Lilian. 1918. Manje's Luz de Tierra Incógnita: A Translation of the Original Manuscript Together with an Historical Introduction. MA thesis. University of California, Berkeley.

Darling, J. Andrew, John C. Ravesloot, and Michael R. Waters. 2004. Village Drift and Riverine Settlement: Modeling Akimel O'odham Land Use. *American Anthropologist* 106:282–95.

Decorme, Gerard, S.J. 1941. *La obra de los Jesuitas mexicanos durante la época colonial (1572–1767).* Book 2, *Las misiones.* Antigua Librería Robredo de José Porrúa e Hijos, México, DF. https://ia902304.us.archive.org/13/items/laobradelosjesuio2deco/laobradelosjesuio2deco.pdf.

Di Peso, Charles C. 1953. *The Sobaipuri Indians of the Upper San Pedro River Valley, Southwestern Arizona.* Amerind Foundation Publication No. 6, Dragoon, AZ.

Di Peso, Charles C. 1956. *The Upper Pima of San Cayetano del Tumacacori: An Archaeohistorical Reconstruction of the Ootam of Pimeria Alta.* Amerind Foundation. Dragoon, Arizona.

Di Peso, Charles C., Daniel S. Matson, and Adamo Gilg. 1965. The Seri Indians in 1692 as Described by Adamo Gilg, S. J. *Arizona and the West* 7 (1): 33–56.

Dobyns, Henry F. 1959. *Tubac through Four Centuries: A Historical Resume and Analysis.* Prepared for the Arizona State Parks Board March 15; reformatted by Tubac

Presidio State Historical Park and revised August 1995. http://parentseyes.arizona .edu/tubac/index.html.

Dobyns, Henry F. 1976. *Spanish Colonial Tucson: A Demographic Study*. University of Arizona Press, Tucson.

Documents. 1833–1901. Documents Relating to San Juan de la Boquillas y Nogales Land Grant (AZ 232). Special Collections, University of Arizona Libraries, Tuscon.

Doyel, David E. 1977. *Excavations in the Middle Santa Cruz River Valley, Southeastern Arizona*. Contributions to Highway Salvage Archaeology in Arizona, No. 44. Arizona State Museum, University of Arizona, Tucson.

Edwards, John, compiler, general editor. 2004. Conquistadors: The Struggle for Colonial Power in Latin America, 1492–1825. Manuscript. Primary Source Microfilm; British Library Edition. Primary Source Microfilm, Thomson, Gale, TM, Woodbridge, CT; London.

Ezell, Paul H. 1955. De Anza Letter Reveals Various Indian Problems. *Tucson Arizona Daily Star*, February 24, 114:55.

Ezell, Paul H. 1961. The Hispanic Acculturation of the Gila River Pimas. *American Anthropologist* 63 (5): pt. 2; also *American Anthropological Association Memoir* 90. Mensa, WI.

Fink, T. Michael. 1998. John Spring's Account of "Malarial Fever" at Camp Wallen, A.T., 1866–1869. *Journal of Arizona History* 39 (1): 67–84.

Flint, Richard, and Shirley Cushing Flint. 2005. *Documents of the Coronado Expedition, 1539–1541: They Were Not Familiar with His Majesty nor Did They Wish to Be His Subjects*. Southern Methodist University Press, Dallas.

Fontana, Bernard L. 1993. An Administrative and Political History of the San Xavier District of the Tohono O'odham Nation. Prepared for the San Xavier District, Tohono O'odham Nation.

Forbes, Jack D. 1960. *Apache, Navaho, and Spaniard*. University of Oklahoma Press, Norman.

Forest Service. 2000. *Who Named the Mountains? Coronado National Forest*. USDA Forest Service, Southwest Region. https://www.ltrr.arizona.edu/~sheppard/sop /WhoNamedTheMountains.pdf.

Franklin, H. H. 1980. *Excavations at Second Canyon Ruin, San Pedro Valley, Arizona*. Arizona State Museum Contribution to Highway Salvage Archaeology in Arizona, No. 60, Tucson.

Gerald, Rex E. 1968. Spanish Presidios of the Late Eighteenth Century in Northern New Spain. *Museum of New Mexico Research Records*, Number 7. Museum of New Mexico Press, Santa Fe.

Geronimo, Ron. 2012. Comments in Telling the O'Odham Side of History in the Pimería Alta. Video. YouTube, November 16. https://www.youtube.com/watch?v=nCrBoP5XouI&feature=emb_share&fbclid=IwAR0aR9WLyHV8JjU8VTYmde5ujE2I7NQ1Y9KVCcBoU_3zQdcu_YVV962HAJQ.

González R., Luis. 1977. *Etnología y misión en la Pimeria Alta, 1715–1740: Informes y relaciones misioneras de Luis Xavier Velarde*, edited by Giuseppe María Genovese, Daniel Januske, José Agustín de Campos, and Cristóbal de Cañas. Universidad Nacional Autónoma de México, México, DF.

Gray, A. B. 1856. Survey of a Route for the Southern Pacific R.R., on the 32nd Parallel. Wrightson and Co.'s ("Railroad Record,") Print, Cincinnati.

Hackenberg, Robert A. 1964. Changing Diet of Arizona Indians. *Journal of American Indian Education* 3 (3): 27–32.

Hackenberg, Robert A. 1974a. *Aboriginal Land Use and Occupancy of the Pima-Maricopa Indians*. In *Pima-Maricopa Indians*. Vol. 1, edited by David A. Horr, 25–350. Garland Publishing, New York.

Hackenberg, Robert A. 1974b. *Aboriginal Land Use and Occupancy of the Papago Indians*. In *Papago Indians*. Vol. 1, edited by David A. Horr, 23–308. Garland Publishing, New York.

Hackenberg, Robert A. 1983a. Pima and Papago Ecological Adaptations. In *Southwest, Handbook of North American Indians*. Vol. 10, edited by Alfonso Ortiz, 161–177. Smithsonian Institution, Washington, DC.

Hall, Theodore B. 1936. Letter from Sells Agency, Sells, AZ, March 24, to William Zimmerman Jr., Washington, DC. In NAPSR, RG 75, SIA, Folder "069.0 G&S Tribal Constitution and Indian Organization, 1935–1939." Box 58.

Hammond, George P. 1929. Pimería Alta after Kino's Time. *New Mexico Historical Review* 4 (3): 220–238.

Hammond, George P. 1931. The Zúñiga Journal: Tucson to Santa Fe, the Opening of a Spanish Trade Route 1788–1795. *New Mexico Historical Review* 6 (1): 40–65.

Harlan, Mark E. 2009. Translation of a Document Relating the Events of the 1776 Las Mesitas Battle between Capitan of the Santa Cruz de Terrenate Presidio, Don Francisco Tovar, and the Apache by Antonio María Bucareli y Ursua. Manuscript on file with the author, Albuquerque.

Harlan, Mark E. 2017. Protohistoric Arrowhead Variability in the Greater Southwest. Chapter 9 in *Fierce and Indomitable: The Protohistoric Non-Pueblo World*, edited by Deni J. Seymour, 115–137. University of Utah Press, Salt Lake City.

Harlan, Mark E., and Deni J. Seymour. 2017. Sobaipuri-O'odham and Mobile Group Relevance to Late Prehistoric Social Networks in the San Pedro Valley. In *Fierce and Indomitable: The Protohistoric Non-Pueblo World*. University of Utah Press, Salt Lake City.

Hastings, James Rodney. 1961. People of Reason and Others: The Colonization of Sonora to 1767. *Arizona and the West* 3 (4): 321–340.

Haury, Emil, 1976. *The Hohokam: Desert Farmers and Craftsmen, Excavations at Snaketown, 1964–1965*. University of Arizona Press, Tucson.

Henderson, Richard N. 1957. Field Notes of Mescalero-Chiricahua Land Claims Interviews with various Chiricahua Tribal Members. Papers in possession of Deni Seymour.

Hoover, J. W. 1935. Generic Descent of the Papago Villages. *American Anthropologist* 37 (2): 257–264.

Huckell, Bruce B. 1984. Sobaipuri Sites in the Rosemont Area. In *Miscellaneous Archaeological Studies in the Anamax-Rosemont Land Exchange Area*, edited by M. D. Tagg, R. G. Ervin, and B. B. Huckell, 107–130. Arizona State Museum Archaeological Series 147 (4). Tucson.

Ives, Ronald L. 1973. Father Kino's 1697 *Entrada* to the Casa Grande Ruin in Arizona: A Reconstruction. *Arizona and the West* 15 (4): 345–370.

Ives, Ronald L., and Henry Ruhen. 1955. Mission San Marcelo del Sonoydag. *Records of the American Catholic Historical Society of Philadelphia* 66 (4): 201–221.

Joseph, Alice, Rosamond B. Spicer, and Jane Chesky. 1949. *The Desert People: A Study of the Papago Indians*. University of Chicago Press, Chicago.

Karns, Harry J. 1954. *Luz de tierra incognita*. Arizona Silhouettes, Tucson.

Kessell, John L. 1965. Father Eixarch and the Visitation at Tumacácori, May 12, 1775. *Kiva* 30 (3): 77–81.

Kessell, John L. 1966. "The Puzzling Presidio San Phelipe de Guevavi, Alias Terrenate." *New Mexico Historical Review* 41 (1): 21–46.

Kessell, John L. 1970. *Mission of Sorrow: Jesuit Guevavi and the Pimas, 1691–1767*. University of Arizona Press, Tucson.

Kessell, John L. 1976. *Friars, Soldiers, and Reformers: Hispanic Arizona and the Sonora Mission Frontier 1767–1856*. University of Arizona Press, Tucson.

Kessell, John L., and Fray Bartholomé Ximeno. 1964. San José de Tumacácori—1773: A Franciscan Reports from Arizona. *Arizona and the West* 6 (4): 303–312.

Kinnaird, Lawrence. 1958. *The Frontiers of New Spain: Nicolás de LaFora's Description, 1766–1768*. Quivira Society, Berkeley.

Kino, Eusebio Francisco. 1698a. *Favores celestiales de Jesús y de María Santísima y del gloriosísimo apóstol de las Indias, San Francisco Xavier, experimentados en las nuevas conquistas y nuevas conversiones del nuevo reino de la Nueva Navarra de esta América septentrional incógnita y paso por tierra a la California, en treinta y cinco grados de*

*altura, con su nuevo mapa cosmográfico de estas nuevas y dilatadas tierras, que, hasta
ahora habían sido incógnitas, dedicados a la Real Majestad de Felipe V, muy católico
rey y gran monarca de las Españas y de las Indias.* Microfilm of original, Office of
Ethnohistorical Research, Arizona State Museum, Tucson. [This document is
believed to have been written somewhere between 1698 and 1710. The author has
cited 1698a throughout the text for ease of reference.]

Kino, Eusebio Francisco. 1698b. Breve Relación, Archivo General de la Nación
(AGN), Background: History, Vol. 16, Record, 17, Fol. 301–303v. Handwritten copy
dating to 1792, Archivo General de la Nación. México, DF.

Kino, Eusebio Francisco. 1698c. *Relación Diaria.* Relasion Diaria de la entrada al
nortuesta que fue de Yda y Buelta mas de 300 leguas desde 21 de setiembre hasta
18 de Otubre de 1698. Descubrimiento del desemboque del rio grande hala Mar
de la California y del Puerto de Sa. Clara Reduction de mas de 4000 almas de las
Costas Bautismos de mas de 400 Parbulos 1698. Con Enseñanzas y Experienzias.
Historia, Vol. 393, 1680–1792, Archivo General de la Nación, México, DF.

Kino, Eusebio Francisco. 1698d. *Del Estado Gracias al Señor Pasifico y Quieto.* [Thanks
to the Lord for the peaceful and quiet state of this extensive Pimería and of the
Province of Sonora.] Microfilm of original. Office of Ethnohistorical Research,
Arizona State Museum, Tucson.

Langellier, J. P., and D. B. Rosen. 1996. *El Presidio de San Francisco: A History under
Spain and Mexico, 1776–1846.* Arthur H. Clark, Spokane, WA.

Last of Indian Braves Tell Story Out of Rich Long Life. 1931. *Silver Belt,* 4-1.

Last of Sobaipuri Tribe Passes with 'Red Evening'; Words Left to White Man:
Toibio [*sic*] Aragon, 85, Laid to Rest last Night at San Xavier Mission Which His
Forefathers Built—Service Is Simple. 1930. *Tucson Citizen,* March 14.

Loendorf, Chris, Craig Fertelmes, David H. Dejong, M. Kyle Woodson, and
Barnaby V. Lewis. 2019. Blackwater Village at the Turn of the Twentieth Century:
Akimel O'Odham Perseverance and Resiliency. *Kiva* 85 (1): 25–48.

Loendorf, Chris, and Glen E. Rice. 2004. *Projectile Point Typology Gila River Indian
Community, Arizona.* Gila River Indian Community Anthropological Research
Papers No. 2, Sacaton, AZ.

Manje, Juan Mateo. 1720. Luz de Tierra Incógnita en la América Septentrional y
diario de las exploraciones en Sonora. Microfilm of original, Bancroft Library,
Berkeley, CA.

Masse, W. B. 1980. The Peppersauce Wash Project. Highway salvage manuscript,
edited by Gayle Hartmann. Arizona State Museum Archives, Tucson.

Masse, W. B. 1981. A Reappraisal of the Protohistoric Sobaipuri Indians of Southeastern Arizona. In *The Protohistoric Period in the North American Southwest,* AD

1450–1700, edited by David R. Wilcox and W. Bruce Masse, 28–56. Arizona State University Anthropological Research Papers No. 24, Tempe.

Matson, Daniel S., and Bernard L. Fontana. 1977. *Friar Bringas Reports to the King: Methods of Indoctrination on the Frontier of New Spain, 1796–97*. University of Arizona Press, Tucson.

Matson, Daniel S., and Bernard L. Fontana. 1996. *Before Rebellion: Letters and Reports of Jacobo Sedelmayr, S.J.* Arizona Historical Society, Tucson.

McCarty, Kieran 1997. *A Frontier Documentary, Sonora and Tucson, 1821–1848*. University of Arizona Press, Tucson.

McGuire, Randall H., and Elisa Villalpando C. 1993. *An Archaeological Survey of the Altar Valley, Sonora, Mexico*. Arizona State Museum Series 184. Arizona State Museum, Tucson.

McQuigg, Henry J. 1913. Letter from San Xavier Indian Agency, Arizona, Tucson, AZ, January 22, to the commissioner of Indian Affairs. In NAPSR, RG 75, SIA, Folder "Commissioner of Indian Affairs, July–December 1914," Box 6.

McQuigg, Henry J. 1914. Letter from San Xavier School, Arizona, Tucson, Arizona, September 1, to the commissioner of Indian Affairs. In NAPSR, RG 75, SIA, Folder "Commissioner of Indian Affairs, July–December 1914," Box 6.

Medina, Roque de. 1779. Presidio de Santa Cruz de Terrenate: Roque de Medina, Presidiales de la Provincia de Sonora. Cavalleria. Extracto de la Revista de Inspección. February 7–March 3. Inspection report. Archivo General de Indias, Seville, Spain; GUAD 272.

Mission 2000 Database. National Park Service database. https://www.nps.gov/tuma/learn/historyculture/mission-2000.htm.

Moorhead, Max L. 1975. *The Presidio: Bastion of the Spanish Borderlands*. University of Oklahoma Press, Norman.

National Park Service. 2007. Los Santos Ángeles de Guevavi. http://www.nps.gov/tuma/historyculture/guevavi.htm.

Navarro García, Luis. 1964. *Don José Gálvez y la Comandancia General de las Provincias Internas del Norte de Nueva España*. Prólogo de José Antonio Calderón Quijano. Publicaciones Universidad de Sevilla. Escuela de Estudios Hispanoamericanos, 148. Consejo Superior de Investigaciones Científicas, Seville, Spain.

Nentvig, Juan. 1764. Descripción geográfica, natural y curiosa de la provincial de Sonora, año 1764. Archivo General de la Nación (AGN). México, DF.

Nentvig, Juan. 1863. *Rudo Ensayo*. Buckingham Smith Version. St. Augustine, FL.

Oblasser, Bonaventure. 1931. Carnacion Tells Her Tale. *Arizona Historical Review* 3 (4): 97–98.

O'Conor, Hugo, 1952. *Informe de Hugo de O'Conor Sobre de las Provincias Internas de Norte, 1771–1776. Prologo por Enrique González Flores y Anotaciones de Francisco R, Almada.* Editorial Cultura, T.G., S.A. México, DF.

O'Conor, Hugo, ed. and trans. Donald C. Cutter. 1994. *The Defenses of Northern New Spain: Hugo O'Conor's Report to Teodore de Croix, July 22, 1777.* Southern Methodist University Press, Dallas.

Officer, James E. 1987. *Hispanic Arizona, 1536–1856.* University of Arizona Press, Tucson.

Ortiz, Alfonso, ed. 1979. *Handbook of North American Indians.* Vol. 9, Southwest. Gen. ed. William C. Sturtevant, Smithsonian Institution, Washington, DC.

Pacheco Zevallos, Francisco. 1686. Confession of Canito, September 14. "Criminal contra y Yndio llamado Canuto por haber sido traidor á la Real Corona, 1686." Archivo Histórico del Hidalgo de Parral, Chihuahua, México. Microfilm copy in the University of Arizona Main Library, film 0318, reel 1686B, fr. 758–803, Tucson.

Phillips, David A. 2008. The End of Casas Grandes. Paper presented to the symposium the Legacy of Charles C. Di Peso: Fifty Years after the Joint Casas Grandes Project, at the 73rd annual meeting of the Society for American Archaeology, March 27, Vancouver, BC. https://www.unm.edu/~dap/End-of-Casas-Grandes.pdf.

Pickens, Buford L. 1993. *The Missions of Northern Sonora: A 1935 Field Documentation.* University of Arizona Press, Tucson.

Polzer, Charles W., and Ernest J. Burrus. 1971. *Kino's Biography of Francisco Javier Saeta, S.J.* Sources and Studies for the History of the Americas, vol. 9, edited by Charles W. Polzer and Ernest J. Burrs. Jesuit Historical Institute, Rome and St. Louis, MO.

Pradeau, Alberto Francisco, and Robert R. Rasmussen. 1980. *Rudo Ensayo: A Description of Sonora and Arizona in 1764, by Juan Nentvig, S.J.* University of Arizona Press, Tucson.

Radding, Cynthia. 1998. *Contested Ground: Comparative Frontiers on the Northern and Southern Edges of the Spanish Empire,* edited by Donna J. Guy and Thomas E. Sheridan, 52–66. University of Arizona Press, Tucson.

Ramírez de Salazar, Francisco. 1692a. Diary of military campaign, March 5–27, Document 1. Autos de guerra contra los indios rebeldes. Archivo Histórico del Municipio de Hidalgo del Parral, Mf. rl. 1692a fr. 0166-0187. University of Arizona, Tucson.

Ramírez de Salazar, Francisco. 1692b. Diary of military campaign, March 5–27, Document 2. Autos de guerra contra los indios rebeldes. Archivo Histórico del Municipio de Hidalgo del Parral, Mf. rl. 1692a fr. 0166-0187. University of Arizona, Tucson.

Ramírez de Salazar, Francisco. 1692c. Diary of military campaign, March 5–27, Document 3. Autos de guerra contra los indios rebeldes. Archivo Histórico del Municipio de Hidalgo del Parral, Mf. rl. 1692a fr. 0166-0187. University of Arizona, Tucson.

Ramírez de Salazar, Francisco. 1692d. Diary of military campaign, March 5–27, Document 4. Autos de guerra contra los indios rebeldes. Archivo Histórico del Municipio de Hidalgo del Parral, Mf. rl. 1692a fr. 0166-0187. University of Arizona, Tucson.

Ravesloot, J. C., and S. M. Whittlesey. 1987. Inferring the Protohistoric Period in Southern Arizona. Chapter 7 in *The Archaeology of the San Xavier Bridge Site (AZ BB:13:14) Tucson Basin, Southern Arizona.* Archaeological Series 171, 81–98. Cultural Resource Management Division, Arizona State Museum, University of Arizona. Prepared for the Arizona Department of Transportation, Contract 84-37; Project ER-19-1(97), Tucson.

Reyes, Antonio de los. 1772. Del Estado Actual de las Missiones que en la Gubernacion de Sonora Administian los Padres del Colegio de Propaganda Fide de la Santa Cruz de Queretaro. The State of Sonora Provinces by the MRP Fr. Antonio Reyes, on April 20, 1772, Santa Cruz de Queretaro, letter K, leg. 14, no. 18.

Roberts, Heidi, and Richard V.N. Ahlstrom. 1997. Malaria, Microbes, and Mechanisms of Change. *Kiva* 63 (2): 117–135.

Rocha y Figueroa, Gerónimo de la. 1780a. Diario de los reconocimientos hechos en la frontera de la provincia de Sonora en de la superior orden del 19 de abril del presente año del señor comandante general de las provincias internas de Nueva España por el teniente de infantería e ingeniero extraordinario de los reales ejércitos Don Gerónimo de la Rocha y Figueroa. [Diary of the reconnaissance made in the frontier of the Sonoran province under the superior order of April 19 of these years by orders of the general commander of the Provincias Internas of New Spain . . . by the engineer of the royal armies Gerónimo de la Rocha y Figueroa.] Unpublished manuscript, Houghton Library, Harvard University, Cambridge, MA.

Rocha y Figueroa, Gerónimo de la. 1780b. *Mapa de la frontera de Sonora para el establecimiento de la linea de presidios.* Woodbridge, CT: 2003. Microfilm, reel 55 of 105. MS. No. Add. 17661 A. Original in British Library, London.

Rocha y Figueroa, Gerónimo de la. 1780c. Diario y derrota de los reconocimientos ejecutados en la Frontera de la Provincia de Sonora para el Establecimiento del Presidio de Fronteras y translación del de Santa Cruz . . . [Diary and route of the reconnaissances carried out on the border of the province of Sonora for the establishment of Fronteras Presidio and the movement of the one of Santa

Cruz . . .] Manuscript obtained from Houghton Library, Harvard University, MS Sparks 98, Papeles varios de América vol. 7, no. 3.

Rocha y Figueroa, Gerónimo de. 1784. *Mapa del terreno que ha de vatir la Expedición que deve executarse contra los Apaches Gileños, March 18, 1784*. AGI location: Gobierno, Audiencia de Guadalajara, 103-5-4. Huntington Library filing location: Karpinski Collection, Box 15, #552.

Russell, Frank. [1908] 1975. *The Pima Indians*. University of Arizona Press, Tucson.

Sauer, Carl O. 1934. *The Distribution of Aboriginal Tribes and Languages in Northwestern Mexico*. University of California Press, Berkeley.

Seymour, Deni J. 1987. *Sobaipuri Settlement along the Upper San Pedro River Valley, Arizona*. Paper presented at the 53rd Annual Meeting of the Society for American Archaeology, Phoenix.

Seymour, Deni J. 1989. The Dynamics of Sobaipuri Settlement in the Eastern Pimería Alta. *Journal of the Southwest* 31 (2): 205–222.

Seymour, Deni J. 1990. Sobaipuri-Pima Settlement along the Upper San Pedro River: A Thematic Survey. Report submitted to the Bureau of Land Management.

Seymour, Deni J. 1991. A Cultural Resources Inventory of the Proposed Guevavi Ranch Preserve, Santa Cruz County, Arizona. SWCA, Inc. Environmental Consultants, Tucson.

Seymour, Deni J. 1992. Archaeology of the Plain and Subtle. Poster presented at the Third Southwest Symposium, Tucson, Arizona. January 1992.

Seymour, Deni J. 1993a. Piman Settlement Survey in the Middle Santa Cruz River Valley, Santa Cruz County, Arizona. Prepared in fulfillment of contractual requirements for a research grant awarded by Arizona State Parks.

Seymour, Deni J. 1993b. In Search of the Sobaipuri Pima: Archaeology of the Plain and Subtle. *Archaeology Southwest Newsletter* 10 (4): 1–4.

Seymour, Deni J. 1993c. *A Cultural Resources Inventory of the Proposed Guevavi Ranch Preserve, Santa Cruz County, Arizona*. SWCA Archaeological Report No. 91-43. Tucson.

Seymour, Deni J. 1995. Behavioral Approach to the Recognition of Inconspicuous Apachean Sites. Paper presented at the 68th Annual Pecos Conference, Gila Wilderness, New Mexico. (See Appendix A, "Conquest and Concealment.")

Seymour, Deni J. 1997. Finding History in the Archaeological Record: The Upper Piman Settlement of Guevavi. *Kiva* 62 (3): 245–260.

Seymour, Deni J. 2002. Conquest and Concealment: After the El Paso Phase on Fort Bliss. Conservation Division, Directorate of Environment, Fort Bliss. Lone Mountain Report 525/528.

Seymour, Deni J. 2003. Sobaipuri-Pima Occupation in the Upper San Pedro Valley: San Pablo de Quiburi. *New Mexico Historical Review* 78 (2): 147–166.

Seymour, Deni J. 2004. A Ranchería in the Gran Apachería: Evidence of Intercultural Interaction at the Cerro Rojo Site. *Plains Anthropologist* 49 (190): 153–192.

Seymour, Deni J. 2007a. Delicate Diplomacy on a Restless Frontier: Seventeenth-Century Sobaípuri Social and Economic Relations in Northwestern New Spain, Part I. *New Mexico Historical Review* 82 (4): 469–499.

Seymour, Deni J. 2007b. A Syndetic Approach to Identification of the Historic Mission Site of San Cayetano del Tumacácori. *International Journal of Historical Archaeology* 11 (3): 269–296.

Seymour, Deni J. 2007c. An Archaeological Perspective on the Hohokam-Pima Continuum. *Old Pueblo Archaeology Bulletin* No. 51 (December): 1–7.

Seymour, Deni J. 2008a. Despoblado or Athapaskan Heartland: A Methodological Perspective on Ancestral Apache Landscape Use in the Safford Area. Chapter 5 in *Crossroads of the Southwest: Culture, Ethnicity, and Migration in Arizona's Safford Basin*, edited by David E. Purcell, 121–162. Cambridge Scholars Press, Cambridge, MA.

Seymour, Deni J. 2008b. Delicate Diplomacy on a Restless Frontier: Seventeenth-Century Sobaípuri Social and Economic Relations in Northwestern New Spain. Part II. *New Mexico Historical Review* 83 (2): 171–199.

Seymour, Deni J. 2009a. The Canutillo Complex: Evidence of Protohistoric Mobile Occupants in the Southern Southwest. *Kiva* 74 (4): 421–446.

Seymour, Deni J. 2009b. Evaluating Eyewitness Accounts of Native Peoples along the Coronado Trail from the International Border to Cibola. *New Mexico Historical Review* 84 (3): 399–435.

Seymour, Deni J. 2009c. Father Kino's "Neat Little House and Church" at Guevavi. *Journal of the Southwest* 51 (2): 285–316.

Seymour, Deni J. 2009d. Distinctive Places, Suitable Spaces: Conceptualizing Mobile Group Occupational Duration and Landscape Use. *International Journal of Historical Archaeology* 13 (3): 255–281.

Seymour, Deni J. 2010a. Beyond Married, Buried, and Baptized: Exposing Historical Discontinuities in an Engendered Sobaípuri-O'odham Household. Chapter 12 in *Engendering Households in the Prehistoric Southwest*, edited by Barbara Roth, 229–259. University of Arizona Press, Tucson.

Seymour, Deni J. 2010b. Archaeological Insights into the 1698 Victory of the Sobaípuri O'odham over the Enemies of the Sonoran Province. *Old Pueblo Archaeology Center Bulletin*. December issue.

Seymour, Deni J. 2011a. *Where the Earth and Sky Are Sewn Together: Sobaípuri-O'odham Contexts of Contact and Colonialism*. University of Utah Press, Salt Lake City.

Seymour, Deni J. 2011b. *Data Recovery on Sobaipuri and Spanish Colonial Sites along the Middle and Lower San Pedro River on Bureau of Land Management Lands.* Report submitted to the Bureau of Land Management in fulfillment of Permit No. AZ-000455. On file at the Bureau of Land Management and Arizona State Museum, Tucson.

Seymour, Deni J. 2011c. 1762 on the San Pedro: Reevaluating Sobaípuri-O'odham Abandonment and New Apache Raiding Corridors. *Journal of Arizona History* 52 (2): 169–188.

Seymour, Deni J. 2011d. Dating the Sobaípuri: A Case Study in Chronology Building and Archaeological Interpretation. *Old Pueblo Archaeology Bulletin* 67 (September):1–13.

Seymour, Deni J. 2012a. Isolating a Pre-differentiation Athapaskan Assemblage in the Southern Southwest: The Cerro Rojo Complex. Chapter 5 in *From the Land of Ever Winter to the American Southwest: Athapaskan Migrations, Mobility, and Ethnogenesis*, edited by Deni J. Seymour, 90–123. University of Utah Press, Salt Lake City.

Seymour, Deni J. 2012b. "Big Trips" and Historic Apache Movement and Interaction: Models for Early Athapaskan Migrations. Chapter 17 in *From the Land of Ever Winter to the American Southwest: Athapaskan Migrations, Mobility, and Ethnogenesis*, edited by Deni J. Seymour, 377–409. University of Utah Press, Salt Lake City.

Seymour, Deni J. 2012c. Santa Cruz River: The Origin of a Place Name. *Journal of Arizona History* 53 (1): 81–88.

Seymour, Deni J. 2014. *A Fateful Day in 1698: The Remarkable Sobaípuri-O'odham Victory over the Enemies of the Sonoran Province.* University of Utah Press, Salt Lake City.

Seymour, Deni J. 2015a. Sobaipuri-O'odham: Sonoita Creek Spanish Colonial Period Village Identified. *Arizona Archaeological Council Newsletter* 39 (1): 45–55.

Seymour, Deni J. 2015b. Behavioral Assessment of a Pompeii-Like Event and Its Battlefield Signature. Chapter 2 in *Explorations in Behavioral Archaeology*, edited by William H. Walker and James M. Skibo, 8–21. University of Utah Press, Salt Lake City.

Seymour, Deni J. 2016a. Defining the Jocome and Their "Gifts of Little Value." *Kiva* 82 (2): 137–172.

Seymour, Deni J. 2016b. Captain Francisco Tovar's 1776 Battle of Las Mesitas—A Revised Perspective. Paper presented at the Arizona History Convention, Yuma.

Seymour, Deni J. 2017a. Who Are the Sobaipuri O'odham? Video prepared by the Sobaipuri O'odham Heritage Research Group at San Xavier del Wa:k. YouTube. https://www.youtube.com/watch?v=4khqVQOPw8w.

Seymour, Deni J. 2017b. Perceiving the Protohistoric: When Weak Signatures Represent the Strongest Cases. Chapter 11 in *The Strong Case Approach in Behavioral Archaeology*, edited by M. B. Schiffer, C. R. Riggs, and J. J. Reid, 139–157. University of Utah Press, Salt Lake City.

Seymour, Deni J. 2017c. Protohistoric Projectile Points and Other Diagnostics: A Pan-regional Southern Southwestern Perspective. *Journal of Arizona Archaeology* 4 (2): 132–149.

Seymour, Deni J. 2018. Padre Kino's Footsteps: Tumacácori. Sobaipuri O'odham Heritage YouTube Research Video #7. https://www.youtube.com/watch?v= WtBVpCi5ZhY&t=118s.

Seymour, Deni J. 2019a. Finding Father Eusebio Kino's San Xavier del Bac. *International Journal of Historical Archaeology* 23 (3): 772–805.

Seymour, Deni J. 2019b. San Xavier del Wa:k's Late Eighteenth Century Fortified Village Revealed in Early Imagery and Texts. *Kiva* 85 (2): 161–185.

Seymour, Deni J. 2020a. "Submerges . . . Coming Out Again and Then Flowing": What Historical Documents Tell Us about the Character of the Santa Cruz River. *Kiva* 86 (3): 349–371.

Seymour, Deni J. 2020b. "A Distinction without a Difference": Primary Narrative Texts in Historical Inquiry. *Routledge Handbook of Global Historical Archaeology*, edited by Charles Orser, Pedro Funari, Susan Lawrence, James Symonds, and Andrés Zarankin, 458–477. Routledge, London and New York.

Seymour, Deni J. 2020c. Land of the Buzzard Clan and Their Mobile Neighbors: Exploring the Protohistoric in the Southern Southwest. *Journal of Arizona Archaeology* 7 (2): 179–199.

Seymour, Deni J. 2020d. Captain Tovar's 1776 Battle of Las Mesitas: A Revised Perspective, *Sierra Vista Herald*, May 15.

Seymour, Deni J. 2021. Anza Route and Campsites in Southern Arizona. Video. YouTube, July 18. https://www.youtube.com/watch?v=mardW_Q9RIY.

Seymour, Deni J., 2022a. Unveiling Tucson's Birthplace: The Sobaipuri O'odham Village of San Cosme del Tucsón. *Journal of Arizona History* 63 (2): 115–152.

Seymour, Deni J. 2022b. "To Take Death from the Enemy": The Juh-Cushing Battle Site. *New Mexico Historical Review* 97 (4) (forthcoming).

Seymour, Deni J. 2023. They Fought like Lions: Santa Cruz de Terrenate Presidio, 1775–1780. Book manuscript.

Seymour, Deni, with Tony Burrell, and David Tenario. J. 2022a. The Wa:k O'odham and Their Akimel O'odham Heritage, Chapter 6 in *Borderlands Histories: Ethnographic Observations and Archaeological Interpretations*, edited by John Carpenter and Matthew Pailes, 85–110. University of Utah Press, Salt Lake City.

Seymour, Deni, Tony Burrell, and David Tenario. J. 2022b. Lost Songs of the Buzzard Clan: Heritage and Historical Identity at San Xavier del Wa:k. Manuscript.

Seymour, Deni J., and Oscar Rodríguez. 2020. *To the Corner of the Province: The 1780 Ugarte-Rocha Sonoran Reconnaissance and Implications for Environmental and Cultural Change.* University of Utah Press, Salt Lake City.

Seymour, Deni J., and Ron Stewart. 2017. Naming Arizona's San Pedro River. *Journal of Arizona History* 58 (1): 89–98.

Seymour, Deni J., and Chris Sugnet. 2016. Thematic Inventory of Terminal Prehistoric, Protohistoric, and Historic Expeditionary Sites in Southeastern Arizona. Draft report on file with the author. [This report is updated routinely because the research is ongoing.]

Smith, Buckingham. 1863. Rudo Ensayo: Tentativa de una prevencional descripción geographica de la Provincia de Sonora, sus términos y Confines; ó mejor, colección de materiales para hacerla quien lo supiere mejor. Munsell, Albany, NY. https://babel.hathitrust.org/cgi/pt?id=loc.ark:/13960/t8cgohn4w&view=1up&seq=9&skin=2021.

Smith, Fay Jackson, John L. Kessell, and Francis J. Fox, SJ. 1966. *Father Kino in Arizona.* Arizona Historical Foundation, Phoenix.

Soba Puris Once Ruled Tucson Area: Encarnacion Mamake, Only Survivor, Taken by Death. 1931. *Tucson Citizen,* December 21.

Spicer, Edward H. [1962] 1981. *Cycles of Conquest: The Impact of Spain, Mexico, and the United States on the Indians of the Southwest, 1533–1960.* University of Arizona Press, Tucson.

Stern, Peter, and Robert Jackson. 1988. Vagabundaje and Settlement Patterns in Colonial Northern Sonora. *Americas* 44 (4): 461–481.

Thomas, Alfred Barnaby. 1932. *Forgotten Frontiers: A Story of the Spanish Indian Policy of Don Juan Bautista de Anza, Governor of New Mexico, 1777–1787.* University of Oklahoma Press, Norman.

Thomas, Alfred Barnaby. 1941. *Teodoro de Croix and the Northern Frontiers of New Spain, 1776–1783.* University of Oklahoma Press, Norman.

Treutlein, T. E., trans. 1945. "The Relation of Philipp Segesser." *Mid-America* 27 (3) (n.s. 16:3): 139–187.

Treutlein, T. E., Translator. 1965. *Missionary in Sonora, the Travel Reports of Joseph Och, S.J.* California Historical Society, San Francisco.

Underhill, Ruth M. 1938. A Papago Calendar Record. *University of New Mexico Bulletin. Anthropological Series* 2 (5). University of New Mexico Press, Albuquerque.

Underhill, Ruth M. 1939. *Social Organization of the Papago Indians.* AMS Press, New York.

Underhill, Ruth M. 1941. *The Papago Indians of Arizona and their Relatives the Pima*. United States Bureau of American Ethnology, Division of Education. Haskell Institute, Lawrence, Kansas.

Underhill, Ruth M. 1946. *Papago Indian Religion*. Columbia University Press, New York.

Underhill, Ruth M. 1968. *Singing for Power: The Songs of the Papago Indians of Southern Arizona*. University of California Press, Berkeley.

Underhill, Ruth M. 1969. The Autobiography of a Papago Woman. *Memoirs of the American Anthropological Association*, Number 46. American Anthropological Association, Menasha, WI, Kraus Reprint Co., New York.

Underhill, Ruth M. 1974. Acculturation at the Papago Village of Santa Rosa. In *Papago Indians I: American Indian Ethnohistory, Indians of the Southwest*, compiled and edited by David Agee Horr, 309–348. Garland Publishing, New York.

Underhill, Ruth M. 1979. *Papago Woman*. Waveland Press, Inc. Prospect Heights, IL.

Voss, Barbara L. 2008. *The Archaeology of Ethnogenesis: Race and Sexuality in Colonial San Francisco*. University of California Press, Berkeley.

Webb, Robert H., Julio L. Betancourt, Raymond M. Turner, and R. Roy Johnson. 2014. *Requiem for the Santa Cruz: An Environmental History of an Arizona River*. University of Arizona Press, Tucson.

Wells, E. Christian. 2006. From Hohokam to O'odham: The Protohistoric Occupation of the Middle Gila River Valley, Central Arizona. *Gila River Indian Community Anthropological Papers No. 3*, Sacaton, AZ.

Wilcox, David. 1986. The Tepiman Connection: A Model of Mesoamerican-Southwestern Interaction. In *Ripples in the Chichimec Sea: New Considerations of Southwestern-Mesoamerican Interactions*, edited by Frances J. Mathien and Randall H. McGuire, 135–153. Southern Illinois University Press, Carbondale.

Williams, Jack S. 1986. The Presidio of Santa Cruz de Terrenate: A Forgotten Fortress of Southern Arizona, *The Smoke Signal*, combined issues 47 and 48, 129–148. Tucson Corral of the Westerners, Tucson.

Wilson, John P. 1987. *Islands in the Desert: A History of the Upland Areas of Southeast Arizona*. United States Forest Service, Las Cruces, NM.

Wilson, John P. 1999. Peoples of the Middle Gila: A Documentary History of the Pimas and Maricopas, 1500's–1945. Researched and written for the Gila River Indian Community, Sacaton. https://bajaarizonahistory.files.wordpress.com/2019/05/wilson-peoples-of-the-middle-gila-text.pdf.

Winter, Joseph C. 1973. Cultural Modifications of the Gila Pima: AD 1697–AD 1846. *Ethnohistory* 20 (1): 67–77.

Winters, Harry J., Jr. 2012. 'O'odham Place Names: Meanings, Origins, and Histories, Arizona and Sonora. Nighthorses, Tucson.

Wyllys, R. K. 1931. Padre Luís Velarde's Relacíon of Pimería Alta, 1716. *New Mexico Historical Review* 6 (2): 111–157.

Ximeno, Fray Bartholomé. 1772. An unsigned letter book copy of Father Ximeno's report in Informes de los Padres de Sonora, 1772, Documents Relating to Pimería Alta, 1767–1800, Fra Marcellino da Civezza Collection, Film 305, in the University of Arizona Library, Tucson.